Sex, Sensibility and the Gendered Body

Edited by

Janet Holland
Senior Research Lecturer
Institute of Education
London

and

Lisa Adkins
Lecturer in Sociology
University of Kent
Canterbury

MACMILLAN

First published 1996 by
MACMILLAN PRESS LTD
Houndmills, Basingstoke, Hampshire RG21 6XS
and London
Companies and representatives
throughout the world

ISBN 0–333–65001–8 hardcover
ISBN 0–333–65002–6 paperback

A catalogue record for this book is available
from the British Library.

10 9   8   7   6   5   4   3   2   1
05 04 03 02 01 00 99 98 97 96

Printed and bound in Great Britain by
Antony Rowe Ltd
Chippenham, Wiltshire

EXPLORATIONS IN SOCIOLOGY
British Sociological Association conference volume series

From the same publishers

Contents

Preface and Acknowledgements

This book consists of essays originally delivered as papers at the 1994 British Sociological Association (BSA) Annual Conference, on the theme of 'Sexualities in Social Context', held at the University of Central Lancashire, 28–31 March 1994. It is one of three volumes produced from the papers given at that conference. The companion volumes are: *Sexual Cultures: Communities, Values and Intimacy*, edited by Jeffrey Weeks and Janet Holland, and *Sexualizing the Social: Power and the Organisation of Sexuality*, edited by Lisa Adkins and Vicki Merchant.

The conference was one of the largest ever held by the BSA, and these three volumes offer a distillation of the 258 papers which were presented. The editors of all three volumes had great difficulty in making a representative selection of the papers, and we would like to thank the forbearance and patience of all the contributors while we reviewed each paper and came to our often painful decisions about them. The editors of this volume would particularly like to thank the contributors for the speed and efficiency with which they responded to editorial comments and revisions. More broadly, we also wish to thank all the participants at the conference, both those who gave papers and those who participated in the various streams. We feel that all those who participated gained enormously from the intellectual vitality and excitement that was apparent there. We hope that this volume and its companions reflect some of that excitement, and that they contribute to the growing recognition of the significance of sexuality in understanding the social dynamics of contemporary societies.

That the conference was such a success is due to the efforts of countless people. We would like to thank members of the British Sociological Association staff for their support throughout this venture. We are also grateful for the support given by staff at the University of Central Lancashire both before and during the conference itself. The editors of this volume owe a great gratitude to their colleagues at the Institute of Education, University of London and the Open University, and at the University of the West of England. We owe personal debts to our immediate partners and friends; they know who they are.

We dedicate this volume to the many young sociologists who attended the BSA Conference, many for the first time. Their enthusiasm

for the subject, and for the theme of the conference, gave us great
hope for the future of our discipline.

JANET HOLLAND
LISA ADKINS

Notes on the Contributors

Lisa Adkins is Lecturer in Sociology at the University of Kent and previously at the University of the West of England. Her research interests are focused on the sociology of gender, especially sexuality, the labour market and the family. Recent publications include *Gendered Work: Sexuality, Family and the Labour Market* (1995) and *Questioning Sex: French Materialist Feminism*, edited with Diana Leonard (1996).

Patricia Allatt is Professor at Teeside Business School. Her research includes burglary, drugs prevention, the family and youth labour markets, and, within the 'ESRC 16–19 Initiative', the development of economic and political identities, with publications in Spain and Finland. Her publications include *Youth Unemployment and the Family* (1992, with S. M. Yeandle).

Pam Carter is Senior Lecturer in Sociology at the University of Northumbria. She has published in the fields of social work and higher education. Her book *Feminism, Breasts and Breastfeeding* was published by Macmillan in 1995.

Gail Darke is currently in her second year as a PhD student at the University of the West of England, where she is continuing her masters research into female sexuality and the menopause.

Anne Edwards is Deputy Vice-Chancellor of Flinders University of South Australia, and was formerly Professor of Sociology in the Department of Anthropology and Sociology, Monash University, and a senior member of the Centre for Women's Studies at Monash. She has been in Australia since 1968, having previously lived in England. Her academic interests and publications are mainly in the areas of critical social policy and the welfare state, social theory and social control, the law, feminist theory, gender, and women's studies. Major publications include: *Regulation and Repression: The Study of Social Control* (1988) and *Women in a Restructuring Australia: Work and Welfare* (co-edited with Susan Magarey, 1995).

Debbie Epstein lectures in Women's Studies and Education in the Centre for Research and Education on Gender (CREG) at London University's Institute of Education. Recent publications include: *Changing Classroom Cultures: Anti-racism, Politics and Schools* (1993), and *Challenging Lesbian and Gay Inequalities in Education* (1994). *Schooling Sexualities: Lesbian and Gay Oppression, Identities and Education*, which she has co-authored with Richard Johnson, is to be published shortly.

Janet Holland is Senior Research Lecturer in the Social Science Research Unit, Institute of Education, London, and Lecturer in Education at the Open University. She has general research interests in sexuality, education, youth, gender, and class and has published widely in these areas. Recent publications with members of the Women Risk and AIDS (WRAP) team include: 'Coming to Conclusions: Power and Interpretation in Researching Young Women's Sexuality' (1994) and 'Power and Desire: The Embodiment of Female Sexuality' (1994); and, with Maud Blair, an edited collection: *Identity and Diversity: Gender and the Experience of Education* (1995).

Sophie Laws is Principal Officer for Research and Development for Save the Children Fund's UK and European Programmes Department. Her previous publications include *Issues of Blood: The Politics of Menstruation* (1990) and (with Janet Black) *Living with Sickle Cell Disease* (1986).

Chris Mann is based in the Department of Education, University of Cambridge. She is currently researching sociological and psychological issues related to young people, education, and the contemporary family. She has published articles that focus on both early findings from this research and research methods appropriate for such sensitive areas as the family.

Jennifer Mason is Senior Lecturer in Sociology in the School of Sociology and Social Policy, University of Leeds. She has spent many years researching family, kin, and gender relationships. Her publications include *Negotiating Family Responsibilities*, co-authored with Janet Finch (1993).

Linda McKie is Senior Lecturer in Health Education at the University of Aberdeen. She has research and teaching interests in the sociology of health and illness, women's health, and the sociology of food and eating. Her publications include editing and contributing to *Researching Women's Health: Methods and Process* (1995) and articles on women's views of cervical screening, food, diet and body image, and the evaluation of health promotion.

Diane Richardson is Senior Lecturer in the Department of Sociological Studies at the University of Sheffield and was recently a Visiting Scholar in Women's Studies at Harvard. Her books include *Women and the AID Crisis* (1989), *Safer Sex* (1990), and *Women, Motherhood and Childrearing* (1993). She is currently editing *Theorizing Heterosexuality*, and writing *Social Theory, Social Change and Sexuality*.

Carol Smart is Professor of Sociology at the University of Leeds and was formerly Senior Lecturer at the University of Warwick. She teaches courses on 'Sexuality and the Body' and is currently researching issues of household transition on divorce and separation. Major publications include *Feminism and the Power of Law* (1989), *Regulating Motherhood* (1992) and *Law, Crime and Sexuality* (1995).

Introduction

JANET HOLLAND and LISA ADKINS

Sexuality is moving from the margins of sociological awareness, from being ignored to becoming central to an understanding of the social. The body is moving in parallel,[1] emerging from outer darkness and the terrors of essentialism, an 'absent presence' in sociology (Shilling, 1993), to a locus of attention and debate. The body and its social construction are entwined, no simple conceptual dualism will allow us to distinguish the biological body from the social meanings attached to it. And that physical body and those social meanings are gendered. Radical feminists have long argued that the female body and sexuality are a site of control and potential contestation; lesbians and gay men have struggled with the pervasive power of normative heterosexuality; feminist critiques of Foucault's gender blindness have indicated that discourse can be gendered. From these political and intellectual struggles new understandings of the multiple interrelationships between bodies, sexuality, and identities are emerging.

Identity and sexual politics and a healthy dose of postmodernism have then released our multiple identities and sexualities into consciousness and the light, revealing a hollow space for heterosexual identity. Heterosexuality, it seems, is on the line. As Smart argues in her provocative chapter in this volume, doing (practice) should be distinguished from being (identity), and despite its omnipresence, heterosexuality can be seen as merely a fleeting subjectivity. It has not been discursively constructed in the same way that Foucault (1981) suggests the homosexual identity was in medical discourse, Walkowitz (1980) the prostitute through the Contagious Diseases Acts, and Faderman (1985) the lesbian. It is often denied or subverted by its apparent exemplars, particularly feminists (see the influential collection edited by Wilkinson and Kitzinger, 1993) but is invisible in its ubiquity. As the chapters in this collection and the companion volume *Sexualizing the Social* demonstrate, although normative heterosexuality can be deployed in the construction of gender identity and difference – and indeed the reverse – heterosexual identity needs to be decoupled from gender identity if we are to understand either.

The chapters in this book come from different perspectives and a variety of angles to shake loose gender and sexuality. The focus is on

1

women: the kaleidoscope of roles they play or in which they are cast: mother, sister, daughter, wife, carer, patient, miscreant, sexual object, childbearer, ex-childbearer. Excavations of these roles and castings reveal a particularly tense intersection of gender and (hetero)sexuality played out over the female body. Aspects of control and constraint of bodies, social (external) and individual/personal (internal) and their interaction, and potential resistances are explored, often simultaneously, in many of the chapters. Gendered identity, (hetero)sexuality, embodiment and control are then the major themes emerging in this collection.[2]

This book is divided into three parts. Chapters in Part I examine the construction of gendered identity in relation to the family. Those in Part II consider the medicalisation and control of the body, and in Part III the construction of heterosexuality comes under scrutiny.

PART I   THE FAMILY AND GENDERED IDENTITIES

Chapters in Part I explore the ways in which gender identity is constructed both within the family and in support of the family through cultural representations. Mason sensitises us to the limitations and limits of generalisation about gender in a subtle and supple discussion of care and responsibility in family and kin relationships, drawing on, criticising and developing concepts introduced by Gilligan, Ruddick, Tronto and Sevenhuijsen. She is intent to uncouple caring as a 'labour' of 'love', hard physical work, from the moral and emotional dimension of care. She builds on the feminist, sociological and social policy debates which identified the practical, physical and labour-intensive activity of caring, to extend labour to thinking and feeling. Her development of the moral dimension of caring draws on the work of Gilligan and Ruddick, commenting that although both assert that they do not want to make sweeping essentialist claims about women's inherent nature and morality, they are both interpreted as doing exactly that and, in their use of the category 'woman,' implying too simple a construction of gender difference. In each of their formulations women are seen to develop an ethic of care and responsibility, and Ruddick argues that maternal practice inculcates a particular kind of moral thinking in those who do it.

Tronto has criticised these authors for fitting too well with a longstanding politics of morality which privilege a particular category of woman – white, middle-class women, and others have seen their position as capable of supporting a conservative notion of women as fitted to be carers. Mason, too, rejects the idea of carers as necessarily women, caring as part of the gendered identity of women, although empirically it is often women who take up this role. Caring for her, drawing on her work with Janet Finch, is a relational, multi-dimensional activity, involving morality, feeling and thought. And the important conceptual step she makes is to define caring as neither labour nor love, but sentient activity and active sensibility. Sentient activity identifies thinking and feeling as activities, a way of engaging with others and with the social world, not a type of felt emotion. And active sensibility is the activity of feeling and accepting a responsibility for some-one else, a commitment to another. This involves being alert to their needs, and meeting those needs, often in a way not explicitly recognised by donor or recipient. Mason suggests that sentient activity and active sensibilities are developed relationally in specific families, with specific relatives or family members, although within social and cultural contexts, and so are not generalisable. They do, however, she would contend, 'provide us with a sensitive mechanism for exploring the relevance of gender and other dimensions of social experience and context'.

Allatt is concerned with the construction of gendered identity in support of the family through ideology, particularly in popular cultural representations. She analysed two women's magazines during the Second World War, when, she argues, the traditional inegalitarian structures of gender and class were challenged both materially and symbolically, and political processes became more visible for exploration. The disruption of the war exposed the frailty of the boundaries between the masculine, public domain of war, work and politics and the feminine, private domain of home and family. The two magazines were selected to highlight contrasts in their readership, who differed by class, education, age, and family life-course stage. Allatt proposes from her analysis that the ideological messages embedded in the romantic stories and other items in the two magazines were tailored to meet the challenges posed to the maintenance of the traditional family structure of bread-winner husband and home-based wife–mother in two different social strata. The political intent was to maintain relations of domination and subordination between the sexes and the existing distribution of resources. *True Romances* met the task of persuading young working-class women to accept the harsh realities of their lives and, through the construction of a model of female behaviour, to construct a particular type of male worker. *Good Housekeeping* persuaded the middle-class wife back into the home in a context of egalitarianism, when she had possibly had a taste of independence in war work.

The ideological work required of the material in *True Romances* is first to address the contradictions and threats posed by poverty, romance and women's rational economic behaviour in choice of marriage partner – i.e. *not* a poor working-class male; and, second, to control women within marriage in poverty through an exaltation of the domestic division of labour. Through her analysis of romantic fiction, articles and other material in the magazine, Allatt identifies the various mechanisms through which she sees this ideological sleight of hand as being accomplished. The approach in *Good Housekeeping*, for older married middle-class women, was to elaborate the paradox of continuities within change and the domestication of the public domain. For the first, women are seen as the carriers of eternal verities, particularly in relation to the private domain of family and home, and the magazine reaffirmed the deeper truths and inevitability of the life cycle. For the second, the outside world is trivialised as a site of power, not worth the effort of entry, and power is translated into the housewife role.

Threaded through the material and the analysis are elements of the requirements of heterosexuality in the two class contexts, and features of the embodiment of appropriate femininity. These are exemplified in two of the transformations accomplished by the material in *True Romances*. The first is the transformation of physical power in the form of sexual violence, from the romantic violence of courtship to the domestic violence of marriage, in the event that wives reject the domestic or sexual services they are expected to provide. The second is the displacement of beauty, from outer to inner and structural to personal. The young working-class woman's beauty is fleeting and fragile, soon lost in the drudgery of poverty but in the romance stories this physical loss is attributed to personal failure rather than inherent in the structural demands of a woman's life.

In the rhetoric of the recent public campaign of vilification of teenage mothers we witness further ideological sleight of hand through which the material conditions of young women's lives are transformed into an attack on their sexuality. And in this instance we have an example of the disappearing heterosexual male. As Richardson points out in her chapter in this volume 'it is almost as if women became pregnant through parthenogenesis', in the focus on teenage pregnancy rather than conception. Here, in a pincer movement on the teenage mother, gender and sexuality are totally and inappropriately enmeshed in an attempt to control the female body; and the heterosexual couple in a family is extolled as the ideal parenting arrangement for a healthy society. Laws decries the way in which policy appears to be generated on this basis. Policy makers employ media campaigns and manipulate public opinion through misinformation or 'economy with the truth', demonstrating in this concerted attack on teenage mothers complete irresponsibility towards children. The objective seems to be to eliminate the existence of these children by changing adult behaviour through economic pressure. The public and Press debate rarely focuses on the children of lone parents, except in the attack on their upbringing without the presence of a father. Laws systematically demonstrates that actual and proposed policy is in contradiction of the articles of the UN Convention on the Rights of the Child (ratified 1991), denies children their rights, and places them at risk.

Laws draws attention to articles in the UN Convention on the Rights of the Child which cover discrimination, the right to an adequate standard of living, preservation of identity, parental responsibility and support to parents, protection from abuse and neglect, and from sexual exploitation. All are contradicted by the attack on lone parenting rather than the social conditions in which it occurs, and the approval of any policy which might deter women from becoming lone parents. Examples are policies which make acquiring adequate accommodation even more difficult than it actually is for these mothers, or which generate social and financial pressures to drive women back into relationships with abusive men. And young single mothers themselves are, of course, vulnerable to sexual exploitation.

The developing social and sexual identity of academically successful young women is the focus of Mann's work, this time in the context of changing family structures and relationships (particularly their relationship with their fathers) and changing constructions of masculinity and femininity. The young women were beset by contradictions, in terms of their own educational success and its conflict with models of appropriate feminine behaviour, and the ambivalent and contradictory contribution of parents to their sense of self and identity. The heterosexual male as father emerges in a baleful light filtered through these young women's reported experience. He is absent, and emotionally absent even when present; he favours traditional gender divisions; he is controlling, particularly in relation to sexuality and the body; he is a disappointment – 'a clear theme that is evident throughout my work with young women is the level of disappointment that many girls express when they describe their relationship with their fathers'. The young women in this study are acutely aware of the way the power relations

of gender and age are played out in their relationship with their father
– their language evokes an intimidating figure of authority who holds
them prisoner.

Many of the fathers elide gender and heterosexuality, upholding the
virgin/whore dichotomy, and concentrating their control on their daughter's body. Mann sees the eating disorders which appeared in these
young women's accounts 'almost as an inevitability . . . nearly as predictable as menstruation' as part of the powerful influence of family
men who have not relinquished control of the young woman's body.
One young woman was caught in a series of double binds by her father's
responses to her body: 'When I had puppy fat my dad was teasing me
and saying how fat I was – then when I started losing weight he started
teasing me about being too thin.' His ambivalence about her sexuality
and sexual attractiveness emerges when she is dressed up to go out
one night 'You've got no chest . . . nothing, you're just bones. You
look sick. Disgusting. You don't think anyone's going to look at you
the way you are now.'

The sexualised, female body and its control has increasingly emerged
as we have progressed through the chapters in this section. In the following section it is a major object of concern.

PART II　BODIES, MEDICALISATION AND CONTROL

Drawing on the messages of the medical profession and childcare
manuals, Carter examines the changing construction of breast feeding
over time, changing but always to be recognised within the parameters
of heterosexuality. Although analysing breasts in discourse, Carter highlights the material body: 'Breasts and breast feeding are heavily constructed through a wide range of language, practice and representation.
But at the same time breasts swell, leak, tingle and sometimes appear
to have a life of their own.' This unpredictability of the natural func-
tioning body is something which women find difficult to handle particularly, as Carter points out, in a patriarchal world which treats women's
bodies as inherently problematic. Social control of women's bodies
operates through multiple mechanisms, including the agency of the individual woman (see Prendergast (1995) on the menarche, and Darke,
in this volume, on the menopause). In this instance, fear of unpredictability
and the need for control might lead women to eschew the 'natural'
course of breast feeding for the more predictable bottle. But this leads,

in Carter's narrative, to accusations of 'unnaturalness' and selfishness on the part of the mother, the breast is for the baby (and the 'race') not the mother.

As time progressed, fathers and sexuality began to appear in texts on breast feeding, initially husbands are expected to show 'delicacy and forbearance', but later male sexual 'needs' and women's sensual enjoyment of breast-feeding was discussed. The exhortations in the breast feeding texts were always couched within the context of the heterosexual couple/family, and increasingly a chapter on breast feeding and specific sexual practices would appear, in which distinct models of female and male sexuality emerged. The potential contradictions between the two supposed functions of breasts, sex and breast feeding, were overcome through a particular model of female (hetero)sexuality, and 'discursive linkages between breast feeding and heterosexuality, particularly sexual intercourse'. Breast feeding and heterosex practices are portrayed as similar in terms of the production of hormones and the physical and emotional responses these hormones induce. It is suggested that as a result of arousal during breast feeding, the breast-feeding mother becomes more eager for sexual intercourse; and and, finally, when husbands play with their wives' breasts they are performing a service to mother and child by toughening up nipples and maintaining milk supply. In the light of this analysis, Carter argues that, given its embeddedness in heterosex/ual/ist discourse, it is difficult to retrieve breast feeding as potentially an aspect of autonomous female sexuality, or a vehicle for resistance. She suggests, however, that a reappropriation of the meaning of breasts for and by women might provide a starting point such a retrieval.

McKie's chapter takes us further into the domain of medicalisation and control, and the regulation, surveillance and monitoring of bodies which are central to the creation and maintenance of society (Turner, 1992). She discusses the meaning that screening in general, and cervical screening in particular, have in public health and popular discourses. General practitioners have a financial incentive to encourage women to undergo cervical smear tests, which are regarded uncritically as a good thing, and concomitantly those who resist are seen by health care workers as irresponsible, feckless and non-compliers. These judgements are made without consideration of any negative physical or emotional effects the test may have on women themselves.

McKie and her colleagues undertook group discussions about cervical smear tests with working-class women and found a high degree of similarity in the issues which arose across groups. The researchers found

that a consideration of sex and sexuality in the groups was often triggered by discussion of: men's lack of understanding; the social and
treatment consequences of any abnormalities which might be found;
women's concerns about the gender of the test-taker and related male
problems with male doctors coming into contact with 'their' women's
genitals. In popular discourse, as indeed in medical circles, a positive
smear had implications for sexual identity, suggesting promiscuous sexual
activity. Male partners thought that the smear test could give women
patients and male doctors 'sexual thrills'. 'Concepts of ownership and
control pervaded the discussions; of men owning women through relationships and of men surveying women through the cervical screening
service.' Heterosexuality is constructed, taken for granted, and but-
tressed, and a negative, denigrating image of women is purveyed through
these processes. This reinforces women's feelings of inadequacy and
vulnerability. The ownership of the woman's body in both public and
private domains denies her selfhood. (Issues of ownership of the body
and its relationship to gendered selfhood are also discussed in the companion volume *Sexualizing the Social*.)

The nub of all this intense activity of social control around women's
bodies is the womb, women's reproductive capacity. And when this
fundamental organ loses its reproductive capacity, is she a woman?
Darke argues that the medicalised meaning of the menopause has its
roots in Victorian medico-moral definitions which conflated female
sexuality with 'womanhood'. Constructed upon the norm of heterosexual relations, a woman's worth was measured in terms of her fertility and physical attractiveness to men. The menopause then, becomes
the death of 'womanhood'; and the medical redefinition of this life
event as a hormone deficiency 'disease' in the 1960s offers hormone
replacement therapy (HRT) to stave off this disaster. The meaning of
the menopause and HRT is (and has historically been) constructed through
a range of intersecting and overlapping discourses (medical and popular) which all draw on 'a wider context of dominant constructions of
gender and female sexuality that operate through what McNay calls a
regulatory notion of a "natural" reproductive heterosexuality'. Popular
discourse on the menopause in a range of media reconstitutes information drawn from medical discourse and practice, and formed the basis
of the women in Darke's study labelling of themselves as menopausal.
Alternative feminist explanations are also available in popular discourse,
although not always or necessarily identified explicitly as such.

Darke examines the usefulness of the concepts of practices of the
self – techniques through which individuals actively participate in a

process of self-fashioning (Foucault), and the self as a reflexive project in which the body is a site of choices and options (Giddens) for analysing the way in which the women in her study experience the menopause and HRT. Both modes of construction of self-identity take place within a broad socio-cultural context which constrains the individual, but the latter offers a social interactive context for the formation of the self. Each, however, are limited, since as Darke's material indicates, they are gendered phenomena. Men and women are differently positioned in relation to discourse and the construction of self-identity, and as Darke concludes, 'practices of the self and the reflexive project of the self are tied to wider social constructions of gender and female sexuality, and social class differences'. The unruly material body which resists attempts to reconstruct it are also missing from these modes of analysis. Darke is referring to the body's resistance to individual control, as in frustrating attempts to lose weight gained through menopause. But as Grosz (1990) puts it, while 'the body is internally lived, experienced and acted upon by the subject and the social collectivity' (p. 65), 'its energies and capacities exert an uncontrollable, unpredictable threat to a regular, systematic mode of social organisation. [It is] a site of resistance, for it exerts recalcitrance, and always entails the possibility of a counterstrategic reinscription, for it is capable of being self-marked, self-represented in alternative ways' (p. 64).

PART III THE CONSTRUCTION OF HETEROSEXUALITY

The heterosexual male emerges in the unlikely guise of victim in Richardson analysis of the discourse of AIDS. He is at risk from types of deviant women who may tempt him – sex workers, black African women, drug injectors, promiscuous women – or from gay or bisexual men. He is in danger of losing his traditional male sexual agency in this manifestation, one of a series of contradictions which Richardson identifies as arising in the construction of the heterosexual male in AIDS discourse. There is tension between the image of the heterosexual man as victim of a strong sexual urge, which may lead him into these dangerous liaisons, and his invisibility as a source of danger and infection to others. It is gay and bisexual men and deviant women who represent the danger. Richardson argues that normative heterosexuality, or heteronormativity, is constructed as appropriate, acceptable and not dangerous in AIDS discourse through contrast with 'deviant heterosexuality'. This deviance can be promiscuous sex, heterosexuality challenged by the identity of one or more of the partners, or specific forms of sexual practice, such as anal intercourse. Through these processes of exclusion 'the boundaries of heterosexual inclusion are firmly constructed and by implication, those of safe/normal sex'. Here Richardson moves onto the same ground as Smart in her search for post-heterosexuality, by highlighting the potential for AIDS to disrupt the notion of distinct sexual identities – heterosexual, lesbian, gay – through an emphasis on routes of transmission (types of sexual practice) rather than sexual identities. An analysis of the contradictions in the construction of heterosexuality in AIDS discourse, policy and education, may offer the opportunity to 'destabilise the meaning of heterosexuality and the constructions of gender upon which it is organised'.

Such a destabilisation of the meanings of heterosexuality and constructions of gender would seem to be far from possible in the context of the judicial processing of rape and the rape trial, where the fusion of sexuality, gender, and power takes a dramatic form. As Jackson (1978) has said 'The attributes of masculinity and femininity, learnt from the beginning of childhood and incorporated into expectations of sexual behaviour, provide the motivational and interactional basis of rape.' In this context, the heterosexual male emerges in his usual cultural cloak of action, aggression, assertiveness, self-reliance, and equipped with a powerful biological sex drive. The corresponding heterosexual female is passive, dependent, sexually restrained and accommodating, and if she is not, she can be regarded as sexually provocative, promiscuous, and deviant.

Edwards argues that although there have been changes in the legal system in relation to rape resulting from lobbying by law reform and women's groups, these changes have not touched the fundamental masculinist bias of the system and the process, which leaves women treated as if they were on trial rather than complainants, and men acquitted, particularly in 'consent' cases and non-stranger rape. The fundamental problem is that given 'the way that femininity, masculinity and (hetero)sexuality are constructed and gender relations are organised in a male-dominated social order, it is hard to differentiate between coerced and noncoerced forms of social/sexual interaction'. The law and the criminal justice system operate within a rigid structure of binary logic: the crime was or was not committed, the accused is guilty or innocent, it cannot deal with multiple meanings for any specific human interaction with no way of discerning which is the 'truth'. The problem is particularly acute in non-stranger rape cases, and jurors are being asked to be agents of change in a process of societal redefinition of rape in a context of the restrictive framework of the law of rape, and an inflexible binary logic which 'governs both the criminal judicial system and cultural understandings of gender and sexuality'. The chapters by Richardson and Edwards have examined, in quite different contexts, the way in which the normative social construction of heterosexuality can be realised in discourse and institutionalised in practice to endanger women and put them at risk of damage. Although the same underlying theme can be identified in Epstein's chapter, she takes a step back to focus on a specific aspect of the hard cultural work, which 'goes into the maintenance of the oppositional, binary "gendered possibilities" available to us' and the 'presumption of heterosexuality as both "normal" and normative' upon which it is based'. She builds her argument on what Judith Butler (1990) has called the 'heterosexual matrix' which includes the institutionalisation of compulsory heterosexuality and the discursive field which shapes our understandings of gender in terms of binary opposites, 'that grid of cultural intelligibility through which bodies, genders and desires are naturalized' (Butler, 1990, p. 151). Decoupling sexual identity and gender once more, Epstein wants to reconceptualise sexual harassment as sexist harassment, regarding the harassment of women and gay men as 'a kind of pedagogy of heterosexuality and a key way in which heterosexuality is institutionalised'.

Epstein highlights the complexity of social relations and sexist harassment, arguing that forms of harassment which are experienced shape and are shaped by the particular social locations of both harassed and harassers, giving examples of black and disabled women. Deviance from heterosexuality is punished, and lesbians and gay men interviewed in her studies reported being harassed because they were seen as not feminine enough or not sufficiently like real boys. To avoid harassment they might heighten their own homophobic or even heterosexual activities, and gay young men might engage in the normative masculine objectification and harassment of women. Thus are the boundaries of heterosexuality policed and heterosexist harassment of gay men and women constitutes a pedagogy of heterosexuality, schooling them (us) into gender appropriate sexuality.

In this collection of chapters, we have traced the multiple constituents of the construction of heterosexuality, particularly female heterosexuality, through discourse, institutionalisation, and the lived experience of the material body, through social control and individual agency, and through the permeation of power. The pressure of normative heterosexuality has been palpable. In this context, can we agree with Smart that there is no self-conscious heterosexual identity? Or can we see the multiplicity and elusiveness which meets a closer examination of heterosexual subjectivity as an opportunity to leap with her into post-heterosexuality and embrace plurality and diversity. Can we dismantle the institutionalised privilege of the heterosexual life-style; deconstruct the powerful, silent essentialism of the 'ubiquitous heterosexual subject position'; de-code particular acts as heterosexual, depriving penetration, for example, of its symbolic power by wrenching it out of a heterosexual matrix of meanings; and so 'destabilise heterosexuality and the constructions of gender upon which it is organised'.

NOTES

1. Although the sociology of sexuality generated the current concern with the body, as ever the binary has taken over (see Edwards, Chapter 9) and the two are frequently separated.
2. See *Sexual Cultures* and *Sexualizing the Social* (the companions to this volume) for a contextualisation of these themes in terms of the emergence, development and recent shifts in the sociology of sexuality.

REFERENCES

Butler, J. (1990) *Gender Trouble: Feminism and the Subversion of Identity* (London: Routledge).
Faderman, L. (1985) *Surpassing the Love of Men* (London: The Women's Press).
Foucault, M. (1981) *The History of Sexuality*, vol. I (Harmondsworth: Penguin).
Grosz, E. (1990) 'Inscriptions and Body-maps: Representations and the Corporeal', in Threadgold, T. and Cranny-Francis, A. (eds) *Feminine Masculine and Representation* (London: Allen and Unwin).
Jackson, S. (1978) 'The Social Context of Rape: Sexual Scripts and Motivation', *Women's Studies International Quarterly*, 1: pp. 27–38
Prendergast, S. (1995) 'With Gender on my Mind': Menstruation and Embodiment at Adolescence', in J. Holland and M. Blair (with S. Sheldon) (eds) *Debates and Issues in Feminist Research and Pedagogy* (London: Macmillan).
Shilling, C. (1993) *The Body and Social Theory* (London: Sage).
Turner, B. (1992) *Regulating Bodies: Essays in Medical Sociology* (Routledge: London).
Walkowitz, J. (1980) *Prostitution in Victorian Society* (Cambridge: Cambridge University Press).
Wilkinson, S. and Kitzinger, C. (1993) *Heterosexuality* (London: Sage).

Part I
The Family and Gendered Identities

1 Gender, Care and Sensibility in Family and Kin Relationships

JENNIFER MASON

INTRODUCTION

This chapter explores concepts of care and responsibility for others in the context of family and kin relationships. There has been a great deal of research activity and scholarship on these issues, particularly since the 1970s, and much of it centres on a distinction between the ideas of *caring about*, involving feelings and emotions of a non-active nature, and *caring for*, involving care or servicing labour which is conceptualised in a more active fashion. Whilst the distinction between caring about and caring for has been a useful one, I am going to suggest ways of moving beyond it. I shall argue that there is a way of caring in family and kin relationships which takes up a great deal of the time and energy of those who do it (usually but not exclusively women), and which does not sit comfortably within either of these formulations. I approach this task by focusing on aspects of care which have conventionally been defined as caring about, especially those connected with thinking, feeling, and emotion, because I think it is these which have been under-theorised in recent scholarship. I shall begin by drawing on various intellectual debates which have addressed these issues to some extent, and then go on to apply and develop some of the key ideas in relation to my own work on family and kin relationships. I shall argue that much caring for family and kin involves what I am calling *sentient activity* and *active sensibility*, and that these imply that we should rethink conventional distinctions between activity, thought, and feeling in our conceptualisation of care.

15

CARING AS A LABOUR OF LOVE

The first debate on which I want to draw begins with questions about care and, in particular, its nature and social organisation, the relationship between 'formal' and 'informal' care, and the connections between care and gender divisions. Feminist scholars, mainly from Britain and Scandinavia, initiated debates around these questions in the late 1970s and have played the major role in them since that time. There is now a large and important body of work from feminist sociology and social policy relating to these questions, and we know that a high proportion of the formal and informal caring activities of British and Scandinavian societies are performed by women in service of others (see, for example, Finch and Groves, 1983; Waerness, 1984a, b; Land and Rose, 1985; Dalley, 1988; Ungerson, 1990; Graham, 1991; Thomas, 1993). The achievements of this scholarship are many and include the generation of a great deal of research activity, not all of it feminist in orientation, whose products tell us much about the labour, social divisions, social consequences, and lived experiences of caring (e.g. Finch and Groves, 1983; Ungerson, 1987, 1990; Lewis and Meredith, 1988; Arber and Gilbert, 1989; Qureshi and Walker, 1989; Graham, 1991; Glendinning, 1992; Twigg and Atkin, 1994).

One of the most important achievements of this body of scholarship, taken as a whole, was the acknowledgement that caring can and does involve practical, physical, and labour-intensive activity in support of others. This has underpinned the distinction between caring for and caring about, which became a key item on the agenda of feminist researchers in the 1980s. Although debates about care have moved onto new terrain since then, this theme remains relevant to my concerns. Many of the contributors to the Finch and Groves *A Labour of Love?* collection (1983), for example, were keen to distinguish caring about someone, in the sense of being fond of them or loving them, from caring for someone, in the sense of the often hard physical grind of looking after them. All too often, it was argued, the latter element was made invisible or subsumed under the former. Hilary Graham's contribution to the Finch and Groves volume pointed out that this had everything to do with gender relations, because caring for someone in the physical sense could be, and was, socially constructed as a natural extension of women's caring psyche. The claiming of the term *labour* for informal unpaid caring was therefore central to these feminist debates about the material and ideological processes through which the relations of caring, and the division of labour which produced them, were played out.

Graham — domestic labour subsumed
and made invisible

Graham's essay 'Caring: A Labour of Love?' exposed the invisibility and appropriation of women's labour in unpaid caring relationships and had a deservedly major impact, not only on the conceptualisation of care and on feminist understandings of care for family and kin, but also on campaigns for public recognition of this hidden form of labour. Her analysis distinguished the labour and love elements of care analytically, but she argued that a feminist understanding of care should explore how these are intertwined in the familial work which women do, which uniquely involves informal, unpaid physical labour in the service of others to whom one is intimately connected or related (Graham, 1983).

As the debates continued through the 1980s and into the 1990s, it became clear that many feminist scholars, including Graham herself, would not be satisfied with a conceptual understanding of *care in general* which was actually grounded in an analysis of what Graham has called *'home-based-kin-care' in particular* (Graham, 1991). That base, it was argued, was too specific a starting point for the formulation of ideas about the caring activities which are carried out in a society more generally (including formal and informal or public and private caring). Furthermore, it was grounded in a feminism generated through the experiences and social location of white women which consequently failed to grasp fully the complex relations of difference between women, especially those based on 'race' and social class (Ungerson, 1990; Graham, 1991). Thus, as feminists more generally debated questions of difference and argued more energetically about whether or not women's existence was determined in the last instance by their position in the 'family', so debates about care took on these questions too.

I have no argument with either of these developments in feminism and, indeed, if our concern is to theorise the concept of care in general and the complex processes of social and economic relations which produce, sustain, and depend upon it, then Graham's argument that we should begin from a broader base than (white) home-based-kin-care is entirely legitimate and convincing. However, I want to suggest that a move away from examining the complex intertwining of labour and love in caring relationships seems less useful if our concern is to conceptualise care for family and kin. Graham's earlier work gives us scope for exploring aspects of care which are to do with feeling and interpersonal connection as well as aspects which are to do with labour. Although I shall argue later that neither labour nor love constitute the most appropriate analytical categories for understanding care for family and kin, the idea that feelings and thought should be part of the frame is one I wish to retain.

CARING AS MORALITY AND ETHICS

I want now to turn to a different debate which begins with more philosophical questions about care and its connections with gender; specifically, do women have a distinctive morality and ethics which is based
on care and responsibility for others? A consideration of the idea that
moralities are gendered, and a discussion of what have become known
as ethics of care, takes us away from sociological scholarship and into
areas addressed by feminist psychologists, feminist political scientists,
and feminist philosophers. Where the sociological and social policy
debates about care as a labour of love have focused on material and
ideological processes – a kind of political economy of care – debates
about care as morality and ethics turn the spotlight onto processes of
reasoning, of perceiving, 'knowing', and acting.

Given my suggestion that feeling and thinking should be part of the
frame for the analysis of care in family and kin relationships, then the
importance of this very large and diverse body of scholarship for my
purposes cannot be overstated, but I cannot do justice to the whole in
this discussion. Instead, I shall briefly consider the relevance to my
concerns of the writings of four key scholars: Carol Gilligan, Sara
Ruddick, Joan Tronto and Selma Sevenhuijsen.

Carol Gilligan's contribution has its origins in object-relations perspectives on gender development in psychology, and her work *In a
Different Voice* opened up a controversy within and outside feminism
about whether and in what ways morality might be gendered (Gilligan,
1982; for aspects of the debate see, for example, Gilligan, 1986; Gilligan
et al., 1988; Porter, 1991; Davis, 1992; Larrabee, 1993). Her work was
developed initially as a critique of Kohlberg's theory of the stages in
moral development (Kohlberg, 1981, 1984). Put simply, Gilligan argued for the existence of a different moral voice to the one developed
by Kohlberg. His version had a hierarchy of moral stages constructed
in relation to the ability to reason in an abstracted fashion about justice and rights. Gilligan suggested that Kohlberg's formulation systematically positioned men as superior moral reasoners, and women as
deficient. Her different voice was based instead on the idea of an
ethic of care, responsibility, and relationships, where moral reasoning
is done and judgements arrived at contextually rather than on the basis
of universal abstract principles. She argued that the voice was empirically, but not essentially or inherently, gendered. The social conditions of women's development and women's lives, and the kinds of
activities women tend to do in their relations with others, create the

conditions for the development of an ethic of care and responsibility. 'Sensitivity to the needs of others and the assumption of responsibility for taking care lead women to attend to voices other than their own and to include in their judgement other points of view' (Gilligan, 1982, p. 16).

The importance of Gilligan's ideas for my concerns is that she is focusing attention on moral viewpoints, acts of moral reasoning and judgement which are grounded in ideas about care and responsibility, although she does not formulate these specifically in a family and kinship context. Her suggestion that women are, on the whole, more active and accomplished *care* reasoners than men clearly needs to be given serious consideration. Nevertheless, there are a number of reasons why it is unwise to take Gilligan's ideas on board wholesale. Before I discuss these, I want briefly to examine Sara Ruddick's ideas about what she calls 'maternal thinking', since many of the cautionary points about Gilligan apply also to Ruddick.

Where Gilligan's interests are in the psychology of individual moral development, Sara Ruddick's concern is more obviously grounded in philosophy, with the idea that maternal practice – the practice of mothering work – inculcates a certain kind of moral thinking in those who do it. There are three key elements in maternal practice which produce maternal thinking: preservative love, fostering of growth, and training of children. According to Ruddick, these mothering practices can in principle be done by women or men, although empirically it is usually women who do them. So she has in common with Gilligan's different voice the idea that these dimensions of moral/maternal thinking are to do with care and responsibility for others, and that they are empirically but not essentially gendered. Ruddick moves quite rapidly from her ideas about the development of maternal thinking to a more generalised argument about the possibility for a benevolent and emancipatory 'feminist maternal peace politics'[1] (Ruddick, 1989). In that sense, she also has in common with Gilligan the aim of generalising from her focus on specific forms of care and care thinking or reasoning, to the nature of care and morality in general. It is probably for this reason that, although both Gilligan and Ruddick deny that they wish to make sweeping and essentialist claims about women's inherent nature and morality, they are, nevertheless, interpreted as doing precisely that. Indeed, while Ruddick's work is clearly relevant to my concerns, particularly in its insistence that we should be interested in the activity of *thinking*, and that we should see maternal thinking as concerned with responsibility and care for others and as socially constructed through

the social practice of mothering, it has a number of further limitations
in common with Gilligan's different voice.

In fact, some of the most thoroughgoing criticisms of Gilligan and
Ruddick have centred on the way each of them uses the category *woman*
which implies, it is argued, too simple a construction of gender difference. Although both writers are strenuous (if not always convincing)
in suggesting that the moral voice and the maternal thinking which
they identify are not inherently, innately, naturally or essentially attributes of women (as opposed to men), they are perhaps less careful
to explore differences within and beyond these gender categories. Hence,
both authors have been accused of implying that their analyses apply
more universally to all women than is justified, and also of failing to
engage with other ways in which moralities based on care and responsibility might develop. As Tronto argues 'the construction of women as
moral has, throughout American history, been especially reserved for
women who are White, or native-born, and middle class'. In Tronto's
view, Gilligan's idea that women have a different moral voice fits too
well into a longstanding politics of morality which grants a form of
partial moral privilege only to some – that is, White and middle class
– women (Tronto, 1993, p. 85).

In part, these criticisms relate to methodological problems in the
work of Gilligan and Ruddick, since essentially it is being suggested
that they are generalising, or universalising, too readily from empirical work which is, in different ways, rather too limited to support such
generalisations. My first response to the methodological criticism is to
be supportive of Gilligan and Ruddick, in that at least they do attempt
to derive their analyses from empirical research – a practice which is
all too uncommon in much contemporary social theorising. Nevertheless, I think it is fair to say that many of the most interesting asser-
tions which both of them make are not well supported by empirical
argument or 'evidence', even in their own terms. Ruddick is quite candid
about this, pointing to a very thorny epistemological problem concerning how it is that researchers can 'know' what mothers are thinking,
and requesting that the reader grants epistemological credibility for
her practice of 'making it up' (Ruddick, 1989, pp. 61–4).[2]

If Ruddick and Gilligan's different versions of the construction of
gender, morality, and thinking are not fully convincing methodologi-
cally, there have also been controversies about how far they (or a
misreading of them) lend weight to conservative views about women's
moral superiority and therefore their fitness for caring. Although feminist theorists like Gilligan and Ruddick certainly need to be aware

that their ideas can be misused in a political context to justify and celebrate a division of labour between the sexes which consigns all caring responsibilities to women, it is also important to avoid what Sevenhuijsen refers to as 'a feminist discourse that equates "difference" with conservatism and opposes it to equality as sameness. It is . . . the same way of thinking that evaluates "gender" in a negative mood, as something that has to be overcome as soon as possible' (Sevenhuijsen, 1993, p. 147; see also Davis, 1992). There are other difficulties with the idea that women are always good at caring, or even that maternal thinking or an ethic of responsibility straightforwardly produces good caring, and I shall return to a discussion of these in my final section.

Joan Tronto has produced a sophisticated argument about the politics of morality which says that we should not see any moral theorising as outside the sphere of politics, and instead we should scrutinise the strategic role of moral boundaries such as that apparently drawn between morality and politics by asking, for example, 'who is included and who excluded by drawing these moral boundaries? What are the consequences of this set of moral boundaries?' (Tronto, 1993, p. 11). She analyses historically the ways in which boundaries between morality and politics have been constructed, and argues that the only way to remove ourselves from stalemates such as the sameness/difference – equality/conservatism one, is to change the boundaries which have produced them. Her agenda is thus 'to offer a vision for the good society that draws upon feminist sensibilities and upon traditional "women's morality" without falling into the strategic traps that have so far doomed this approach' (Tronto, 1993, p. 3). A discussion of how well she achieves this aim is outside the scope of this chapter, but it is important to establish that these are the intellectual and political bases of her work.

What is relevant about Tronto's work for my purposes is the concept of care which she develops, and which she proposes should form the basis of our rethinking of these moral boundaries. She begins by disentangling what she sees as four interconnected 'phases' of caring activity, namely: *caring about*, which involves recognising that care is necessary; *taking care of*, which involves working out how to respond to care needs; *care-giving*, which involves directly meeting care needs; and *care-receiving*, which involves recognising 'that the object of care will respond to the care it receives'. She says that we can connect these caring activities or practices to moral notions or qualities like attentiveness, responsibility, competence, and responsiveness (Tronto,

1993, pp. 106–7; 127–34). This approach to conceptualising care is helpful, in my view, chiefly because it sees caring as multi-faceted and involving a range of different types of activity – moral, practical, and sentient. It is a version which suggests that activity, work, thinking, and feeling are bound up together in rather complex ways around the moral practice of care, and I shall go on to argue that in this sense it has a clear resonance for family and kin relationships. However, because Tronto herself wants to theorise care and ethics of care *in general* – in other words she wants to produce a framework for understanding all caring activities, not just those which are carried out in a family or kinship context, nor indeed those which are carried out between individuals or groups of individuals – her categories of caring and the moral qualities which relate to them end up feeling rather bland. This is precisely because, in order to be applicable to all types of caring, her categories inevitably have to express only the lowest common denominator. One is left with the feeling that what she has produced is a descriptive typology rather than an analytical framework. In particular, her idea of 'care-receiving' as the response of 'the object of care to the care it receives' (which is her attempt to recognise that caring involves the 'cared for' as well as the 'carer') nevertheless conjures up an image of an extraordinarily passive receiver of care.

She has to use this terminology, because her concern with all caring activity means that receivers of care may be not only people but nations, polities, environments, and so on. However, the result is a categorisation which is wholly inadequate for exploring the significance of the personal and relational context of caring between family and kin members.

The final contribution I want to discuss in this section comes from Selma Sevenhuijsen (Sevenhuijsen, 1991, 1993). Sevenhuijsen has, in common with Tronto, a concern with care and ethics of care which is grounded in feminist political science. However, Sevenhuijsen's recent arguments about how we might understand care suggest some very fruitful possibilities both for seeing care as relational, and for keeping thinking and feeling in the analytical frame. In describing the nature of care, Sevenhuijsen argues that it is:

> a cognitive and a moral activity in itself, an idea that is difficult to grasp when care is conceptualised in the dichotomy of labour and love. Care is not just the changing of nappies, cleaning the house or looking after the elderly. Also, when we see care as an activity, it is still basically about needs: not just the 'meeting of needs', but more

relational activity
self-other

the ability to 'see' and 'hear' needs, take responsibility for them, negotiate if and how they should be met and by whom. Care is fundamentally a relational activity, in which self-other feelings and connections are central and certainly so when the caring activity concerns intimate and proximate strangers, or when caring for the self is at stake. (Sevenhuijsen, 1993, p. 142)

Sevenhuijsen's version of care as a *cognitive and moral activity*, which is not simply about meeting physical 'needs', and which is *relational*, allows what I think is the most fruitful possibility in the literature I have reviewed so far to conceptualise care for family and kin (although her arguments are developed in a wider context). She is arguing that care is not simply about feeling, neither is it simply about labour or a set of tasks. In that sense, the conceptualisation of care as labour or as love will not do.

CARING AND THE NEGOTIATION OF COMMITMENTS TO FAMILY AND KIN

Debates about philosophies of care and the moral nature of caring activity have been conducted, for the most part, outside the discipline of sociology, drawing on different intellectual traditions.[3] Nevertheless, I believe that some of the themes discussed in the previous section are indeed relevant to sociological understandings of care in relation to family and kin. In this section I want to begin to spell out how I propose to make connections between these different intellectual traditions, by introducing a discussion of the analysis of the negotiation of responsibilities and commitments between kin in Britain which I have developed jointly with my colleague Janet Finch. Our work has certainly been concerned with moral activities in a relational context, and with caring, although we have approached these issues with analytical tools which are distinct from those used by political philosophers like Sevenhuijsen and Tronto. To begin with, our work has started from an exploration of family and kin relationships, rather than from questions about care *per se*.[4]

Our primary interest is in the ways in which people take responsibility for and/or support each other, in a wide variety of senses, in family and kin relationships. We have explored the negotiation of responsibilities amongst adult kin and the workings of obligation and commitment in that context (Finch and Mason, 1993). The analysis which we have developed does not isolate caring specifically, because we are interested in a wide range of supportive (and non-supportive) family and kin relationships and exchanges; for example, financial, practical, and emotional support as well as personal care. Indeed, our data suggest both that a wide range of types of assistance and support pass between kin, and also that a wide range of kin become involved in giving, receiving, and negotiating them. So, for example, although relationships between parents and their adult children are clearly an important source of support, we have many examples of kin in more distant genealogical relationships giving and receiving help. Similarly, although there is certainly a tendency for the women in our study to have been more closely or regularly involved in personal care relationships with kin, we have many examples of men's involvement in personal care too.

Our work explores, from a variety of angles, how such assistance comes to be transacted. We reject the idea that these patterns are determined by the 'structural' positions of family members, since they cannot be explained straightforwardly by either gender or genealogy. Indeed, there is a great deal of variation in the types and amounts of support which pass between kin, which suggest that any 'structural' explanation of this kind will be inadequate. We also reject the idea that these patterns are derived from rules of family obligation, in part for the same reason, that there is too much variation in people's everyday practice. Also, however, our research explores in some detail whether or not it is possible to identify a 'normative consensus' in Britain about rules of kin support or about whether there should be a gendered division of labour in the provision of support and, in the analysis, no very clear consensus emerges (Finch and Mason, 1987, 1990, 1991).

This means that the patterns of supportive relationships which people become involved in with their relatives cannot be explained either by their structural or genealogical positions, or by the notion that they follow normative rules of obligation which spell out what they should do. Instead, we have developed a set of arguments about how responsibilities are negotiated between relatives. Central to these arguments is the concept of commitment and a framework for understanding how commitments develop between kin. We have suggested that commitments are established through processes of *negotiation* which take place in social and personal relationships, within a broader social and cultural context, over time. Negotiations, which can be implicit as well as explicit, are about more than 'material' aspects of responsibilities to kin, such as exchanges of goods, services, and support. They are also about 'moral' aspects of responsibilities and, in particular, we have argued that the ways in which negotiations are carried out have implications for people's moral identities and reputations. In this sense, exchanges of goods and services are not reckoned purely in material terms, but also have moral dimensions. An individual becomes committed to giving certain forms of help to another, or to responding positively if and when a need is perceived to arise, as a consequence of long and often complex processes of negotiation rather than, for example, because they are following a set of cultural rules of kinship obligation, or as a consequence of their gender or their genealogical position. Gender, genealogy, ethnicity, social class, and so on, are likely to be influential contexts and experiences in the process, but in ways which are not straightforward (and certainly not as though they were 'variables'). Certainly, we have observed that women more often than men (although not exclusively so) become locked into long-term commitments to relatives.

We have borrowed elements from Howard Becker's concept of commitment to help us to formulate our ideas (although Becker, 1960, does not discuss responsibilities of kinship or gender specifically). In particular, Becker argues that commitments become consolidated over time because it becomes 'too expensive' for people to withdraw from them. Our version says that some people get committed materially and morally to certain courses of action in relation to specific other people in their families and kin groups, and to withdraw would entail material or moral risks (for example, to one's reputation within one's family). This accumulation of commitment may happen gradually, but such commitments are likely to *feel* very powerful because they have apparently been developed through one's own choices, actions, and decisions, rather than having been obviously imposed from 'outside', even though negotiations do not take place in a social and cultural vacuum, and negotiators are rarely in a position of social equivalence to one another.

This analysis of the negotiation of commitments between family and kin members makes at least three contributions to my current discussions about care. First, our analysis of the ways in which commitments develop says that they are specific, negotiated, and relational. In this sense there are parallels with Sevenhuijsen's ideas that care is a relational activity, although our analysis takes us further in understanding that not only are activities performed relationally, but that commitments to care *develop* relationally. Secondly, the concept of

commitment encapsulates a variety of activities which may involve
doing physical care or supportive tasks, but also moral aspects of commitments to others. In the context of caring commitment, this suggests
that the activity of care may be multi-dimensional and cannot usefully
be subsumed under the categories of labour or love. Thirdly, and relating to the second point, our analysis implies that feeling and thinking may be important components both of the activity of care and the
relational process through which it develops. Although we do not isolate thinking and feeling specifically, because we have been concerned
with the activity of acknowledging a commitment, or behaving as though
you feel committed to a relative, our discussion suggests that feeling
and thinking are certainly relevant. For example, our analysis of negotiations over time suggests that some people become quite deeply committed to specific relatives whilst others do not and, by implication,
people are likely to *feel* more or less committed in that process. We
have suggested that commitments are likely to feel particularly strong
precisely because they have been established through a process of negotiation in relationships with other people. Furthermore, our concern
with moral as well as material aspects of negotiations suggests that we
think more is at stake than simply the material aspects of what relatives do for each other. Our analysis focuses on the negotiation of
moral identities between kin rather than people's moral feelings, and,
indeed, we have strongly rejected an overly simplistic formulation which
supposes that people have static inner feelings or hold attitudes and
beliefs which are more real than negotiated meanings, and which somehow direct their activities. However, a concern with moral aspects of
family and kinship leaves open – although in our research largely un-
explored – the relevance of the dimensions of thinking and feeling.

CARING AS SENTIENT ACTIVITY AND ACTIVE SENSIBILITY

Up to this point I have reviewed aspects of some fairly diverse bodies
of scholarship which intersect around questions about care and responsibility for others. In particular, I have tried to draw out threads which
suggest that care is a multi-dimensional activity, that it is relational
and that it involves *inter alia* morality, feeling, and thought. My aim
in this final section is to make some proposals about how we might
conceptualise these dimensions in the context of family and kin relationships.

I think we should begin by rejecting the idea that feeling, thought, mind, or emotion are inner, natural, essential states or essences of self, and by rejecting what Stanley and Wise have argued are unhelpful 'binary and oppositional notions of "the self" and its relationship to "the body" and "mind" and "emotions"' (Stanley and Wise, 1993, p. 195). Similarly, as Sevenhuijsen (1993) has argued, I think we should avoid thinking that there is a dichotomous relationship between labour and love. Instead, I want to suggest two ways of understanding care and responsibility for others in family and kin relationships which avoid these kinds of binaries and dichotomies, but which pay serious attention to the relevance of thinking and feeling in the activity of care, instead of seeing these as by-products or motivational states of mind. I am calling these *sentient activity* and *active sensibility*, and I shall suggest that although they are analytically distinct, in practice in family and kin relationships they are likely to be intricately interconnected.

In using the term 'sentient activity' I am referring deliberately to thinking and feeling as *activities*. This focus on activity is intended to move us away from the idea that thinking and feeling are merely to do with sentiment and non-activity, but also to avoid the dichotomous conclusion that sentient activity is mental *labour*, or indeed any other kind of labour. Examples of sentient activities in relation to care and responsibility for family and kin might be:

attending to . . .		needs . . .	
noticing . . .		health . . .	
hearing . . .		wellbeing . . .	of
being attuned to . . .	the	behaviours . . .	specific
seeing . . .		likes and dislikes . . .	others
constructing . . .		moods . . .	
interpreting . . .		individuality . . .	
studying . . .		character . . .	
exercising an interest in . . .		relationships . . .	

or:

thinking through . . .	
working out . . .	relationships between oneself
organising . . .	and others
planning . . .	relationships between others
orchestrating . . .	

It is possible to find many empirical examples in research on caring in family and kin relationships to suggest that these kinds of activities do get done – usually by women – and that sentient activity is a meaningful conceptualisation. In our study of commitments between family and kin, Janet Finch and I noted a tendency for some women to be seen as especially good at noticing the needs of others. The quotation below is an illustration of this. It is from a woman who is talking about support given by her adult son and daughter following a period of hospitalisation:

> Jane [daughter] seems to *know* what wants doing, and do it. I mean Jack [son] would come over and cook a meal and bring the food with him. But he hasn't much sense of reality as to what sort of meal you want. He fancies himself as a cook, I mean, he came over and brought a huge joint of meat, you know a big joint of beef and things to cook it with, all the trimmings and things. Well, when you've not been very well that isn't what you want. What do you do with all the meat that's left? You know, sort of not thinking. Whereas Jane would think what you'd like, and she's perhaps taken more note over the years as to the sort of things I would eat and like.

Another set of examples comes from Marjorie DeVault's fascinating discussion of 'feeding' the family. In material terms, feeding involves shopping for food, providing food, and cooking food in families, but in sentient terms it involves a great deal more. Her study gives close scrutiny to what I would call the sentient activities involved in shopping and cooking, such as: noticing, interpreting, and responding to the needs of others; juggling dietary requirements and individual preferences; working these into some form of shopping and eating plan often whilst shopping in relation to what provisioning choices are actually on offer; attempting to synchronise the timetables of family members in relation to eating; and orchestrating social relations around mealtimes. DeVault does a very good job of exposing these invisible activities, and points out that 'when one person takes responsibility for the work [sic], others rarely think about it. Even the one who does it – because so much of her thought about it is never shared – may not be fully aware of all that is involved' (DeVault, 1991, p. 142). Thus to outsiders, and even to oneself, the extent and nature of sentient activity taking place may be systematically underestimated or misjudged.

Of course, research on domestic and household labour has often touched on these kinds of 'servicing' activities, and indeed on emotional labour (e.g. Delphy and Leonard, 1992), but what is particularly interesting about DeVault's study is her concern that none of the words 'work', 'labour' or 'care', adequately capture the kinds of activity to which she refers (although she does, nevertheless, retain them). Some studies which identify similar activities performed in a different context also pose a challenge to conventional understandings of servicing and domestic labour. For example, in their recent study of relationships between teenagers and their parents around questions of health, Brannen *et al.* note that the mothers (and much more rarely the fathers) in their sample engaged in a lot of 'worrying' about the activities and wellbeing of their teenage children. Brannen and her colleagues see this worrying as important – not a side issue – and as activity rather than more straightforwardly as an emotional state, yet it would clearly be inappropriate to try to squash it into the conceptual straitjacket of domestic labour (Brannen *et al.*, 1994). A similar ambiguity arose in my own study, conducted some years ago, on gender relations in long-term marriages. I argued that the wives in my study took responsibility for supporting the wellbeing and health of their husbands, and specifically for smoothing their transitions into retirement. In practice, this regularly involved structuring their husbands' time, and 'having a conscience' about going out and leaving husbands at home during the day. It was premised upon fairly careful and very long-term monitoring by wives of their husbands' states of mind, health, and happiness. I struggled for words to describe this, and settled upon terms like 'worry work' and 'mental labour' which I now find inadequate (Mason, 1987, 1989a, b).

In all of these examples I have selected strands which tell us about what I now want to call sentient activity in the care and support of others, but each of the studies was also replete with examples of hard physical activity performed in that context. I am certainly not wishing to suggest that the activity of caring is predominantly sentient or cerebral, and there is a large body of evidence which points to the gruelling and exhausting physical activity which may also be involved (Finch and Groves, 1983; Ungerson, 1987; Lewis and Meredith, 1988; Qureshi and Walker, 1989; Graham, 1991; Glendinning, 1992; Twigg and Atkin, 1994). However, an overemphasis on physical activity in our definitions of care – as though care equates to physical labour – risks underplaying the significance and potentially gruelling nature of sentient activity. In practice, it is very likely, of course, that people – and the research would suggest in particular women – routinely engage in both sentient and physical caring activity.

I am arguing that the kinds of sentient activities I have identified should not be excluded from sociological scrutiny as though they were 'mere' caring thoughts, *states* of feeling, attitudes, personality traits, or even moralities which people have or hold statically and passively in relation to others. The idea that sentient activity is *activity* is too readily dismissed if we view care in what Sevenhuijsen has called the 'dichotomy of labour and love', where really only labour counts as activity. Quite simply, I want to suggest that sentient activity is neither labour nor love. My reasons for wishing to avoid a conceptualisation of sentient activity as love should be clear, as it leads us into unhelpful analytical distinctions between feeling states on the one hand and activities on the other. It also leads us to suppose that caring and responsibility for others should be viewed in the frame of only one, positive, type of feeling or emotion – namely love – whereas my conceptualisation makes no prior assumptions about connections between the activities and the *classification* of one's feelings for the other. In other words, I am referring to a way of engaging with others, or connecting with others, and with the social worlds, rather than a type of felt emotion.

I want to avoid the conceptualisation of sentient activity as labour or work for the same initial reason, that is that it suggests an unhelpful polarisation between physical activity on the one hand and feeling on the other. More than that, however, given the sociological discourse within which the notions of labour and work have been constructed and articulated, to claim this status for sentient activity means engaging with what I see in the context of my enquiry as diverting questions about whether or not the *raison d'être* of sentient activity has anything to do with economic production.

Once sentient activity is acknowledged to be activity, it also becomes clear that to a greater or lesser extent it is skilled activity which one needs training in order to be able to engage in. This means we need to confront how it is that this form of activity gets constructed, and how the skills are developed. In a variety of ways, much of the research which has a bearing on this suggests that the kinds of domestic, family, household, and bodily work which are predominantly associated with women – for example, housework, cooking, mothering, and childcare – and which are done for or in service of others, provide such a training. I think that we can accept that these types of work do give the workers the opportunity to develop skills in attentiveness to people's needs, likes, preferences, and so on. However, this is likely to be only a partial explanation of the performance of sentient activity, since it does not help us to identify other ways in which sentient activity skills might develop, nor does it tell us why some women might become sentient actors in caring relationships with relatives while others do not, nor, importantly, *why people may engage in sentient activity in caring relationships with some relatives but not others.* In other words, accounting (if partially) for the acquisition of skills does not explain why people do or do not exercise them and tells us little about why people should feel that the responsibility for exercising these skills is theirs.

In order to understand this, I think we need to see sentient activity in combination with what I am calling *active sensibility.* What I mean by active sensibility is the activity of feeling a responsibility for someone else, or a commitment to someone else. This involves taking a responsibility on board as something which is your own, which you will deal with, and I want to suggest that this involves activity of feeling. I should distinguish my version of active sensibility from the more common understanding of, for example, non-active felt sensibilities (the common usage of 'offending one's sensibilities' draws on the latter non-active form). Despite these connotations, 'sensibility' does seem to capture the essence of what I wish to describe, in the sense that I am referring to a relationally and socially constructed 'predisposition' to draw a connection between self and specific others, and to take on a responsibility to care.

The analysis which Janet Finch and I have produced of the development of commitments to kin gets close to my notion of active sensibility in the sense that it focuses on the acceptance of responsibilities for each other between kin (Finch and Mason, 1993). As I pointed out earlier, our analysis deals with the acceptance and acknowledgement of responsibilities and commitments, rather than directly confronting the activity involved in feeling a commitment, but the latter is implied (if not straightforwardly) in the former. Most important here is our point that commitments are likely to feel particularly strong, and particularly personal, precisely because they are developed through negotiations in relationships with specific others, rather than as a more passive response to, for example, one's genealogical position (for example, 'I am a daughter, therefore I have this set of responsibilities'), or to rules of kinship obligation (for example, 'it is morally appropriate to provide this response to this particular set of circumstances and needs', or 'there are cultural rules which say I ought to feel committed here') (Hochschild, 1979).

This suggests that active sensibility makes sense only in the context of the ways in which relationships and commitments get constructed. I would suggest that ideas about the development of commitments through

negotiations about moral and material aspects of kin support which
Janet Finch and I have developed are a good starting point for exploring this process of construction. Although these involve focusing on
individual relationships, they also imply that we should see these as
located within social and cultural contexts. So, for example, we have
argued that just as material constraints and opportunities shape what
responsibilities people are able to accept for their family and kin in
their negotiations, so too cultural notions of, say, what constitutes a
good family reputation for a woman or a man will have some influence on (although will not directly determine) negotiations about moral
reputations and identities in families.

CONCLUSION

In conclusion then, I am suggesting that if we reconceptualise these
aspects of care as sentient activity and active sensibility, we move
beyond dichotomies between caring for and caring about, or loving
and labouring, and we join those scholars who are beginning to rethink conventional sociological distinctions between activity, thought
and feeling (see, for example, Stanley and Wise, 1993). It is vital to
grasp the point that sentient activity and active sensibility cannot be
equated with the notion of caring for, since such an equation both
misses the point that these are activities not feeling states, and plays
into the hands of those who would misinterpret the argument to be
saying that caring about someone (a feeling state) is as good as caring
for them (a form of labour, in the original interpretation).

Central to my argument is the idea that sentient activities and active
sensibilities are developed and carried out relationally, with specific
relatives or family members, within specific social and cultural contexts. This locates my arguments within a sociology of personal relationships, rather than a sociology of work or of care. I have argued
that a relational understanding of these aspects of care is needed to
explain both the nature of this caring activity (especially that it is about
connection with specific others), and the active feeling of responsibility which encourages some people to exercise sentient activity skills
in support of some others. It also provides us with a more sensitive
mechanism for exploring the relevance of gender and other dimensions of social experience and context, than a focus on these as variables, determining factors or even cultural prescriptions permits.

A relational approach, grounded in a sociology of personal relationships, has certain implications for the wider significance of my arguments, since essentially I am suggesting that sentient activities and active sensibilities in relation to family and kin are constructed and performed parochially, in specific relationships albeit within social and cultural contexts. This means that I could not possibly argue, neither would I wish to, that this particular process underpins the construction of gender difference, or gendered moralities, more generally. Sentient skills developed in this way are not necessarily and inevitably transferable to different contexts such as care of other people, or care of the environment, or world peace, as for example Ruddick would have us believe. Someone who regularly notices and attends to the needs of specific others cannot automatically be regarded as being able or willing to do this in general, for any other, although they may of course have a head start over those who have never done this for anyone. My formulation of active sensibility suggests, on the contrary, that this activity of feeling a responsibility is unlikely to get transferred wholesale to other contexts and relationships. If, therefore, it is observed that women do appear to care more than men about/for other people, the environment, and world peace, then we either need to seek explanations which are not grounded in parochial family and kin responsibilities, or to demonstrate how these different types of caring become connected. Even in the context of family and kin, I think we should resist any broad brush or universal interpretations of the social patterning of sentient activity and active sensibility if they take no account of the different relational and cultural experiences of social actors. It is through the media of specific relational contexts that we should understand and explore the significance of, for example, cultural and gender differences. Only in this way can we produce a sensitive analysis of the ways in which gender relations, caring relations, and family relations intersect *relationally* to produce differences between women, for they surely exist, as well as between women and men, and indeed between men.

NOTES

1. In this sense Ruddick's work can be viewed as connected to feminist standpoint epistemology, which suggests that women's experiences and in particular the types of labour they perform for others helps to develop in them a particular – superior – world view, and a privileged epistemological

position. Different versions of these types of ideas have been produced by, for example, Hartsock (1983), Rose (1983, 1986), and Smith (1988).
2. Again, Ruddick's arguments here derive from feminist standpoint epistemology.
3. The most notable exception is the 'sociology of emotion', which includes some important ideas about emotional labour, emotion work, and the sociological analysis of feeling, especially love (see, especially, Hochschild, 1975, 1979, 1983; Bertilsonn, 1986; James, 1989; Cancian, 1990; Duncombe and Marsden, 1993; Jackson, 1993). However, for the most part this work does not engage with the themes I have drawn out of debates on ethics of care – especially the idea of care as moral activity – and instead focuses on the labour involved in managing or regulating other people's feelings, or on the analysis of feelings of affection and love, especially in hetero-sexual relationships. Some of this work appears to draw an implicit distinction between 'real feelings' which are supposedly not amenable to sociological analysis, and emotional behaviours or discourses, which are. As I go on to argue, I think this distinction is unhelpful in the analysis of care.
4. This work has been published in various forms (see, especially, Finch and Mason, 1993), and is based on an ESRC funded project called 'Family Obligations: Social Construction and Social Policy', grant no. GOO232197, 1985–9. The study had a two-stage research design, involving: (a) a large scale survey (978 respondents, randomly sampled) designed to ascertain whether or not there was a consensus about what relatives should do for each other. The survey used vignettes which posed hypothetical situations concerning third parties, and invited respondents to indicate what should be done in those situations; (b) a qualitative study involving 120 interviews with 88 people (theoretically sampled), 40 of whom had a spouse or cohabiting partner in the study and 58 of whom had kin other than a spouse in the study. These interviews were semi-structured, and were designed to generate data about people's own family responsibilities and commitments in practice.

REFERENCES

Arber, S. and Gilbert, N. (1989) 'Men: the Forgotten Carers', *Sociology*, **23**: 1, pp. 111–18.
Becker, H. S. (1960) 'Notes on the Concept of Commitment', *American Journal of Sociology*, **66**: pp. 32–40.
Bertilsonn, M. (1986) 'Love's Labour Lost? A Sociological View', *Theory, Culture and Society*, **3**: 2, pp. 19–35.
Brannen, J., Dodd, K., Oakley, A. and Storey, P. (1994) *Young People, Health and Family Life* (Milton Keynes: Open University Press).
Cancian, F. M. (1990) *Love in America: Gender and Self-development* (Cambridge: Cambridge University Press).
Dalley, G. (1988) *Ideologies of Caring: Rethinking Community and Collectivism* (London: Macmillan).
Davis, K. (1992) 'Toward a Feminist Rhetoric: The Gilligan Debate Revisited',

Women's Studies International Forum, **15**: 2, pp. 219–31.

Delphy, C. and Leonard, D. (1992) *Familiar Exploitation: A New Analysis of Marriage in Contemporary Western Societies* (Cambridge: Polity Press).

DeVault, M. L. (1991) *Feeding the Family: The Social Organisation of Caring as Gendered Work* (London: University of Chicago Press).

Duncombe, J. and Marsden, D. (1993) 'The Gender Division of Emotion and "Emotion Work": A Neglected Aspect of Sociological Discussion of Heterosexual Relationships', *Sociology*, **27**: 1, pp. 221–41.

Finch, J. and Groves, D. (eds) (1983) *A Labour of Love: Women, Work and Caring* (London: Routledge & Kegan Paul).

Finch, J. and Mason, J. (1987) 'Gender and Family Obligations', unpublished paper presented to Lancaster Women's Studies Research Group, January.

Finch, J. and Mason, J. (1990) 'Gender, Employment and Responsibilities to Kin', *Work, Employment and Society*, **4**: 3, pp. 349–67.

Finch, J. and Mason, J. (1991) 'Obligations of Kinship: Is There Normative Agreement?', *British Journal of Sociology*, **42**: 3, pp. 344–68.

Finch, J. and Mason, J. (1993) *Negotiating Family Responsibilities* (London: Routledge).

Gilligan, C. (1982) *In a Different Voice: Psychological Theory and Women's Development* (London: Harvard University Press).

Gilligan, C. (1986) 'Reply', *Signs*, **11**: pp. 324–33.

Gilligan, C., Ward, J. and Taylor, J. (eds) (1988) *Mapping the Moral Domain* (Cambridge: Harvard University Press).

Glendinning, C. (1992) *The Costs of Informal Care: Looking Inside the Household* (London: HMSO).

Graham, H. (1983) 'Caring: A Labour of Love?', in J. Finch and D. Groves (1983), op. cit.

Graham, H. (1991) 'The Concept of Caring in Feminist Research: The Case of Domestic Service', *Sociology*, **25**: 1, pp. 61–78.

Hartsock, N. C. M. (1983) 'The Feminist Standpoint: Developing the Ground for a Specifically Feminist Historical Materialism', in S. Harding and M. B. Hintikka (eds) *Discovering Reality: Feminist Perspectives on Epistemology, Metaphysics, Methodology and Philosophy of Science* (Dordrecht: D. Reidel).

Harding, S. (1986) *The Science Question in Feminism* (Milton Keynes: Open University Press).

Hochschild, A. R. (1975) 'The Sociology of Feeling and Emotion: Selected Possibilities', in M. Milkman and R. Kanter (eds) *Another Voice* (New York: Anchor).

Hochschild, A. R. (1979) 'Emotion Work, Feeling Rules and Social Structure', *American Journal of Sociology*, **85**: pp. 551–75.

Hochschild, A. R. (1983) *The Managed Heart: The Commercialisation of Human Feeling* (London: University of California Press).

Jackson, S. (1993) 'Even Sociologists Fall in Love: An Exploration in the Sociology of Emotions', *Sociology*, **17**: 2, pp. 201–20.

James, N. (1989) 'Emotional Labour: Skill and Work in the Social Regulation of Feelings', *The Sociological Review*, **37**: 1, pp. 15–42.

Kohlberg, L. (1981) *Essays on Moral Development*, vol. 1 (San Francisco: Harper & Row).

Kohlberg, L. (1984) *Essays on Moral Development*, vol. 2 (New York: Harper & Row).

Land, H. and Rose, H. (1985) 'Compulsory Altruism for some or an Altruistic Society for All?', in P. Bean, J. Ferris and D. Whynes (eds) *In Defence of Welfare* (London: Tavistock).

Larrabee, M. J. (ed.) (1993) *An Ethic of Care: Feminist and Interdisciplinary Perspectives* (London: Routledge).

Lewis, J. and Meredith, B. (1988) *Daughters who Care: Daughters Caring for Mothers at Home* (London: Routledge & Kegan Paul).

Mason, J. (1987) 'Gender Inequality in Long Term Marriages', unpublished PhD thesis, University of Kent.

Mason, J. (1989a) 'No Peace for the Wicked: Older Married Women and Leisure', in M. Talbot and E. Wimbush (eds) *Relative Freedoms* (Milton Keynes: Open University Press).

Mason, J. (1989b) 'Reconstructing the Public and the Private: The Home and Marriage in Later Life', in G. Allan and G. Crow (eds) *Home and Family: Creating the Domestic Sphere* (Basingstoke: Macmillan).

Porter, E. J. (1991) *Women and Moral Identity* (Sydney: Allen & Unwin).

Qureshi, H. and Walker, A. (1989) *The Caring Relationship: Elderly People and their Families* (Basingstoke: Macmillan).

Rose, H. (1983) 'Hand, Brain and Heart: Towards a Feminist Epistemology for the Sciences', *Signs*, **9**: pp. 73–90.

Rose, H. (1986) 'Beyond Masculinist Realities: A Feminist Epistemology for the Sciences', in R. Bleier (ed.) *Feminist Approaches to Science* (New York: Pergamon Press).

Ruddick, S. (1989) *Maternal Thinking: Towards a Politics of Peace* (London: The Women's Press).

Sevenhuijsen, S. (1991) 'The Morality of Feminism', *Hypatia*, **6**: 2, pp. 173–91.

Sevenhuijsen, S. (1993) 'Paradoxes of Gender: Ethical and Epistemological Perspectives on Care in Feminist Political Theory', *Acta Politica*, **2**: pp. 131–49.

Smith, D. (1988) *The Everyday World as Problematic: A Feminist Sociology* (Milton Keynes: Open University Press).

Stanley, L. and Wise, S. (1993) *Breaking Out Again: Feminist Ontology and Epistemology* (London: Routledge).

Thomas, C. (1993) 'De-constructing Concepts of Care', *Sociology*, **27**: 4, pp. 649–69.

Tronto, J. (1993) *Moral Boundaries: A Political Argument for an Ethic of Care* (London: Routledge).

Twigg, J. and Atkin, K. (1994) *Carers Perceived: Policy and Practice in Informal Care* (Buckingham: Open University Press).

Ungerson, C. (1987) *Policy is Personal: Sex, Gender and Informal Care* (London: Tavistock).

Ungerson, C. (ed.) (1990) *Gender and Caring: Work and Welfare in Britain and Scandinavia* (Hemel Hempstead: Wheatsheaf).

Waerness, K. (1984a) 'The Rationality of Caring', *Economic and Industrial Democracy*, **5**: pp. 185–211.

Waerness, K. (1984b) 'Caring as Women's Work in the Welfare State', in H. Holter (ed.) *Patriarchy in a Welfare Society* (Oslo: Universitetsforlaget).

2 The Political Economy of Romance: Popular Culture, Social Divisions and Social Reconstruction in Wartime

PATRICIA ALLATT

INTRODUCTION

Women's magazines and similar forms of popular culture have been variously conceived as forms of escapism, a means of disarming challenge to the *status quo* through the vicarious satisfaction of needs and desires, or, in the case of women's magazines, a paradoxical format embodying women's work and leisure.

As escapist literature, women's magazines are seen as a means whereby their readers, predominantly women, can mentally suspend themselves from the humdrum and drudgery of everyday life, a view reflecting what Giddens (1992, p. 45) calls 'the counter-factual thinking of the deprived'. Thompson (1988) similarly interprets the significance a woman attaches to soap opera, watched 'in the context of the family household [as that of enabling her] to distance herself from domestic demands, ... from the social relations in which she is embedded, ... and to experience vicariously a form of pleasure or control which is absent from her ordinary life'. Even when the hint of challenge appears, the focus remains on escapism. Thus, drawing upon Radway's (1984) study of romantic novels, he notes, that 'satisfying needs and desires in the mode of the imaginary may also disarm critical impulses and reconcile her to the status quo' (Thompson, 1988, p. 378); while Buswell (1989) sees magazines as providing escape from reality or superficial enjoyment whilst readers remain cynical about the message projected.

In contrast, writers such as Winship (1978, p. 137) draw attention to the real and mundane in women's magazines, highlighting the paradox within their format of stories and practical advice as one which simultaneously reflects the family as a place of leisure and renewal whilst constituting the location of work for married women.

37

This chapter takes up the contradictions posed by the real and the imaginary other ways. It shows how the paradox of romance (or the imaginary satisfaction of needs and desires) and the realities of the everyday world are differently combined in two women's magazines, *True Romances* and *Good Housekeeping* (hereafter, when extracts from these magazines are cited, the abbreviations *TR* and *GM*, respectively, will be employed), to meet different challenges to the *status quo*. It reveals how the dualities and paradoxes, implicitly or explicitly present in the critiques noted above, place women's magazines in the realm of ideology. In this sense, their content of romantic stories and other items is highly political, concerned with the power relations of domination and subordination between the sexes and the distribution of resources. This chapter examines this political theme by focusing on mechanisms which sustained the tenacity of the traditional single-role family structure of bread-winner husband and home based wife–mother during the Second World War, a time when inequality was under challenge. It shows how the elements of a familistic ideology were differently honed to meet challeges arising from different parts of the social structure.

MESSAGES

As Molotoch (1975) observed, power is a process, requiring constant maintenance in the routines of daily life. Ideology, moreover, is not a unitary concept, but made up of diverse and contradictory elements (Althusser, 1972). In these terms, women's magazines fall within a wider orchestration of a familistic ideology, facets of which are embedded in the explicit and implicit messages which bombard individuals with precepts of normality and how normal life should be lived.

Such messages emanate from many sources – for example, the law, social policy, education, children's literature, and marriage manuals – and the familism infusing them is well documented (Allatt, 1981a). They also carry behavioural sanctions whose effect is problematic but whose variety and potential are recognised in their type, severity, authority, and level of consciousness. For example, the law and social policy (Allatt, 1981b; Land, 1976), with recourse to financial penalty or reward and ultimately deprivation of freedom, draw upon different and heavier sanctions than do religious tracts or children's comics operating at the level of cultural consciousness. Thus, while the state can exercise legal and economic controls over behaviour, the stories, advice, articles, and advertisements in women's magazines appeal to internal feeling states, insidiously constructing frames of reference which orientate the reader to particular ways of interpreting events and behaviour.[1] Their power lies in their apparent triviality; for they fuel those implicit background assumptions regarded as 'too true to warrant discussion' but which inform 'more coherent meanings' (Douglas, 1975, pp. 3, 4), and that category of discourse which Barthes (1973, p. 11) describes as *'what-goes-without-saying'* [italics in original].

Messages are directed at different audiences; for within an ideology the representation of normality is not an undifferentiated entity (Althusser, 1972). Hence, to have any hope of impact, a message must engage with its audience's social world, as editors of women's magazines are well aware (Grieve, 1964). Consequently, since the social circumstances and experience of societal groups differ – by age, gender, stage in the life course, domestic career, social class – so messages must be tailored. As Gramsci (1971) notes, within an embracing ideology the content of messages is differently honed to sustain and shape the different common senses of the various strata of a society.

This chapter illuminates the place of romance in the cultural reproduction of the traditional power structures of gender and class relations during the Second World War, a time when underlying assumptions were exposed by the war effort and inequality was publicly challenged on many fronts. It first describes the factors which called the *status quo* to account and explains the selection of the two magazines and the method of analysis. It then shows how the challenges grounded in the different social positions and circumstances of the readerships were met within the texts of the magazines.

CHALLENGES TO TRADITIONAL POWER STRUCTURES

In her history of women's magazines, White (1970) excludes the period of the Second World War because of its abnormal and hence, she argues, unrepresentative character. Here, in contrast, that abnormality provides the theoretical and methodological basis for selection. During these six years, 1939–45, the traditional inegalitarian structures of class and gender were challenged both materially and symbolically. Consequently, far from being a period to be dismissed because unrepresentative, it is one in which political processes are made visible for exploration.

Periods of social disruption dislodge individuals from their social niches (Kornhauser, 1960). For the single-role family structure of bread-winner husband and home-based wife–mother, the upheaval of war exposed the material and conceptual frailty of the boundaries between the masculine, public domain of war, work, and politics and the femi-nine, private domain of home and family.

The war atomised the family unit through conscription, women's war work, child care provision outside the home, and evacuation, a situation exacerbated by bomb damage to housing stock. Further, fol-lowing the Blitz of 1940, the provision of communal feeding in local authority British Restaurants and industrial canteens, and the expan-sion of the school meals service (Price, 1981), encroached upon, drawing into the public domain, that function *par excellence* – wifely service in the provision of meals – which underpinned the ideology, indeed the spirituality, of the family and the power relations within it (Allatt, 1981a; Murcott, 1983).

This dislocation was accompanied by changes in the objective experi-ences of women, new patterns of daily life which were conducive to, at least, a questioning of hitherto accepted ways and assumptions. Demands by the war economy for women, and appreciation of them, in formerly male-defined jobs (Douie, 1949; Bullock, 1967) and en-forced separation from husbands in the armed forces or working away from home in key occupations, gave women a new or renewed experi-ence of social and economic independence which many had not ex-pected to taste again once married. Moreover, irrespective of entry into the labour force, women had to assume responsiblity for family affairs previously held to be the sphere of men. Additionally, some experienced a new independence in the regularity, irrespective of its adequacy, of the dependents' allowances compulsorily deducted from servicemen's pay.

Most critically, this dislocation was set within a moral context of egalitarianism, for the war embraced armed forces and civilians alike. Hence, to engender commitment to 'the people's war', one war aim addressed the old inequalities. It was symbolically encapsulated in the term 'Post-War Reconstruction' and the image of a better post-war society 'for which we were fighting' (*Picture Post*, 1943; Directorate of Army Education, 1944, p. 65). A sense of egalitarianism infused the national debate, largely in terms of class but also for many women's organisations and individual women, in terms of gender (Beveridge, 1942, Appendix G; Allatt, 1981a; *Picture Post*, 10 May 1941, 14 Novem-ber 1942, 28 November 1942, etc.). Moreover, as Phyllis Bentley (1943) noted in her pamphlet 'Women in the Post War World', written for the Forces' Education Programme, the very logic of the concept of equality connotes its extension to women (Allatt, 1983). Such a configuration of factors renders these years a laboratory in which to explore the tenacity of cultural values and social structures in times of apparent social change.

THE RESEARCH

Women's magazines are directed at discrete audiences and the two here were selected to highlight contrasts. The readerships differed by social class, education, age, and stage in the family life-course. *Good Housekeeping* was aimed at the educated, middle-class, married woman and *True Romances* at young, predominantly unmarried, northern, working-class mill girls.

However, notwithstanding their contrasting economic and social worlds, the lives of these readerships were embedded in a shared and overarching familistic ideology. This raised two questions: first, within this commonality what distinctive threats did the different social milieu pose to the traditional family structure and, second, what distinguished their accommodation in the two texts?

Every issue of the two magazines was read for the six months immediately following the Beveridge Report of November 1942[2] and nonfiction for a further six months up to November 1943. All contents,[3] excluding the advertisements,[4] were thematically analysed for items which, however remotely, might have some bearing on the marital relationship at any of its stages. Since an element might appear infrequently, and the aim being to capture the entirety of the familism a magazine presented to its readers, sampling was rejected. For the same reason, an element was accorded the same importance in the analysis whether appearing once or many times.

The following shows how romance was articulated for each audience, tailoring familism to their different circumstances in ways that lent support to the traditional social divisions of class and gender. Taking Giddens (1992) definition of romance as 'the creation of a mutual narrative biography' the chapter first describes the readerships and then the processes within the romantic stories, associated articles, and advice as they construct the shared futures of these women with their men.

TRUE ROMANCES

Two surveys of the period (Spring-Rice, 1939; Slater and Woodside, 1951) and Jephcott's (1942, 1948) studies of the reading habits of girls between the ages of 14 and 20 give insight into the lives of the readers of *True Romances*. Jephcott describes the poverty and general economic insecurity in which working-class girls grew up, in the shadow of the economic depression of the 1930s, and their paucity of individual possessions. The lives of their mothers and older sisters offered models of marital and family relationships that were harsh and unenviable in the constant struggle against poverty, models graphically described in the surveys of the 1930s and 1940s (Spring-Rice, 1939; Slater and Woodside, 1951). Although these girls might wish to be, as one 14-year-old expressed it, 'a lady with of course the means' (Jephcott, 1942, p. 38), they could only vaguely hope that their lives would be better than their mothers. Yet marriage was imminent, many marrying before the age of 21.[5] Seen by both girls and boys as a full-time career for a girl, girls only contemplated working after marriage, not for a belief in the value of their job or personal independence, but 'if a husband's pay isn't enough' or to put a 'good home together'. Gendered inequalities, moreover, were woven into the texture of their lives.

> She grows up in the knowledge that the boy does not do any housework, has better pay and more pocket money than they have and they accept its concomitant that the woman is an inferior person to the man. (Jephcott, 1942, p. 39)

In addition to poverty's effects on the marriage relationship were its ravishes upon health, physique, and beauty. Thus Spring-Rice (1939, p. ix) writes:

> It is often heartbreaking to see how rapidly a pretty, attractive girl grows old after a few years of marriage. She loses her looks and ceases to take pride in her appearance; minor ailments are neglected, her temper frayed, and household worries weigh unnecessarily heavily.

This fate contrasts with the time and effort young girls devote to their personal appearance, and the belief they hold of the priority boys give to physical attractiveness, as well as its implicit economic potential.

[T]he 'poor' girl's personal appearance is her main stock-in-trade. Her face literally *is* her fortune: and a girl can more quickly be a success through this than by her job. (Jephcott, 1948, p. 63; italics in original)

Yet Slater and Woodside (1951) note how men took an ambivalent attitude towards physical attractiveness in women once they are wives.

As well as the toll poverty exacts, these studies also point to women's role in the mediation of male work identity. While, for working-class girls, an appropriate marriage is one to a good provider, Jephcott voices concern about girls' prejudice against certain types of male work. '[T]heir pervasive selective influence against the traditional occupation' (Jephcott, 1948, p. 80) and the social inferiority both girls and boys attach to pit work are seen as raising wider social and economic problems.

Themes and Strategies

Not unexpectedly, against this background the stories in *True Romances* exhibit strong elements of escapism: handsome heroes apparently unattainable but eventually won; anti-heroes and anti-heroines ultimately defeated; independent, beautiful heroines as well as modest ones rewarded with love.

Yet a striking feature of these texts is the dominance and pervasiveness of economic themes, reflecting the survey findings. Unsurprisingly, given the need to 'speak' to the readership, such themes in women's magazines, and the neglect of the structural location of poverty and unemployment, have been noted by others (Carter, 1977; Fowler, 1979). The texts, however, also contain what has hitherto been overlooked – a dense interweaving of economic, familistic, and romantic themes which draw a host of elements into a distinctive configuration. Economic themes include stories which variously focus on the desire to marry a rich man, types of wealth, contrasts between miser and spendthrift, advantages of security versus romance, economic irresponsibility and the hollowness of economic achievement. There are comments on money as a trust, pensions, rejection of riches, abhorrence of debt, disconnected meters, unpaid bills, and families short of food and clothes; stories of more affluent main characters are enacted against a hinterland of the poor and humble: the gardener's family, the slum evacuee, families in desperate need of medical attention.

In the autobiographical form these narratives take, economic strands are interwoven with such familistic elements as age of marriage, sex, beauty, incest, sexual rivalry, illegitimacy, love, romantic and domestic violence, and a range of female stereotypes. The thrust is two-fold. Messages are not confined to persuading women to accept the harsh circumstances of their lives as Carter (1977) suggests. The texts also, through a model of female behaviour, construct a specific type of male worker, retaining them in their class position as a supply for the economic system. This is done in two ways: first by ensuring a pool of women prepared to marry working-class men on low wages, and, second, by using women's domesticity to mediate the work ethic of the working-class male.

The cultural reproduction of this working-class male is wrought by controlling women at two stages of the life-course: at the stage of marital choice and then within marriage. The first set of controls addresses the contradictions and threats posed by poverty, romance, and women's rational economic behaviour in choice of marriage partner. The second controls women within marriage in circumstances of poverty by exalting the domestic division of labour. The following examines each of these stages of the domestic career.

Choosing a Mate

Notwithstanding the apparent acceptance of marriage's inevitability, and given the models of marriage surrounding them, rational economic behaviour would dictate that girls adopt strategies to escape this fate, especially when such rejection is supported by the idea of romance itself. For a major threat to familism lies in the contradiction between the ideal and the real world. It is latent in the economic themes listed above, the mean economies and hurtful poverty of marriage, the early loss of youthfulness, the routine drudgery, monotony, and the dullness of husbands and the married state.

The contradiction, however, is countered in several ways. One is to surround the married state with mystery, whose riddle can only be solved by entering that state itself. Thus, marriage to a poor man 'would mean the same economies my parents practiced, the same hurtful poverty my two married sisters lived in'. 'Love dies in poverty', argues one young man. 'Let them [her sisters] have their stodgy unexciting men, if they looked no further for romance . . . and their dull and boring married lives' (*TR*, 30 May 1943, pp. 22, 23).

Yet, in ways bewildering to the narrators of these stories, 'scant'

suppers stretch to accommodate an unexpected guest, 'rare and beautiful marriages [are] completely happy in spite of not much money, not
much security, and lots of hard work'. 'Dangers of marriage and the
difficulties of life' are juxtaposed with the spirituality of windows in
the setting sun, 'which bloomed like beacons in the gathering dusk,
beacons of home and hearth, love and family devotion' (*TR*, 29 May
1943, p. 40).

In this accommodation of ideal and the real world, romance itself
undergoes conversion. Romantic love, a key component of our culture
but which raises contradictions within the ideology of familism, is recognised in magazine and story titles and retained in some of the characters' married lives. Yet marital choice cannot rest on this alone.

> Could I hope to build a real marriage out of deep affection?. . .
> I tried desperately to sell myself the idea that second best – the
> loving relationship that should exist between Ricky and me, a home,
> children – were better far better than nothing at all . . . something
> inside me that had been terribly young and honest and idealistic,
> died a secret bitter death. . . . I knew – and I'd always known – that
> I was not one of the lucky, level headed people in the world who
> could learn to love a man.   (*TR*, 26 May 1943, pp. 33, 34)

This heroine is released from the choice. Another, however, by rejecting the path of 'settling down to a safe comfortable life' finds
herself on one leading to illegitimacy, potential incest, and attempted
murder. It is this case which directs attention to the concept of female
economic rationalism.

Denial of Economic Rationalism

Despite the poverty in which they lived, escape through rational economic behaviour is denied these girls. Logically, the avenues holding
the promise of greater economic security lie in marriage out of one's
class, out of one's age group or personal economic and occupational
ambition. Yet these are tacitly forbidden categories; all three under-
mine an ideal model of the family which promotes marriage to the
working class male and are accordingly dealt with.

Some heroines, wanting 'more than a steady provider', who refuse
to live in poverty, are determined to 'fall in love with a rich man'
(one in order to look after parents) and are not prepared to put up
with the life their parents led. They look for this to be tempered by

romance and 'to be swept off their feet', but while some marriages are of this kind, such good fortune does not fall to those who actively seek it. Moreover, the marriages that are condoned are to men of a similar age. The economically independent gold-digger who makes wealthy men the basis of her income and comfortable life style forfeits true love; and the girl who contemplates marrying a man old enough to be her father nearly ends up doing just that.[6]

Where economic ambition depends upon sexual conquest, a woman's key resource is her beauty. But cultivation of this, as well as cultivation of personal, individualistic skills, are hedged with warnings. Men might find beautiful, talented girls fun, but will marry the retiring plain ones – a reminder of the ephemeral nature of beauty and a warning not to invest too much in this fragile commodity, so easily destroyed by domestic life. Marriage, however, is the imperative, and even the economic independence of professional women cannot compensate for that indefinable loss accompanying singlehood, culturally bolstered by rejection of the 'scrawny old maid'.

Marriage and Transformations

On marriage, the high profile given to the denial of economic rationality is superseded by the sexual division of labour and acceptance of the appropriate conjugal pattern. Again, directives come into play.

A deep sense of shock assails these starry eyed heroines on realising what marriage to a low wage earner entails. Reik (1965, p. 20), from a psychoanalytic perspective, writes, 'Women's task in the field of love is, in reality, twofold: To get men and to keep them', and this, indeed is a theme in the stories. From this evidence, however, it could equally be argued that the problem for men (and society) is to get women to choose appropriate men and to keep women within marriage once they discover what it is like:

> Working like a slave all day. . . . I thought I'd go mad with the continual round of cleaning, cooking, washing, ironing and other chores. There was not time for glamour or good times. There didn't even seem to be time for love. . . . Was this marriage? If it was I wondered why they called it the exalted state. (*TR*, 23 April 1943, pp. 14, 15)

> Yes, it was our home but I was beginning to hate it. I felt like something caged with clipped and crippled wings against the bars. (*TR*, 8 January 1943, p. 15)

You chose this life, and then you set yourself against it. Why you chose it I don't know. (*TR*, 8 January 1943, p. 42)

A baby – to thwart my plans for escape. (*TR*, 23 April 1943, p. 16)

I'm old, worn out, hideous. That's what your farm has done to me. (*TR*, 8 January 1943, p. 42)

I didn't intend to forfeit beauty for a yoke of bondage; it was too great a price to ask of anyone! (*TR*, 23 April 1943, p. 36)

Fowler (1979, p. 106) argues that such reflections of the real world permit identification deriving from the everyday life with which the reader must struggle, and inspire a desire to complete the story to see how they are resolved. Romantic love, she argues, is frequently the mainspring of these stories because it bears the promise that individuals can, together, transcend the structural contradiction. Such mutual attempts to meet the problem are certainly found in the stories of *True Romances*. They are, however, not confined to mutual endeavours but are accompanied by controlling mechanisms directed at women.

Married women experience a series of transformations. First, women realise the errors of their ways through a 'Damascus' experience, when the scales fall from their eyes. They see the moral rightness of their restricted domestic role and its purpose in their guardianship of a fragile male work ethic. They recognise that their appropriate domestic contribution sustains a willing male worker, and in some cases will change an irresponsible male into one. Thus a wife (in this case a middle-class wife in a marriage which had suffered economically because the husband had lost the will to work) overcomes both her desire for romantic togetherness and her rejection of married domestic drudgery.

This is my home, I thought. Tomorrow, John will leave me in the morning to go to his own business which he has firmly established, tomorrow evening he will come back to me. He has his work and I have mine. I put my apron on singing as I went. (*TR*, 18 March 1943, p. 35)

There are, however, more overt controls. A less rosy picture than the one above is offered by Giddens (1992). For he notes that once romance has gone, partners, especially where divorce is difficult, become reconciled to long-term marriage though it might mean years of unhappiness. And, although not particularly rewarding, an effective marriage 'could be sustained by a division of labour between the sexes, with the domain of the husband that of paid work and the wife that of the home' (Giddens, 1992, p. 46). What remain unexplained, however, are the mechanisms through which this division itself is achieved and sustained, particularly important in a context of structural and physical inequality.

Thus the second transformation of note is that of physical power in the form of sexual violence – from the romantic violence of courtship to the domestic violence of marriage. In these stories the romantic violence of courtship signifies affection, when 'strong hands bite deeply into [women's] shoulders', or when a heroine speaks of 'lips pressing again and again over mine assuring me with their violence as his words had failed to do' (*TR*, 25 March 1943, p. 35). Marriage, however, can transform this into explicit domestic violence should wives reject the domestic or sexual services they are expected to provide. 'Steve caught my arms in an iron grip and shook me. His face was dark and congested. A little forked vein sprang out on his forehead' (*TR*, 8 January 1943, p. 42). Moreover, the absence of domestic work itself endangers marriage. A bored wife venturing outside the home flies back to the haven offered by a dull husband and takes on domestic tasks (hitherto performed by domestic help) to escape the sexual violence threatened by predatory males in the outside world.

The third transformation is the two-dimensional displacement of beauty – from outer to inner and structural to personal. The fragility of beauty was noted earlier. Real beauty, however, as defined here, is not external and physical but an inner quality cultivated through devotion to domestic duties. Yet if, as de Beauvoir (1949) argues, a woman's identity is intimately linked with her physical appearance, and this is viewed as a measure of her intrinsic value, loss of beauty means loss of both identity and worth. In these stories such physical loss is attributed, accompanied by moral overtones, to personal failure rather than as inherent in the structural demands of a woman's life. Such physical and structural displacement, a key technique in the workings of an ideology, is metaphorically encoded (Brandes, 1981) in the idiom 'letting yourself go'.

I've worked like a horse in this place, and, instead of appreciation I have to listen to insults. . . . I looked pretty before I married you. But look at me now! I've stood all I'm going to! I'm going away! 'Well!', Dick shouted, 'Whose fault is it if you can't find time to be a real wife? Who asked you to let yourself go to seed? You should have married a rich man who had money to burn'. (*TR*, 23 April 1943, p. 36)

In sum, the interweaving of economic, romantic and familistic themes for a poor working-class female audience produces a complex model of familistic behaviour deeply related to an economic hierarchy and a gendered society. Dismissing economic rationality and promoting domestic labour through a series of controlling mechanisms comprise the dynamic sustaining a male work ethic and keeps both men and women in their place.

GOOD HOUSEKEEPING

The readers of *Good Housekeeping* present different challenges to traditional familism and the power relations of gender. Poverty threatened the ideal family structure amongst the readership of *True Romances*; for the middle-class readers of *Good Housekeeping* the challenge arose from the logic of egalitarianism and the changing social patterns of wartime. This audience, moreover, was educated; articulate feminists, voicing these issues in a range of public arenas, came from this class. It was an audience, therefore, that had to be wooed through an apparently reasoned and balanced argument.

A further aspect of social change relevant to middle-class women, was the decline in the number of domestic servants (only partly due to their absorption into war work). It meant there had to be a greater involvement of middle-class women in domestic work in the home. *Good Housekeeping* itself started publication to address this change, attempting to give housewifery a professional underpinning.

On first reading, *Good Housekeeping* seemed liberal and educational. Unlike *True Romances*, which included little non-fiction, *Good Houskeeping*, carried both romantic stories and several regular feature articles. Moreover, through both fiction and features it alerted its readers to the social disruption of war, its challenge to the old order and the debates about post-war reconstruction. The flavour is reflected in extended pieces on, for example, social insurance, evacuation, housing, education, and army training.

Within this ambience of societal and personal change, the texts convey a sense of individual engagement in a wide-ranging public debate and the possibilty of achieving planned change for a better post-war world through the efforts of the individual citizen. The mood is captured in an editorial on the Beveridge Report on social insurance, exhorting women to read and discuss the report and accompanied by a picture of a woman reading it:

> 'Freedom from want cannot be forced on a democracy or given to a democracy. It must be won by them.' Are you reading, thinking, talking, *working* to win this freedom and more particularly to achieve the aims of the Beveridge Plan? (*GH*, February 1943; Italics in original)

This embracing of change and the informed rhetoric and comment, however, is interlaced with more traditional themes. The liberalising atmosphere is countered by other messages directed towards the maintenance of a traditional gendered division of labour in the middle class household. Of central concern is the role of women when their men return from the forces – will women be willing and content to relinquish the new freedoms experienced in both paid employment and in the management (especially economic management) of domestic affairs? Articles in the magazine, especially those offering advice, centre on how to keep women within, or return them to, the domestic boundaries of the home and to resume their appropriate role within it. Because, however, of the nature of the readership, and in contrast to the texts of *True Romances*, this theme of domesticity has to be set within the promise of a less hierarchical and more egalitarian post-war world. Hence, paradoxically, the traditional hierarchical relations of gender and domesticity are articulated round the theme of change.

Continuities within Change: Out of Time

The controlling mechanisms are illustrated by focusing on two: continuities within change and the domestication of the outside world.

In *Good Housekeeping*, one strategy of containment is to locate change within historical and universal perspectives, in contrast with *True Romances* where timelessness is evoked by the virtual absence of historical references and even little mention of the war. Giddens (1992) has noted that while men have been viewed as the carriers of history and change, women are seen as ahistorical, that is, pushed into timelessness because of the cyclical patterning of the lives of all women.[7] Yet in *Good Housekeeping*, women are also conceived as carriers; it is, however, as carriers of eternal verities, and, as such, women symbolically (as well as biologically) confirm their placement in the domain outside time.

These verities, therefore, are not the highly regarded universals of the public domain, such as justice and freedom; they are, rather, the values associated with the private domain of family and home. They are sustained by mystical elements which draw upon reflection and untestable states of inner feeling; and, whilst most forcefully conveyed in the romantic stories, they are also present in feature articles and advice; in some of the latter, change is denied by *fiat*. The circumstances of everyday life in war time opened opportunities and possibilities for the individual to construct a life-*course*, with transitions and turning points holding the potential for individuals to influence the path they take. But *Good Housekeeping* continues to reaffirm the deeper truths and inevitability of the life *cycle*, with its repetitive, non-individualistic patterns and deterministic overtones.

There are several elements in this process. Certain values are treated as absolutes and cyclical, and time itself is used as a literary vehicle to transport the reader across a peculiarly timeless history. Literary techniques of flashback, memory, retrospection, and introspection are extensively employed. Selected familistic themes – of marriage, birth, death, children growing up, home, and the embodiment of family in houses and gardens (particularly orchards with their own cyclical symbolism) swing pendulum-like between present, past, and future. This movement in time, moreover, is not only across generations of the same family, but also across generations of unrelated families. In one story, time present, embodied in the young family to whom the narrator, an older woman, is selling her house, evokes past memories not only of her own family when at the same stage of the family cycle, but also of a hypothetical reconstruction of an even earlier past of the owner from whom she and her husband bought the house; simultaneously she speculates about the young family's future. Thus, across this sweep of historical time the cameos share an unchanging pattern of familial time, literally embodied as individual time in the narrator's present musings (Cousins, 1943). In other stories, such shared familism, notwithstanding a social distancing from the vulgarity of lower-class taste or the commonness of a local midwife, lies in the common bond of motherhood, reinforcing an ahistorical womanhood irrespective of social class.

Symbolism underpins the articulation of these values. For example, several stories are based on such traditional themes as the Holy Family or rural life and skills, whilst the symbolism of nature sustains the idea of cyclical continuity.

Families, like nature, have symbols, themselves often unimportant, but representing conquest, tradition and memorable occasions: good luck charms and significant heirlooms, meaning more than any outsider can understand. (St John 1943a)

Thus, rings are handed down the generations, references are made to the classical gods of hearth and home, unquenchable sexual urges – 'the ancient hunger of mankind', double beds won in displays of agricultural skill and which last a lifetime, beams of sunlight irradiating a church during a christening whilst a wealthy and beautiful young woman reflects upon her marriage 'the church filled with a pure, very pale gold light [which] seemed to speak to her' (St John 1943b, p. 91).

The Domestic Dichotomy and Sexual Division of Labour

Symbolism also accommodates the middle-class woman's increased involvement in housework. Here a domestic dichotomy comes into play. Ideally, in these texts, the middle-class housewife is beautiful, gracious, serene, sexually available to her husband throughout marriage, economically dependent upon him, and a mother. She is the competent controller of the home, its servants, and its emotional climate.

However, although in the fiction she is seen performing certain household tasks – polishing furniture, serving breakfast with a smile – the complex of household demands is often split between two figures: the wife and either a cook or maid. Each half carries a different familial message. In the first the emphasis is upon the wife as manager of relationships. The second strikes deeper sacred chords; domestic chores and household drudgery are invested with a spiritual quality, enabling them to be reconciled with the ideal conception of the role of the middle-class housewife, signalling that these too are worthy of her time and effort. The drudgery of housework and child care, for example, are taken up in one story and enveloped in mystique and quasi-religious ritual.

Whatever household gods we had, it was her cherishing that preserved them for us, in the years when the cornerstones had crumbled and weeds grew about the threshold, her tending that kept the family flame upon the hearth. . . . Time was not measured for you by the clock or the calendar, but by the cradle, the pram, the school desk. (Watson, 1943, p. 19)

Such controls over change are accompanied by mechanisms which address challenges to the domestic power structure more directly. In the fiction, threats to continuity and tradition are allowed to play themselves out. In contrast, the features and advice columns, engaging with the real world, explicitly invite readers to view the change and challenge around them as a mere turbulent slice of an all-embracing and overarching eternity.

The monotony, workload, invisibility, and anti-intellectualism of the middle-class housewife's lot is given voice in the non-fiction and subjected to a series of redefinitions. Thus war, unlike poverty, has not exposed the contradictions of marriage, but rather 'obscures straight thinking', producing a tendency to see life outside the family 'through a haze of glamour'; to want a job is a desire for fame and attention rather than freedom, and dissatisfaction with the structure of conjugal relations is a mere irritation.

Furthermore, experience in the real world is redefined as an internal state. Thus, in her advice column, Mary Gray (1942) notes the changes a working wife is experiencing and the questions both those at work and at home are raising about the former conjugal patterns. But Gray (1942, p. 21) counsels that the change 'is only in [her] own mind. It hasn't really happened, you know.' And women who, in their husbands' absence have been living independently and have discovered their competence in formerly defined male skills are enjoined, on his return, to 'be strong'. To 'be strong', however, means that a woman should 'train herself to lean on him again'. For not to do so will sap her husband's ambition, she will lose respect for him and, thereby, endanger the marriage and his will to work. Such advice, maintaining the symbolic and material aspects of a gendered power structure, complements the romanticism in the story of the housekeeper, Martha, who, the family discover, did not marry the unemployed man she loved, and become the economic provider, in order to preserve his dignity.

The war, by giving women unexpected re-entry into paid work and removing husbands from the home, also gave women access to and control over economic resources and material independence. Such a sense of power, felt by women who had tested their strength, had to be tamed if they were to return willingly to domesticity, adhere to their proper domestic role, and allow husbands to reassert their dominance. As one advice column records:

I simply love [being a wage earner again]. Sometimes I wonder if I don't love it too much. I mean what's going to happen when the war is over and Bob is home and I return to domestic bliss again, not forgetting the washing up. . . . I'll have to ask Bob again for everything again. I'll be dependent. (Gray, 1942, p. 21)

The narrator is reminded, paradoxically, that on marriage she renounced independence for happiness and security; and when her husband comes home she must try not 'to steer the whole ship'.

For, as with the heroines of *True Romances*, the role of the middle-class wife, as dependent, is to mediate her husband's economic identity. But the difference between the working-class and middle-class version of the work ethic becomes clear in a daughter's memories of her father.

[He] was always the last to leave the office at the mill, although he owned it and, as uncle Bill said, there was no earthly reason why he should be the first in and the last out. (Nebel, 1943, p. 3)

Thus, whereas the heroines of *True Romances* are not to encourage their men to seek advancement, thereby preserving a supply of working-class labour, the role of the middle-class wife is not confined to merely sustaining the work ethic, but is extended to helping husbands up career ladders, whether explicitly or unwittingly. Thus, when a wife uses her engagement ring, a family heirloom, as collateral for the house she wants, ' "for you and the children," she wailed', she comfortingly reflects on this after her husband's death – from overwork after achieving the directorship of the firm!

But it hadn't been six months before she got it back because Clem was promoted . . . There was something about getting it back that drove him night and day. If it hadn't been for the ring he might never have been made Sales Manager. (Cousins, 1943, p. 93)

The Domestication of the Outside World

Finally, the texts control any hint of a foray into the public domain of power and politics. The strategy employed is redolent of Rogers' (1981) account of the domestication of women in developing countries, whereby aid agencies define the male as the farmer (and hence recipient of resources) although traditionally a female role. In *Good Housekeeping* the redefinition is reversed, but to the same effect. Whereas the woman farmer is defined away, the feature articles of *Good Housekeeping* trivialise the outside world as a site of power, rendering the public domain not worth the effort of entry. Simultaneously, power is translated to the housewife role. The reader is told she is able to control external events while remaining firmly in the private domain of the home. For example, the fact that she has been a good wife will control her distant husband's romantic and sexual adventures. Previous conformity to her domestic role will, it seems, preserve her husband's love for her and ensure his return. Such a model of wifeliness, and her moral education of her children, will also control the venereal disease rampant in the armed forces. The double standard of sexual behaviour for men and women remains unquestioned. Finally, she is enjoined to view her domestic tasks as a minor version of the 'greater housekeeping' of government. Hence, the status of household management is enhanced and power and politics domesticated.

In contrast to *True Romances*, the configuration of elements sustaining the tradition conjugal relationship and the domestic division of labour for middle-class housewives are woven into a different tapestry. Through a range of devices, the paradoxes produced by war are brought under control. The readership of *Good Housekeeping* is assured of the importance of the housewife role and directed towards the view that they have misinterpreted the changes impinging upon their lives.

CONCLUSION

Though challenged by some historians (Calder, 1969), the Second World War is a period which has entered conventional wisdom as a time when women gained new freedoms. The analysis of these magazines, however, suggests that although the disruption of war provided the seedbed for change, forces were at work with the potential to constrain behaviour, symbolically forcing it back into the old mould. The grip that the messages in women's magazines have on readers' minds and the extent to which decisions and behaviour are influenced are difficult to establish, and no attempt has been made to address the problem here. None the less, such texts are major elements in our culture, and at the mimimum form part of that constant up-dating, moderating, adapting, adjusting, and affirming process in public opinion formation that Gramsci (1971) describes.

The chapter examined the traditional conjugal relationship as presented in *True Romances* and *Good Housekeeping*, two women's magazines directed to different audiences at a time when inequalities of class and gender were challenged by the daily experiences of men and women. Within an overarching traditional familistic ideology, elements were selected and tailored to address the challenges to the *status quo* as they arose from the different circumstances of working-class girls and middle-class married women.

For each audience, romantic narratives and the accompanying articles addressed the contradictions inherent in an ideology and its relationship to the real world. This sustained the traditional domestic division of labour and, through wifely mediation, the cultural reproduction of a class-based, male work ethic.

In each case, the strategies of control vary, producing unique configurations. The mechanisms in *True Romances* centre on the control of marital choice and the retention of women within a poverty stricken marriage to sustain the male work ethic. They are articulated round an economic theme closely interwoven with familism and romance. The elements in this control are the mystique of marriage and denial of women's rational economic behaviour in the search for economic security. Within marriage women are contained within the domestic division of labour through a series of transitions and displacements: romantic violence to domestic violence, physical beauty to inner beauty.

In contrast, the text of *Good Housekeeping*, addressing the problems of social change and a questioning, educated audience, draws upon different controls. These are articulated around the paradox of continuities within change and the domestication of the public domain. Again, a series of interpretations is brought into play to address the implications of women's new freedoms and the changing domestic circumstances of middle-class women without domestic servants.

Whilst apparently embracing the spirit of social change and urging women to take part in the debate on post-war reconstruction, the texts none the less carry a deeply traditional message, persuading women to relinquish their new-found independence. Using literary conventions of time and symbolism, the strategies reaffirm the ahistorical nature of women and their mediation of the middle-class male work ethic of career progression. A domestic dichotomy between servant and mistress, hallowing domestic drudgery, integrates this into the middle-class housewife's role. Reinterpretations are brought into play for those who venture outside the home or enjoy their new independence of the male. Finally, the reader is firmly located within the private domain of home through the domestication of the outside world.

In critically different ways the texts address the inherent contradictions of an ideology; and in both cases romance serves to sustain the traditional divisions of class and gender, the accompanying dependence of women and the consequent allocation of power and resources. The contribution of these magazines to social reconstruction for the post-war world is to fit the familistic bits back into the traditional patterns currently being fragmented by war.

NOTES

1. I have argued elsewhere that collectively these messages work to structure and sustain conceptions of the normal family and the traditional gendered power relations within it (Allatt, 1981a, b).
2. The Beveridge Report, *Social Insurance and Allied Services*, published in November 1942, was the key policy document for research on the family in wartime and hence determined the time span for the selection of magazine issues. The Report entered the public imagination as largely radical and egalitarian, and it came to symbolise the spirit of post-war reconstruction. It was, however, deeply familistic, premised on the maintenance of the traditional family structure.
3. The role of advertisements is described elsewhere (Allatt, 1994).
4. The items analysed were: *True Romance* – 44 items of fiction (23 complete stories and three serials), 12 editorials, 11 personal advice, and 24 domestic service articles; *Good Housekeeping* – 26 stories, 11 editorials, 12 personal advice features, 101 feature articles and 96 service articles (domestic, caring, and personal presentation)
5. In England and Wales for the years 1929–39 between 50 000 and 60 000 girls were married each year before they were 21. In 1940 the number doubled to 116 000 and in 1943 remained as high as 82 000. 1940 was a boom year for weddings; more were married at 20 than any other age.
6. The anti-heroine gold digger raises her head as a social policy strand in the cultural web of familism. One of Sir William Beveridge's memoranda to his Committee on Social Insurance reads, 'The social security scheme should not follow the example of the various veteran schemes of the United States, in encouraging marriages of young women with octogenarians or invalids in hope of prolonged widowhood and other benefits' (PRO, 1942, CAB 87/79 reported in Allatt, 1981b).
7. Similarly, Smith (1974, quoted in Stacey, 1981, p. 119) sees women's oppression lying not in the sexual division of labour as such but in 'the relegation of the domestic to that sphere which is outside history'.

REFERENCES

Allatt, P. (1981a) 'The Family seen through the Beveridge Report, Forces' Education and Popular Magazines: A Sociological Study of the Social

Reproduction of Family Ideology in World War II', unpublished PhD thesis, University of Keele.

Allatt, P. (1981b) 'Stereotyping: Familism in the Law', in B. Fryer, A. Hunt, D. McBarnet and B. Moorhouse (eds), *Law, State and Society* (London: Croom Helm).

Allatt, P. (1983) 'Men and War: Status, Class and the Social Reproduction of Masculinity', in E. Gamarnikow, D. Morgan, J. Purvis and D. Taylorson (eds), *The Public and the Private* (London: Heinemann).

Allatt, P. (1994) 'Order Out of Chaos: The Research Endeavour', Professorial Lecture, University of Teesside, 29 June.

Althusser, L. (1972) 'Ideology and Ideological State Apparatuses', in B. R. Coser (ed.), *Education: Structure and Society* (Harmondsworth: Penguin Books).

Barthes, R. (1973) *Mythologies* (Frogmore: Paladin).

Bentley, P. (1943) 'Women after the War', *Current Affairs*, **44**: p. 22, May; War Office Directorate, Army Bureau of Current Affairs.

Beveridge, W. (1942) *Social Insurance and Allied Services (The Beveridge Report)*, Cmd 6404 (London: HMSO).

Brandes, S. (1981) 'Like Wounded Stags: Male Sexual Ideology in an Andulusian Town', in S. B. Ortner and H. Whitehead (eds) *Sexual Meanings: The Cultural Construction of Gender and Sexuality* (Cambridge: Cambridge University Press).

Bullock, A. (1967) *The Life and Times of Ernest Bevin*, vol. II (London: Heinemann).

Buswell, C. (1989) *Women in Contemporary Britain* (London: Macmillan).

Calder, A. (1969) *The People's War: Britain 1939–45* (London: Jonathan Cape).

Carter, A. (1977) 'An I for Truth', *New Society*, **42**: (789), pp. 364–65, 17 November.

Cousins, M. (1943) 'At a Sacrifice', *Good Housekeeping*, 6 May.

de Beauvoir, S. (1981) *The Second Sex*, first published 1949 (Harmondsworth: Penguin).

Directorate of Army Education (1944) *The British Way and Purpose*, Consolidated Edition of BWP Booklets 1–18 with Appendices of Post-War Reconstruction.

Douglas, M. (1975) *Implicit Meanings. Essays in Anthropology* (London: Routledge & Kegan Paul).

Douie, V. (1949) *Daughters of Britain: An Account of the Work of British Women in the Second World War* (London: George Ronald).

Fowler, (1979) '"True to Me Always": An Analysis of Women's Magazine Fiction', *British Journal of Sociology*, **30**: (1), pp. 91–119.

Giddens, A. (1992) *The Transformation of Intimacy: Sexuality, Love and Eroticism in Modern Societies* (Cambridge: Polity Press).

Gramsci, A. (1971) *Selections from the Prison Notebooks*, Q. Hoare and G. Nowell-Smith (eds) (London: Lawrence & Wishart).

Gray, M. (1942) 'Wives without Husbands', *Good Housekeeping*, 24 March.

Grieve, M. (1964) *Millions Made My Story* (London: Gollancz).

Jephcott, A. P. (1942) *Girls Growing Up* (London: Faber & Faber).

Jephcott, A. P. (1948) *Rising Twenty: Notes on Some Ordinary Girls* (London: Faber & Faber).

Kornhauser, W. (1960) *The Politics of Mass Society* (London: Routledge & Kegan Paul).

Land, H. (1976) 'Women: Supporters or Supported?', in D. L. Barker and S. Allen (eds) *Sexual Divisions and Society: Process and Change* (London: Tavistock).

Molotoch, H. (1975) 'Processes of Power', Departmental Seminar, University of Keele.

Murcott, A. (1983) ' "It's a Pleasure to Cook for Him": Food, Mealtimes and Gender in Some South Wales Households', in E. Gamarnikow, D. Morgan, J. Purvis and D. Taylorson (eds) *The Public and the Private* (London: Heinemann).

Nebel, F. (1943) 'The Man Who Promised Not to Tell', *Good Housekeeping*, 2 April.

Picture Post (1943) 'Special Issue: Changing Britain', **18**: (1), 2 January.

Price, M. (1981) 'British Restaurants (1940–1946): From Collectivism to Consumerism', paper given at Women and Housing Policy Conference, University of Kent.

Radway, J. A. (1984) *Reading the Romance: Women, Patriarchy and Popular Literature* (Chapel Hill, NC: University of North Carolina Press).

Reik, T. (1965) 'Lady Jekyll and Mistress Hyde', in H. Holland (ed.) *Why Are You Single?*, revised edn, 1st edn 1949 (New York: Tower).

Rogers, B. (1981) *The Domestication of Women: Discrimination in Developing Societies* (London: Tavistock).

St. John, A. R. (1943a) 'Good Luck, Dear Spoons', *Good Housekeeping*, 6 February.

St. John, A. R. (1943b) 'Godmother Tomorrow', *Good Housekeeping*, 6 March.

Slater. E. and Woodside M. (1951) *Patterns of Marriage* (London: Cassell).

Smith, D. (1974) 'Women, the Family and Corporate Capitalism', in M. Stephenson (ed.) *Women in Canada* (Toronto: New Press).

Spring-Rice, M. (1939) *Working Class Wives* (Harmondsworth: Penguin Books).

Stacey, M. (1981) *Women: Women Power and Politics* (London: Tavistock).

Thompson, J. B. (1988) 'Mass Communication and Modern Culture: Contributions to a Critical Theory of Ideology', *Sociology*, **22**: (3), pp. 359–83.

Watson, M. A. (1943) 'Martha', *Good Housekeeping*, 18 February.

White, C. L. (1970) *Women's Magazines, 1763–1968* (London: Michael Joseph).

Winship, J. (1978) 'A Woman's World: "Woman" – an Ideology of Femininity', Women's Studies Group (Birmingham: CCCS).

3 The 'Single Mothers' Debate: A Children's Rights Perspective

SOPHIE LAWS

The last couple of years have seen a public debate around lone parent-hood, largely initiated by the UK Government. These discussions have featured much greater attention towards the motives of adults than towards the situation of the children of lone parents. This paper aims to examine this debate from the perspective of a concern for children's rights, and specifically in relation to the UN Convention on the Rights of the Child. I will attempt to show that the UN Convention can provide a helpful framework against which to test policy proposals relating to children.

This chapter has arisen out of engagement with the debate through my work in the Policy Division of Save the Children Fund's UK and European Programmes Department.

The first part of this chapter presents 'edited highlights' of the recent debate around lone parenthood, drawn largely from the press coverage. Some of the underlying themes are then examined: the way in which lone parent families have been presented as a threat to others, either through competition for resources, or as a cause of various social problems. The last section looks at the relevance of a number of the articles of the UN Convention on the Rights of the Child (including those on discrimination, standard of living, preservation of identity, protection) to the rights of the children of lone parents.

THE PUBLIC 'DEBATE'

John Redwood, Secretary of State for Wales, started the open season on lone parents with a speech which went as follows:

> One of the biggest social problems of our day is the surge in single parent families. Everyone would wish to help the young family that has suddenly lost a father through death, or if the mother has been

abused or badly treated by the father and the relationship has broken down. What is more worrying is the trend in some places for
young women to have babies with no apparent intention of even
trying a marriage or stable relationship with the father of the child.
In these circumstances it must be right, before granting state aid, to
pursue the father and see whether it is possible for the father to
make a financial contribution, or even a fuller contribution by offering the normal love and support that fathers have offered down the
ages to their families. It would be better for the child and better for
the family and better for the state if more fathers assumed their
natural responsibilities . . . (speech at the Conservative Political Centre
Summer School in Cardiff, 2 July 1993)

The Press joined in enthusiastically:

Britain can no longer afford these mothers. (*Sunday Express*, 26
September 1993)

Ministers keep up campaign against single mothers. (*Independent*,
8 July 1993)

A runaway success: B & B curb on lone mothers leaving home.
(*Sunday Express*, 11 July 1993)[1]

Where daddies are a myth. Low-life Britain today – by the no-hope
single mums and their fatherless children. (*The Times*, 9 July 1993)

Time bomb of lone parenting. (*Sunday Express*, 19 December 1993)

Should we ban benefits for our single mothers? (*Sunday Express*,
12 December 1993)

Headlines over and over again focus on the individual woman, or 'girl',
and her motives. The constant use of the term 'single mothers' when
all lone parents are affected is also notable.
   Round Two followed the announcement that the government planned
to change the homelessness legislation, allegedly in order to prevent
lone parents from gaining priority for council housing.[2]

Pregnant girls will get worst housing. (*Daily Mirror*, 29 November
1993)

Minister: We'll stop the queue-jump mums. (*Daily Mail*, 19 January 1994)

Tories to abolish housing privilege of single parents. (*The Times*, 29 November 1993)

In July 1994, after the consultation period, during which the Government received a record number of critical responses to its proposals, it put out a statement setting out its intentions for the future. Nothing in the statement, nor in the Department of the Environment press release, refers to lone parents or single mothers. However this announcement set off Round Three in the press:

Tory crackdown on single mums. (*Daily Mirror*, 19 July 1994)

Lone mothers lose priority in council housing queue. (*The Times*, 19 July 1994)

Single mothers lose automatic right to housing. (*Daily Telegraph*, 19 July 1994)

Single mothers to join homes queue. (*Daily Mail*, 19 July 1994)

The belief that large numbers of teenage girls get pregnant deliberately to get access to council housing is now widely held in this country, despite lack of evidence. Even more widespread is the belief that lone parents get privileged access to council housing: again, this is not supported by the evidence from Housing Departments (Institute of Housing, 1993). It seemed particularly extraordinary, after the announcement in July 1994, that the press, across the political spectrum, reported developments in such a prejudicial way, even though the government had made no reference to lone parents in its announcement.

The Autumn 1995 party conference season was preceded by a small flurry of threats to cut benefits to lone parents: 'Lilley targets single parents' (*Independent on Sunday*, 13 August 1995). Again the parents are mentioned, but not the children.

Observing the public debate during most of 1993 (Evans, 1993), Government ministers' utterances were so hostile to lone parents that punitive measures were widely anticipated. In November 1993 a confidential Cabinet paper was leaked to the *Guardian* which set forth evidence relating to a range of policy options. It stated that 'The primary objective of any measures taken will be to reduce the burden on public expenditure caused by lone parent families.' However, the evidence it presented gave a complex view of the situation. It appears that the Government thought better of many of the ideas it considered. The embarrassment that dogged John Major's 'Back to Basics' campaign must have been a factor.

Interestingly, though, it was also in November 1993 that a very positive policy initiative was announced – a new provision for parents on family credit or some other benefits to offset some of their childcare costs against earnings.[3] This will be worth up to £28 per week to families. It was an important first sign of recognition that child-care costs should be taken into account when calculating welfare benefits for low wage earners. The allowance was announced as intended to help lone parents, although it is available to some couples as well.

The Child Support Act is, of course, the other important recent policy measure of relevance to these issues. Its effects are complex, and its general approach was welcomed, for example, by the National Council for One Parent Families. However, research by the five largest children's charities which looked from the child's point of view at the effects of the workings of the Child Support Agency to date on a sample of low income families found that none of the children had benefitted (Clarke *et al.*, 1994):

> the implementation of the Child Support Act has done nothing to improve the well-being of children in lone parent families. Indeed, the distress and material losses which were experienced by a number of children were clearly damaging, rather than beneficial to their welfare.

As with all processes of policy formation, there is some distance between what is said and what is done. It is to be hoped that policy makers will continue to consider carefully before acting on the slogans quoted above from the press coverage of this issue. I will next try to draw out some of the themes embedded in the public discussion of this issue.

LONE PARENTS: WHOSE PROBLEM?

The central thesis of the Right in the recent 'debate' around lone parenthood has been that social policy, primarily various provisions of the
welfare state, has created incentives to women and to men which add
up to encourage lone parenthood. The focus is mainly on younger single mothers, whose numerical importance tends to be exaggerated, who
are believed to set out deliberately to raise children alone. Lone parenthood is seen as a social evil in itself, and the heterosexual two-parent
family held up as an unproblematic ideal.

One of the oddities of the public debate is how little focus there has
been on the child. Looking again at the headlines quoted above, all
refer to the mother. It seems unlikely that the *Mirror* would use the
image of a 'blitz' so readily in relation to a story it perceived to be
about children. The 'pregnant girls' who are to get the worst housing
will soon have babies to share that housing with. If Britain 'can no
longer afford these mothers', what exactly does this mean for their
children?

Concern has focused far more on what are seen as dangers to *others*
of lone parenthood. These concerns have been of two main kinds: the
idea that lone parents make excessive claims on public resources, and
the idea that lone parenthood leads to other social ills through incor-
rect upbringing of children and through the supposed effects on men
cut loose from family responsibilities.

Competition for Resources

A central purpose, for the Government, of this focus on lone parents
is to offer the increase in their numbers as an explanation for the lack
of social support experienced by other families. This thinking has been
mobilised in relation to child support, to benefits generally, and to
housing. The Child Support Agency's priorities are explicitly to save
as much money for the Treasury as possible by retrieving from absent
parents the money paid in benefits to parents with the care of children.

There has been much discussion, though so far no action, on the
idea of using the benefits system to penalise lone parents who have a
further child whilst on benefits. In New Jersey, such mothers receive
no more benefit for a further child. Some in Britain have advocated a
similar system, with a directly punitive purpose.

It is on housing, as discussed above, that this thinking has been
most important in this country. Many people have been convinced that

single mothers are getting priority through councils housing them as homeless. Despite the fact that it removes rights from all homeless families, the majority of whom are couples, the new proposals on the homelessness legislation were widely reported as relating primarily to lone parents.

The Housing Minister, Sir George Young, launched this Green Paper by stating that the current law 'in effect penalises those who act responsibly and is seen as a reward for those who, for whatever reason, act irresponsibly' (*Guardian*, 19 January 1994). The image put over is of virtuous couples living for years with their parents, while single mothers get housed. The accusation of irresponsibility amongst homeless families presumably relates to an assumption that people can always act to prevent themselves from becoming homeless. The largest number of lone parents who are housed as homeless are, of course, separated and divorced women – presumably they should act 'responsibly' and remain with their husbands in order to avoid the cost to the state of housing them and their children.

Even the Archbishop of Canterbury, Dr George Carey, joined in with the discussion, and wove together this theme with the other kind of argument, to argue that 'the resulting cost to our society is far greater than can be measured in financial terms'.[4]

To bring the focus back to the children, which is rarely done in this particular type of argument, what is essentially being said is that the children of lone parents are not valued enough to be worth the support from the state that they require. These children are presented as nothing but a drain on the economy.

Cause of Crime, Delinquency, Urban Decay

The other theme of the Right, led by the 'underclass' theorists, blames lone mothers for many of the problems they in fact suffer from. They are seen as responsible for young men's lack of stable ties to family groups, which is seen as increasing their involvement in crime and disorder. The notion of women and children as a civilising influence on working-class men has a long history, and is readily brought into play here.

Lone mothers are further regarded as bad mothers, especially in relation to discipline for their sons. Perceptions that young men in areas of high unemployment are increasingly 'out of control' are attributed to the lack of proper patriarchal authority in the family. Women are seen as inherently unable to exert parental authority.

Finally, the concentration of lone parents in some areas of council housing is seen as the cause of the hopelessness felt by many in these areas. A circular argument blames the poorest families for their own poverty, rather than looking at issues such as unemployment.

Again, focusing on the children, the obvious response to this type of concern, one might have thought, would be to provide services to compensate for perceived deficits in particular groups of parents' abilities to raise their children to society's standards. However, what is being discussed instead is an attempt, through economic pressure, to change adults' behaviour so radically that such children cease to exist.

WELFARE OR RIGHTS?

Although we may observe greater concern for the secondary effects on others, the case against lone parenthood must rest in some sense on a claim that it negatively affects children's welfare. Louie Burghes' latest report (1994) examines the evidence on the outcomes for children, and finds the research basis of many of the claims made questionable.

In recent years most debate about how children should be raised has taken place within a discourse about the welfare, or the 'needs' of children. Adults argue similarly in relation to individuals and to whole groups of children about 'what is good for them'. The notion of welfare in itself is highly subjective, and these arguments are, by their nature, intensely value-laden.

Because children are such a disempowered group, their own views are rarely held to be relevant, let alone central, to the question of what is good for them. This is changing to some degree in professional discourse in the UK, with the Children Act of 1989 requiring local authorities to 'give due consideration to' the 'wishes and feelings' of children ('having regard to his or her age and understanding') in decisions concerning them.

Alongside this trend, an increasing interest in the idea of children's rights has developed (cf. Freeman, 1983; Newell, 1991; Children's Rights Development Unit, 1994). The remainder of this chapter is an attempt to apply the language of children's rights to the current debate about lone parents.

I will only discuss briefly the philosophical basis of such an approach (see James and Prout (1990) and Archaud (1993) for fuller discussions) – my aim is rather to experiment with it in relation to a particularly confused and confusing debate. The language of rights may give a stable framework to a discussion in which competing ideologies otherwise find no common ground.

It has been argued that children cannot be said to have rights, precisely because they are not adults and have not yet entered into the contract with the state which, in classical terms, confers such rights. However, this argument could surely be made in relation to any less powerful group. Advocates of children's rights frequently refer to the development of the idea of women's rights as an analogy. The strength of the comparison, as with ideas of the rights of disabled people, lies precisely in the paradigm shift involved, from, for example, moralistic ideas about a woman's place, or medicalised views of disabled people, to a rights framework.

The analogy stands also in that it is important to note that to acknowledge the rights of children does not mean denying that adults have rights too, just as rights for disabled people do not mean denying the rights of carers or others.

It is interesting that although these ideas have had relatively little attention in this country, children's rights have been recognised at the international level. The UN Convention on the Rights of the Child was adopted by the General Assembly of the United Nations on 20 November 1989, and ratified with five reservations by the UK Government in December 1991.

The path to a UN Convention was a long one, and one source of it was the declaration of children's rights drafted in 1923 by Eglantyne Jebb, who founded the Save the Children Fund. This was adopted by the League of Nations the following year. The impulse for this came, in part, out of public concern for the hardships suffered by children in the defeated countries after the First World War.

In looking at the UN Convention, it should be noted that its definition of a child goes up to the age of 18, so some lone parents themselves would count as children. Thus in some cases the rights of the child apply to both mother and child – in some, to the father as well.

It is important, though, not to overstate the numbers of teenage mothers. Only a small proportion of all births outside marriage are to girls below the age of 18. There were 4269 births to girls under 16 in 1990, which constitutes only 2 per cent of all births outside marriage.

The great majority of lone parents are older divorced, separated or widowed women. For this majority, children's rights are relevant in relation to their children, not themselves.

THE RIGHTS OF THE CHILDREN OF LONE PARENTS

Quite a number of articles of the Convention are of some relevance to
the rights of the children of lone parents. Articles covering discrimination, the right to an adequate standard of living, preservation of identity,
parental responsibility and support to parents, protection from abuse
and neglect, and from sexual exploitation are of particular interest.

Discrimination

Article 2 of the Convention specifies that all rights apply to all children without exception. There is to be no discrimination of any kind,
'irrespective of the child's or his or her parent's or legal guardian's
race, colour, sex . . . *birth or other status*' (my emphasis). Appropriate
measures are to be taken

> to ensure that the child is protected against all forms of discrimina-
> tion or punishment on the basis of the status, activities, expressed
> opinions, or beliefs of the child's parents, legal guardians or family
> members.

The reference to 'birth status' is a direct reference to discrimination
against children born out of wedlock – this is still a feature of some
countries' legal systems. 'Other status', combined with the reference
to the sex of the parent as a basis for discrimination, would cover
discrimination against children of widowed or divorced parents.

Such discrimination of course abounds, nowadays largely in the form
of indirect and informal discrimination. Social and economic forces
combine to create a situation where the children of lone parents are, in
effect, discriminated against, since their parent has no way of bringing
in an adequate income. Social policy could be directed towards miti-
gating this situation, through policies such as support for child-care
provision, a better-structured benefits system to support lone parents
who choose to seek employment, and through the provision of adequate income and accommodation for all children whose parents cannot provide this.

Instead, what is so especially disturbing about the present debate is
that so many commentators appear to feel comfortable to advocate
increased discrimination against these children. It is argued that lone
parenthood itself is the problem, not the social conditions in which it
occurs – thus any policy which *might* deter women from becoming

lone parents is regarded favourably. Such policies are *intended to* intensify social discrimination against the children of lone parents.

For example a *Daily Mail* editorial on the day the Green Paper on homelessness was published (19 January 1994) first quotes opposition speakers, for example Archie Kirkwood for the Liberal Democrats, saying that the Government was ignoring the interests of children 'in a totally heartless way'. It then argues that 'This is thinking no further than your nose. . . . The easier things are made for young unmarried mothers, the more young unmarried mothers we shall have.' Professor A. H. Halsey's work is then invoked to demonstrate how harmful this would be. It is unusual, to say the least, to see policy defended on the grounds that damage to real children today can be justified on the basis of a possible deterrent effect on parents. Part of the explanation must lie in the way in which the focus on the motives, morals, and choices of women appears to obscure any attention to the situation of the children.

The Right to an Adequate Standard of Living

In Article 27:

> States Parties recognise the right of every child to a standard of living adequate for the child's physical, mental, spiritual, moral and social development. . . .

> States Parties, in accordance with national conditions and within their means, shall take appropriate measures to assist parents and others responsible for the child to implement this right and shall in case of need provide material assistance and support programmes, particularly with regard to nutrition, clothing and housing.

Do the children of lone parents in this country have a standard of living adequate for their proper general development? Some clearly do, but a large proportion live in families whose income is inadequate to make this possible (cf. Millar, 1989).

In 1990/1, a total of 1.26 million children in lone-parent families were living in poverty[5] – this amounted to 32 per cent of the 3.9 million children in poverty. The risk of poverty for children in lone parent families is very high – 74 per cent of children growing up in lone-parent families were in poverty. However, it is worth noting that two-parent families where neither adult is in employment had a risk of poverty of 76 per cent.

Ill health is concentrated amongst those with the lowest incomes (Woodroffe *et al.*, 1993). Any step which reduces either the financial or other resources going into households of such families will have a direct and damaging effect on the children's health. It has been well-shown that it is impossible to feed, clothe, and house a family adequately at Income Support level (e.g. Bradshaw, 1990, 1992; Oldfield and Yu, 1993; Oppenheim, 1993). Policies which would reduce benefits below this level, as in New Jersey, would very directly damage children's health.

One group facing particular poverty are very young parents. 16- and 17-year-olds now have no right to Income Support. They are supposed to be guaranteed a place on a youth training scheme, and otherwise their families are supposed to support them. There is much evidence that training places are not, in fact, available to all. It is of particular relevance here to note that pregnant young women have no automatic right to Income Support during the first 29 weeks of pregnancy. A study of Severe Hardship Payments to young people found that 25 per cent of young women making such claims were pregnant (Maclagan, 1993). It is quite clear that the unborn child of a young woman in this position would suffer as a result of the hardship and malnutrition undergone by the mother.

Accommodation is an important element in a child's standard of living. Hardey and Crow's (1991) summary article 'The Housing Strategies of Lone Parents' states plainly that one-parent families do badly in housing:

> Lone-parent households are far less likely than their two-parent counterparts to be owner-occupiers and far more likely to be tenants or to be homeless. Within the rented sector of the housing market, lone parents are more likely to occupy accommodation of inferior quality. In particular, lone mothers are prominent among those groups of disadvantaged people who 'tend to get very much worse council housing: older rather than newer; flats rather than houses; higher floors rather than lower' (Harrison, 1983). Lone parents are also to be found sharing accommodation with relatives and friends, 'living insecure lives involving frequent moves and being at high risk of homelessness'. In addition, lone parents are more likely to live in inner-city than suburban locations.

Bad housing has a very direct impact on children. Whilst the effects of poor housing are compounded by and therefore easily confused with the effects of poverty itself, there is evidence that damp housing adversely affects children's health (Woodroffe *et al.*, 1993).

The hazards for children of temporary accommodation have been extensively reported (e.g. Furley, 1989; Child Accident Prevention Trust/ Save the Children, 1993; Woodroffe *et al.*, 1993). Accidents are more common, cooking is often difficult so diets are poor, playspace is lacking. Constant moves, in themselves, are very difficult for children, with changes of school and difficulties of access to health care and other services being inevitable.

Where better quality housing is secured, high rents or mortgage repayments may lock lone parent families further into the poverty trap.

Preservation of Identity and Conditions for Adoption

Where illegitimate births carry heavy stigma, it has been common practice for single women to be placed under great pressure to give up their babies for adoption. This was the case in this country until recently – the change in attitudes which has made single motherhood a less stigmatised option has come within a generation.

Encouraged by Charles Murray, the right-wing US writer, the Home Secretary Michael Howard and others have advocated turning the clock back. Howard looked back to this situation:

> So the outcome was that girls in that situation frequently put their babies out for adoption as the only way out. From the child's – and the mother's – point of view that may have been the best outcome.[6]

This thinking flies in the face of a crucial tenet of current child-care thinking, enshrined in law in the Children Act 1989, that the welfare of children is best served by directing support to their own families to bring them up, rather than in separating them from their parents, where this is at all possible. This view has emerged largely from the experience of the outcomes for children of state care and adoption in previous generations. It is perhaps for these reasons that other Ministers distanced themselves from Howard's remarks, but he was far from alone in his view.

The UN Convention, too, comments very directly in the articles on name and nationality and on preservation of identity. Article 7 states:

> The child shall . . . have the right from birth to a name, the right to acquire a nationality and, as far as possible, the right to know and be cared for by his or her parents.

Article 8 adds:

> States Parties undertake to respect the right of the child to preserve his or her identity, including nationality, name and family relations as recognised by law without unlawful interference.

The Article on adoption, Article 21, also sets out that:

> States Parties that recognise and/or permit the system of adoption shall ensure that the best interests of the child shall be the paramount consideration. . . .

There is enormous variation worldwide in how family ties are understood. It is most interesting that the Convention states so clearly that such emphasis should be given to enabling the child to be cared for by his or her parents. The focus on the preservation of identity is also of interest here, as it is known that this question has troubled many children who have been adopted or cared for by the state.

Parental Responsibility

Given the wide diversity of family forms to be considered, it is, again, interesting to see the version the Convention gives of parental responsibilities. Article 18 states that:

1. States Parties shall use their best efforts to ensure recognition of the principle that both parents have common responsibilities for the upbringing and development of the child. . . .
2. For the purpose of guaranteeing and promoting the rights set forth in the present Convention, States Parties shall render appropriate assistance to parents and legal guardians in the performance of their child-rearing responsibilities and shall ensure the development of institutions, facilities and services for the care of children.

Note, firstly, that the Convention, like the Children Act, does not see parents as having rights over children, only responsibilities. This represents a break with traditional Western family law in which the rights of the father placed women and children closer to the status of property than to that of persons in their own right.

The emphasis on 'common responsibilities' echoes the concern of nearly everyone engaged in the current 'lone-parents' debate that fathers should shoulder their share of responsibility for children. The phrase is no doubt carefully chosen: it suggests sharing of care and support.

I would suggest that the choice of the word 'common' before responsibilities leads to an image closer to a sharing of all types of responsibilities than to the division of labour advocated as a norm in this country where the man gives financial support to his child/ren and their mother in return for the woman taking primary responsibility for the practical care of the child/ren.

Although situations where the parents' relationship has broken down are not addressed directly, this Article could be read to support policies to facilitate the maintenance of contact between a child and both his or her parents.

Section 2 of Article 18 would encourage such policies as state support for flexible working arrangements, parental leave, maternity leave, childcare provision, and other support to parents in raising children.

The third part of Article 18 goes even further:

> States Parties shall take all appropriate measures to ensure that children of working parents have the right to benefit from child-care services and facilities for which they are eligible.

This Article is clearly key for the children of lone parents. To get out of the poverty trap, short of total social transformation, lone parents need to take up paid employment. This Article addresses some of the barriers which stand in their way.

Protection from Abuse and Neglect

It has been striking to me how rarely the connection is made between discussion of different family forms and the need to protect children from abuse. Although even John Redwood, as quoted above, recognises that some marriages end because of violence, advocates of the traditional family largely fail to face up to the evidence about the prevalence of child abuse within two-parent families (e.g. Kelly *et al.*, 1991).

Social and financial pressures frequently drive women back into relationships with abusive men, even where abuse has been formally acknowledged. Stark and Flitcraft's (1988) evidence on the links between woman battering and child abuse, and other research and experience in relation to child abuse, suggest that in many cases a key issue in protecting a child is that of whether his or her mother can effectively remove him or her from the abuser. Whether the abuser is 'family friend', father, stepfather or uncle, a woman needs a certain level of financial and social independence to be able to do this.

It is difficult to see how social policy explicitly aimed at creating greater pressure on women to marry and be financially dependent on an individual man rather than the state could avoid increasing the risk of exposing children to abusive situations. If the present disadvantage of lone parents in terms of income and housing is intensified, women will inevitably be put under pressure to stay in, or return to, situations where their children are exposed to violence or abuse. To make a special case of those reporting violence, as has been done in the guidance to the Child Support Act, could do little to mitigate these effects. By no means all mothers who have experienced violence, or who suspect abuse of their children, will be willing to openly charge their ex-partners with abuse, whilst they might quietly remove the child if enabled to do so.

Some single parents are, of course, themselves abusive towards their children. It is again difficult to see how the state does anything but worsen this situation if policies are designed to make life more difficult for them.

Sexual Exploitation

The UN Convention shows further concern for child protection in Article 34:

> States Parties undertake to protect the child from all forms of sexual exploitation and abuse.

This article goes on to mention child prostitution and the use of children in pornography.

Sexual exploitation is an issue in relation to the children of lone parents, and to young women who become pregnant at an early age. This issue is recognised in a number of ways within British law and policy. With a heterosexual age of consent set at 16, the law in effect regards all the 8000 or so girls under 16 who become pregnant each year as having been exploited. Research (e.g. Phoenix, 1991) would suggest that many of the young women in question might not agree, but clearly for some young women exploitation is an issue (Family Planning Association, 1993).

It is interesting that there was enough consensus amongst health professionals for a target to be set as part of the English 'Health of

the Nation' strategy for a reduction in teenage pregnancies.[7] Numbers
in fact reduced somewhat between 1990 and 1991.

Young single mothers report being seen by men as particularly vulnerable to sexual exploitation, for example where they are without a
secure home or income. In terms of risk of working as a prostitute,
very young mothers are a particularly vulnerable group. They are likely
to have few saleable skills for conventional employment, and may have
been obliged to cut themselves off from extended family support. They
are also in particularly acute financial need.

Again, the more lone mothers' practical ability to live a decent life
independently with their child is undermined, the more their vulnerability to exploitation is increased. Obviously, where a young mother
is subject to sexual exploitation her child/ren are also endangered in a
whole series of ways.

CONCLUSION

The great strength of the children's rights perspective is that it re-
minds us that children have rights as persons. So often children are
seen only as potential adults and their present reality disregarded. Focusing on the rights of children can bring an interesting perspective to
debates which are generally conducted in terms of conflicts of interest
between different adults.

In looking at children's rights in relation to the recent discussions
about lone-parent families, some might see an argument for asserting
that children have a right to two parents who live with them. However, this is an assertion of an ideal, and not realisable for all children, even if it was a universally agreed principle. It is notable that
the UN Convention makes no such statement. Much thought went into
the drafting of the Convention, especially in relation to what practical
and appropriate measures national governments could be encouraged
to take, in relation to family life and child-care, often seen as private
matters. The UK Government has ratified the UN Convention on the
Rights of the Child, and therefore has accepted its approach. The Convention should be used as a yardstick against which to assess policy
and practice which affects children.

NOTES

1. This article refers to Wandsworth Council's policy, currently against the law, of only offering single mothers temporary accommodation in the hope that they will return to their parents', or presumably partner's, home and cease to seek council housing.
2. The Green Paper 'Access to Local Authority and Housing Association Tenancies' in fact aimed to remove rights from all homeless families. It proposes to replace the right to permanent housing for those accepted as homeless by the local authority with only a limited provision of temporary accommodation for some such applicants. A White Paper, 'Our Future Homes: Opportunities, Choice, Responsibility. The Government's Housing Policy for England and Wales' followed in July 1995, containing most but not all of the Green Paper proposals. Legislation is expected in the 1995/6 term of Parliament.
3. From October 1994, lone parents and couples who are both working and who are claiming family credit, disability working allowance, housing benefit or council tax benefit are able to offset some of their child-care costs against earnings. Only officially recognised forms of childcare, such as registered childminders, private nursery fees or after-school care club costs are allowable.
4. Speech to members of the Church of Scotland in Edinburgh, reported in *The Times*, 11 October 1993.
5. Households below average income, HMSO, July 1993. Poverty is defined using the standard measure as covering those living on less than 50 per cent of average income, after housing costs.
6. Lecture to The Conservative Political Centre in Blackpool, quoted *Sunday Telegraph*, 10 October 1993.
7. 'To reduce the rate of conceptions amongst the under 16s by at least 50% by the year 2000': Department of Health, *The Health of the Nation Key Area Handbook: HIV/AIDS and Sexual Health*, January 1993.
8. OPCS, *Population Trends*, Autumn 1993. The conception rate for under 16s dropped from 10.1 per thousand girls to 9.3 in 1991. Conception rates for under 15s dropped from 21.6 per thousand in 1990 to 19.9 in 1991.

REFERENCES

Archaud, David (1993) *Children: Rights and Childhood* (London: Routledge).
Bradshaw, Jonathan (1990) *Child Poverty and Deprivation in the UK* (London: National Children's Bureau).
Bradshaw, Jonathan (1992) *Household Budgets and Living Standards* (York: Family Budget Unit, Joseph Rowntree Foundation).
Burghes, Louie (1994) *Lone Parenthood and Family Disruption: The Outcomes for Children* (London: Family Policy Studies Centre).
Child Accident Prevention Trust/Save the Children (1993) *Accidents and the Safety of Children in Temporary Accommodation* (London: CAPT/SCF).

Children's Rights Development Unit (1994) *UK Agenda for Children* (London: CRDU).

Clarke, Karen, Glendinning, Caroline and Craig, Gary (1994) *Losing Support: Children and the Child Support Act* (London: Barnardos, The Children's Society, NCH Action for Children, NSPCC and Save the Children).

Evans, Helen (1993) 'Criticism or Childcare?', *Childcare Now*, No. 4, pp. 8–9.

Family Budget Unit (1992) *Social Policy Research Findings No. 31* (York: Joseph Rowntree Foundation), November.

Family Planning Association/Middlesex University with *World in Action* (1993) 'Children who have Children'.

Freeman, M. D. A. (1983) *The Rights and Wrongs of Children* (London: Francis Pinter).

A. Furley (1989) *A Bad Start in Life: Children, Health and Housing* (London: Shelter).

Hardey, M. and Crow, G. (1991) *Lone Parenthood: Coping with Constraints and Making Opportunities* (Hemel Hempstead, Harvester Wheatsheaf).

Harrison, P. (1983) *Inside the Inner City: Life under the Cutting Edge* (Harmondsworth: Penguin).

Institute of Housing (1993) *Homelessness – Tackling the Definition instead of the Problem* (Coventry: Institute of Housing).

James, Allison and Prout, Alan (eds) (1990) *Constructing and Reconstructing Childhood: Contemporary Issues in the Sociological Study of Childhood* (Basingstoke: The Falmer Press).

Kelly, Liz, Regan, Linda and Burton, Sheila (1991) 'An Exploratory Study of the Prevalence of Child Sexual Abuse in a Sample of 16 to 21 year Olds', Final Report to Economic and Social Research Council, London.

Maclagan, Ianthe (1993) *Four Years' Severe Hardship: Young People and the Benefits Gap* (London: Youthaid, COYPSS and Barnardos), March.

Millar, Jane (1989) *Poverty and the Lone-Parent Family: The Challenge to Social Policy*, Studies in Cash and Care (Aldershot: Avebury Press).

Newell, Peter (1991) *The UN Convention and Children's Rights in the UK* (London: National Children's Bureau).

Oldfield, Nina and Yu, A. C. S. (1993) *The Cost of a Child: Living Standards for the 1990s* (London: Child Poverty Action Group).

Oppenheim, Carey (1993) *Poverty: The Facts* (London: Child Poverty Action Group).

Phoenix, Ann (1991) *Young Mothers* (Oxford: Polity Press).

Stark, Evan and Flitcraft, Anne H. (1988) 'Women and Children at Risk: A Feminist Perspective on Child Abuse', *International Journal of Health Services*, **18**: 1, pp. 97–118.

Woodroffe, Caroline, Glickman, Myer, Barker, Maggie and Power, Chris (1993) *Children, Teenagers and Health: The Key Data* (Buckingham: Open University Press).

4 Girls' Own Story: The Search for a Sexual Identity in Times of Family Change

CHRIS MANN

INTRODUCTION

The last twenty to thirty years have seen complicated shifts in many family and household structures. Such shifts are likely to have affected social behavioural norms, concepts of marriage and sexual standards, but we have little information about how they have impinged on the development of young people. My current empirical research focuses on the academic, social, and sexual identities of adolescent girls in sixth forms, and the contribution made to these constructions by relationships within the family. The Economic and Social Research Council's 16–19 initiative (Banks *et al.*, 1992) has suggested that, in Britain, sixth-formers constitute an elite, regardless of their class background, and that they tend to share similar values. The authors suggest that, whatever their class background, the most highly educated in both sexes were found to be most likely to endorse both egalitarianism and sexual liberalism, concluding that for many sixth formers sexism was viewed as a working-class phenomenon;

> At some parties, they just treated the girls as 'objects', like a can of lager! I don't go to those sort of parties – well there is a bit of that, but in the sixth form we tend to talk to girls more. (Banks *et al.*, 1992, p. 102)

By choosing to work only with academically successful girls I hoped to tap the views of some positive and confident young women, living in the modern world, who would be benefiting from that atmosphere of 'egalitarianism and sexual liberalism'. In addition, I hoped these sixth-form girls, poised at the threshold of adulthood, many of whom

would be already anticipating leaving home for further study, would
be able to reflect on the contribution the family had made to their
success. For in the case of sixth formers, the ESRC authors had concluded that, 'Whether relations with parents were perceived as har-
monious or in conflict, they were the principle agents in maintaining
the students' sense of self and identity' as these young people, 'felt at
least partly immersed in their parents' world' (Banks *et al.*, 1992,
p. 100). However, in my research, discussions concerning changing
structures and relational dynamics within families revealed that the 'principle agents' in a family frequently did not speak with one voice. It
became clear that the contribution of parents to the maintenance of the
girl's 'sense of self and identity' and, in particular, her sexual identity, was often ambivalent and sometimes contradictory. Working with
girls who had managed to get at least one aspect of their lives in order
– having so far successfully negotiated the education system – I was
unprepared for the very many negative feelings that these young women
have to cope with and which, in their own estimation, are directly
related to their experiences of the manifestations of gender identity,
and the direct and indirect repercussions of the sexual behaviour of
family members, particularly parents. For instance, a clear theme that
is evident throughout my work with young women is the level of disappointment that many girls express when they describe their relationship
with their fathers. Accordingly, I shall focus here on the father–daughter
relationship, and the ways in which changed relations between parents
may be constructed by young women and integrated into their social
and sexual identity.

RESEARCH DESIGN

The analysis that follows is based on the narratives of about sixty
working-class and middle-class girls, doing full-time A-levels, at sixth-
form colleges, schools, and further education colleges, in East Anglia.
For demographic reasons there were very few black girls in the sample
so, unless specified, the presumption is that the girl is white. This
research adopted a multiple-methods approach, using focus groups,
individual interviews and autobiographical techniques to investigate the
girls' own perceptions of their lives (Mann, 1995). The methodology
is similar to that used so successfully by developmental psychologist
Carol Gilligan, and her colleagues at Harvard, who claim that it, 'is

not that the girls we spoke with are representative of all girls, or some ideal sample of girls, but rather that we learned from this group of girls and young women, and what we discovered seemed worthy of others' attention (Brown and Gilligan, 1992, p. 23). Using Gilligan's voice-centred method of analysis (Brown and Gilligan, 1992, pp. 25–31) I tried to remain aware of the dynamics between the voice of each girl (the map of her own connections and thinking processes), my own voice as a feminist researcher, and the relationship between each girl and myself. My gender and class background (brought up working class – now middle class), the fact that I have a daughter of the same age, and my perceived beliefs, created a resonance with each individual girl that produced this material. With a different researcher, different issues may well have come to light.

FATHERS AND DAUGHTERS

A girl's relationship with her father is only one strand in the great complexity of inter-familial relations that contribute to the construction of social and sexual identity in contemporary times but its significance cannot be underestimated (Sharpe, 1994). Some girls have 'lost' their fathers following divorce (about half of separated men lose contact with their children three years after separation) but even when the father lives in the home he may still be emotionally 'absent'. However, even if fathers have been mainly absent from the family, 'they represent men and masculinity in a way that does not leave their daughters untouched' (Sharpe, 1994, p. 101). Gaskell argues that girls' construction of masculinity, 'is rooted in an ideology which suggests that what men *are* like is what men *must* be like' and that, 'their perceptions are validated by their experiences of patriarchal family structures' (Gaskell, 1992, p. 79). Lees provides us with a description of what, 'men are like' according to girls – it is, 'the predominant view that it is natural for a boy to behave in a downright egotistically dishonest, bolshie, untrustworthy, unfeeling way' (Lees, 1993, p. 18). With that quote in mind it might be enlightening to consider the ways in which some high-achieving adolescent girls construct their fathers. It has to be said that while some girls spoke positively about their fathers the majority shared some of the reservations that I should like to discuss here.

Gender Patterns in the Home

In group discussions most girls seemed aware of equal opportunities issues and demonstrated at least a superficial support for them. They were aware that often fathers did not pass the 'new man' test and handled this in different ways. Some girls brought in psychological concepts either in an effort to explain or, interestingly, with an awareness that the father's behaviour might be seen to need a defence;

> I don't think my dad thinks 'Oh, the role of the woman is in the kitchen' but I think, subconsciously, he *does* think that.

> You see dad's not very *good* with kids. He's not a kid *person*. He can't handle it, he doesn't go near them, touch them or anything.

Several working-class girls, were quick to identify paternal grandmothers as the source of 'the problem' of their father's behaviour, as the older women continue to suggest that women must wait on husbands 'hand and foot', and 'provide men with anything they want'.

> Like when my nan comes to our house she gets my dad some toast. 'Do you want it cut in half?' 'Yes.' 'Do you want it cut in quarters?' 'Yes.' Like my dad does it to wind her up – but she really thinks that we are here to slave – to be slaves for men. Like no way!

Some girls used the terminology of stereotypical gender behaviour with rueful or ironic awareness. Other girls seemed resigned to traditional gender constructs.

> Dad says that women are best at answering phones and doing secretarial things as it's a man's world. My mum helps me with emotional things and dad helps me with practical things. If I've got a 'man' problem, if you know what I mean – not a boyfriend problem – but if the car's broken, or something's broken in my room – he helps me mend it. And that's about all he does. He's a practical man – and that's about it.

Intimacy, Sexuality and Control

It became more difficult for girls to find a discourse for their father's behaviour once the issues became more related to their experience of their father's masculinity in areas of intimacy, sexuality and control.

Fathers have had, until recently, the legitimation of the discourse of patriarchy to support their behaviour. As Giddens (1992, p. 107) describes,

> the idea that children should obey their elders and betters . . . [was] largely a male doctrine, upheld by the rule of the father. The discipline of the father tied the child to tradition, to a particular interpretation of the past; authority in this situation remained largely dogmatic assertion, backed in many instances by physical punishment.

A preliminary analysis of my data suggests that working-class girls from rural backgrounds are still most overtly exposed to authority as 'dogmatic assertion' sometimes backed by physical punishment. However, more sophisticated middle-class girls also experience the masculine 'other' of their fathers in terms of power and control. In one middle-class home a father capitalises on both his physical and his intellectual strength.

> Dad's a big man. He's not aggressive – but he's like physically imposing. He can argue better than me. Anyway I'm not allowed to answer back. But I know lots of big words! I know them 'cos dad uses them on me: 'pedantic' – 'petulant' – all of those! But I don't try to answer back now. I stay in my room most of the time. And then if he sees me – if I'm looking unhappy – he says 'wipe that expression off your face!' When I was younger he was always going on about me being pale and sulky and never smiling – but it wasn't sulking it was. . . . I was just . . . sad.

The language girls use to describe the ways they see the power relationships of gender and age played out with their fathers is significant as 'relations of power are embedded in constructions of masculinity and femininity' (Lees, 1993, p. 18), and the use of language reinforces the gender identities that girls develop. Sarah, a working-class girl from a rural area is locked in a power struggle with her father, who, 'Like – rules – in a way'. She challenges his dominance by arguing and, in her own words, 'showing a lot of guts'. But she knows she has a precarious hold on her personal control.

> I mean he only sort of really frightened me a few times. Like really frightened me. But then I still did it [argued] cos – I suppose its worth it. I wanted to prove a point to him that *I can't be chained up in my own room*. But yet he has really frightened me I must admit. Before. That last row. He really frightened me.

Her language is that of a prisoner held confined by an intimidating figure of authority and it is echoed by other girls.

My dad's got such a hold over me I mean I'm really scar.... I'm not scar.... I mean we get on really well. I'm not scared of him like in a physical sense. It's more mental. I dunno. I just know I'm not going to win. In the end.

My dad would *never* scream or shout, or lose his temper, but he'd just be able to sit there and while *you* were screaming or shouting he'd just be *looking* at you. And he'd sort of torment you that way, d'you know what I mean?

Some girls attempt to adjust the power balance of gender and age to something more equitable, but this process is fraught with difficulty as issues of intimacy come into play. One working-class girl attempted to discuss her relationship with her boyfriend with her father;

One particular time I do remember sitting down with my dad – but it wasn't sitting down as *equals* – it was sitting down as 'I'm your father. I'm going to tell you what to do.' sort of thing. And he just made me feel really small. And every time I spoke I felt as if I was going to cry cos I just felt so hurt that he wasn't going to treat me as an equal and we weren't going to talk about it properly. I just remember feeling that I wouldn't say anything cos I was going to cry if I opened my mouth. And I just ended up listening to him and just saying I was sorry and not meaning it.

It is not surprising that this girl found such difficulty in engaging her father in a conversation about her boyfriend as a key area in which fathers practised control was sexuality. In this context some fathers reinforce parental authority with the legitimation of tradition as found in the discourse of religion and other moralities. One girl's father, a church elder, was emphatic that women were 'separate sexes' that should 'fulfil different roles within the family'.

He says I shouldn't wear earrings, cut my hair, wear short skirts, low necks or make-up. And he's definitely against children before marriage.'

Girls stressed that their clothing needed to be 'decent' if they wished to avoid parental wrath.

My father doesn't understand that you need to dress up, to follow
the fashion, to go out. He sees it all as like ... vanity.

However, not all girls were prepared to accept the father's morality
frame without question and their language drew on other influences,
as Becky, a working-class girl from a rural area, was to describe.

Becky's Story

B: I think the only way that, say my dad, could talk me out of doing
something, is by saying that the Lord didn't want me to do it.
And when he says things like that I really have to stop and think,
you know – is this true, you know? If it's something like, for
instance, sex, then he'll bring the Bible into it and start quoting
verse and stuff.

C: So wouldn't he want you to have sex before marriage?

B: Well he did! When he was sixteen he got his girlfriend pregnant.
I think – I always think – that's my excuse. Well he did it – so
why shouldn't I, sort of thing. I mean I know it's not morally
right but – I mean the Bible's written years and years and years
ago when, you know, it wasn't such a social issue. But now, you
know, it's rammed down your throat, practically, isn't it? And I
don't think I had sex because I feel as if, you know, I have to fit
in. And at one stage I was really like dad, set against having sex
before marriage, but that's before.... I think, that if you love
someone, and it's not just a one-night thing then, you know, it's
fair enough. If you can see a future with that person then I don't
see why you shouldn't.
    My parents don't know! I just think it'd cause unnecessary ten-
sion in the house. Especially when my boyfriend comes over. I
mean my father would probably make it sound like I was just sort
of bed-hopping, or whatever, and make me feel dirty about it.

Becky still holds on to her religious beliefs, but her narrative shows
that she is seeking a discourse to challenge a control of her sexuality
that she finds inappropriate. She is aware that sexual behaviour is now
'a social issue' but the phrase 'rammed down your throat' suggests a
violent antipathy to its high media profile that may well reflect her
family's views. She is also defensive. She is afraid she will be accused of having sex just to 'fit in'. But Becky, studying history, has
been given a new language of intellectual analysis. She can set the

Bible in context and ask herself if her father's interpretations are 'true'. She can also apply peer group discourse to her father's behaviour. By using the term getting 'his girlfriend pregnant' she demonstrates that she has demoted her father from the language, and hence power, of moral ascendancy. And finally Becky is acknowledging the language of the double standard. Becky's father, like many of the boys she knows, will 'make it sound like' her sexuality is reprehensible. Girls who have 'just a one-night thing', who 'bed-hop' are made to feel 'dirty' about it. If her sexuality is being so constituted by all the men in her life then she can counter it with the discourse of romance: if you 'love someone' and 'can see a future with them' then 'it's fair enough'. Lees suggests that, in the language of romance, 'love is crucial to rendering sex a legitimate activity' (Lees, 1993, p. 107) with the result that, 'a girl either suppresses her sexual desire or channels it into a steady relationship' (Lees, 1993, p. 112). She argues that the girl is, in effect, being sexually controlled once more. However, it could also be argued that the language of romance may give a girl breathing space to experiment with her sexuality until she finds a more sophisticated discourse that could accommodate her developing sexual identity in the longer term.

Control of the Body

My data also suggests that a concentration on the 'body', a key characteristic of the sexist discourse of the peer group, is reinforced by this virgin/whore dichotomy upheld in some form by many fathers. Some fathers talk in terms of sexual provocation centred on the body.

> My dad says I wear too much eye make-up. When I go out I show too much of my body and never look respectable. I also provoke attention.

> It's horrible when you've taken pains to get ready to go out and you think you look nice and you walk through to say 'Goodbye and see you later' and they just turn round and say 'God, you look a right mess.' That's what my dad'll say to me. He says 'I'm not having you tarted up going from here.' And it just knocks your confidence completely – and you feel you don't want to go anywhere.

The girls' emphasis is on loss of confidence linked to unacceptable presentation of the body and it has a particular significance in the light of the prevalence of eating disorders. I was amazed that the narratives of these sixth-form girls incorporated eating disorders into a girl's experience almost as an inevitability, as if it was nearly as predictable as menstruation. Evidence of peer group influence is clear in this area, but, as seen in Carol's story, there is also the hidden and powerful influence of family men who have not relinquished control of the girl's body.

Carol's Story

Carol, a working-class girl, whose own mother had once been seriously anorexic, said her father,

> used to tease me and go on about my big bum and stuff. . . . When I had puppy fat my dad was teasing me and saying how fat I was – then when I started losing weight he started teasing me about being too thin.

Girls frequently experience 'teasing' from boys, other girls, and from within the family, but no-one underestimates its power of control. As Carol says,

> If anyone needs to get me back. If anyone teases me and says 'God, put your fat bum down here' I take that personally. Even if they're mucking about I think 'oh my god – another diet'. And I'd do it. And everyone knows it. That's probably why they tease me – they know it gets to me.

Carol's experience of her father is that he will criticise her for getting 'tarted up' and, knowing that it will get to her, 'tease' her about her weight, until in the end she heard the two elements merged,

> One day I got dressed to go out and he just looked at me and he said 'You look disgusting. You look like a kitten. You've got no chest You've got nothing – you're just *bones.*' Cos literally I was all boney here (touches clavicle) and my skin was all pulled. And he said 'You look sick. Disgusting. You don't think anyone's going to look at you the way you are now.'

There is no doubt that complex inter-connections of ideas and experiences must come into play for every individual with an eating disorder. However, one factor held in common by the girls in this study is their high level of academic achievement. Lawrence (1984) has argued that the onset of anorexia is frequently associated with conflicts brought about by educational attainment. She suggests that education offers women a sexual identity that is almost universally disapproved of because it threatens to marginalise the model of womanhood that is centred on mothering. She adds that anorexia also involves, 'an attempt on the part of the woman to take control of her body, and symbolically, her life' (Lawrence, 1984, p. 208). Significantly, findings from this research suggest that, more frequently than in any other area of their lives, girls experience absence of control in their relationship with their fathers. Perhaps the control of diet offers young women some kind of solution when their lives are seizing up with contradictions. Coping with the demands of competitive achievement and the conflicting stereotypes of femininity a high-achieving girl may also feel torn between the impulse to take control of her life and the desire to keep the love and acceptance of her father. If she senses that her father may be personally threatened by her developing sexuality, at the same time as the nature of her sexuality as a highly educated woman becomes socially suspect, she may choose to take control of her life in a way that attempts to avoid confrontation. In this context anorexia may be an unconscious attempt to return to a time when, 'it was possible to be a clever and pretty little girl' (Lawrence, 1984, p. 207).

For many girls the loss of the pre-adolescent relationship they enjoyed with their fathers is a cause of bitter regret. Other girls are aware that the relationship has always been difficult. Both situations cause distress, for, as Sharpe noted, it is frequently the approval of their fathers that girls most desire (Sharpe, 1994). If girls are bruised by oppressive control from their fathers, they are equally hurt by a sense of being insignificant – being 'really small', not being heard, not being recognised. Girls talk about longing for affirmation from their fathers but their words are phrased in a spirit of resignation:

I wish my father had told me what he really thought of me as I was growing up as I really want him to be proud of me but I don't know what he sincerely thinks of me.

In my maths GCSE my dad was the one whose opinion counted – though I wouldn't let myself really admit that. That was the thing that counted, his congratulations, that counted the most. Because he doesn't really – give an opinion on my life – to have that – for me to think, you know, 'maybe he'll be pleased with me if I do well at that'.

My dad. I can sit there and shout at him for half an hour. I'll go on and on and on and shout at the dog if I have to. I'll go (in a put-on loud and petulant voice) 'You're ignoring me!' Then I ask him what I've just said and he'll just say – he won't know what to say. He'll sit there and he'll go 'Yeah, yeah, mm, mm.' I go and see him now. We do *talk* now. He has problems communicating. He doesn't really show any affection really. That bothered me at one point but it doesn't any more.

From my data I would suggest that some of the father and daughter issues discussed here are relevant to the life experience of many young women. Of course girls' relationships with their fathers may be transitory, complex, and unstable but the question must be asked – what will be the implications for the construction of femininity and the sexual subjectivity of young women whose first experience of masculinity takes these forms? In addition, how will girls recreate masculinity and femininity at this time of social change?

CONSTRUCTING SEXUALITY AT TIMES OF SOCIAL CHANGE

I am finding evidence that girls are receiving constructions of masculinity and femininity that are felt to be in flux, not only within their peer groups, but for adult members of their own families. It is becoming clear that at a time of social change girls are daily confronted with contradictions that they have to develop strategies to deal with. I suggest that one of these strategies is to draw on discourse other than that of their peer group, which, despite the greater 'egalitarianism and sexual liberalism' of the sixth form, continues to be based on language that can demean women; the girls still being 'brought down to size by being rendered a bitch, a cow or a cunt' (Lees, 1993, p. 48). Lees argued that, 'Sexual behaviour is formed by powerful social discourses rather than biology' (Lees, 1993, p. 181). For educated girls, discourses could involve the impact of liberalism, feminism, and new moralities. This research showed that the range of discourse in sixth-formers' narratives is often sophisticated and acute, drawing on sociological and psychological concepts that have often found their way into 'everyday' ideas, and that allow them to contextualise their feelings in some sort of theoretical framework. In varying degrees these young women, regardless of their class background, are becoming less, 'limited by the language they have access to' (Lees, 1993, p. 7).

I should now like to draw on the narrative of a young woman that takes into account her experience of relationships, particularly her relationship with her father, within a home in the process of change. In addition, this narrative will show how the constitution of sexual identity frequently depends on the dynamic between relationships in the home and peer group influences outside.

Amy's Story

I met Amy when she was already eighteen, a year older than her contemporaries. I was to discover why Amy's education had been delayed. Following a long period during which her mother had begun to challenge the *status quo* in her home, and which had been characterised by arguments, her father had finally walked out. Amy had taken his departure very badly and had searched for comfort in both reading and counselling. In Amy's narrative awareness of the new ideas and terminology to which she has recently been introduced resonates with earlier meanings as she struggles to make sense of her experience.

My mother gave up everything for us children. She did everything to become the perfect mother – which is very nice for the children but it's not really very good cos we never knew she *had* any needs. And then when she *did* show she had needs – it was *so* – I just couldn't believe it. I was just so shocked. I just – you know – I didn't want to know. That was . . . some years ago. Erm . . . my mother was *both* parents . . . to us . . . my father was very much . . . sort of absent. He *loved* us but he didn't know how to show it. He did when I was little but when I . . . became eleven – that's when we moved here – I became, like, rebellious. Well, the family was going through a bit of a difficult time at that time [laughs ruefully] . . . well the family's been going through a bit of a difficult time ever since [laughs] I mean my parents weren't getting on too well . . . and er . . . at eleven I think I felt rather [shrugs expressively] . . . so I became rather rebellious at school. I wasn't very nice.

I used to be, like, very sweet and do anything for anyone before that. A real doormat. And then because I became more of my own person – or asserted myself more – he found that very difficult to

handle and he wasn't affectionate towards me any more and he didn't
hug me. I used to sit on his lap and I was such a little daddy's girl.
I know people shouldn't have favourites – but I was his. And then,
you know, a complete gap. I couldn't get on with him. He didn't try
with me. And I felt very unloved. Even though my mother . . . was
very loving towards me. And that's when I was about twelve. And
that's when I started to go downhill really. I *hate* to blame it on
him cos it's not really his fault because *his* mother didn't – love
him enough. But because of that I think my self-esteem suffered –
and then my work did.

I think it's very important as you're growing up for both parents
– but especially your father – to . . . to . . . keep being affectionate
to you. Or you think, you know, 'What's wrong?' I don't know
how to. . . . 'Aren't I good enough?' That's the question – 'aren't I
good enough?' So I mean – about twelve to thirteen – I actually
stopped eating for a while. Not seriously anorexic – I mean I sur-
vived. I lost a lot of weight. Couple of stone. I mean – that wasn't
for long. But, you know, I suppose in a way attention seeking. But
I didn't think that at the time. I didn't know what it was at the time.
I just wanted to be a little girl again. To be loved by my father. To
be accepted, really.

Here we see Amy struggling with traditional stereotypes of the 'good'
woman and trying to set them into her own experience. She has the
language for 'the perfect mother', and 'daddy's little girl' who was so
'very sweet' but while she can see the flaws in the stereotypes she
has to struggle to find words to present alternatives in a positive light.
Faced with the needs of her 'perfect mother' she flounders incoher-
ently. Determined not to be a 'doormat' but to be more assertive she
also falls back on the language of adolescent delinquency – she is no
longer 'nice', the 'ideal girl', but starts to 'go downhill.' Amy is aware
of the negative label 'rebellious' as applied to teenagers, setting the
word in invisible quotation marks as she speaks, but she counters it
with the discourse of personal fulfilment 'I became more of my own
person', and at a later point in her narrative she was to pull in media
terminology for combative feminism – 'I rebelled. I got bull-shitty'
But the verbal acrobatics she was using in an attempt to justify the
legitimacy of her desire for autonomy, her longing to escape the mould
of the 'ideal woman', could not protect her from the perceived masculine identity of the key man in her life, her beloved father.

As she constructs his masculinity, she uses the terminology of current psychology. He is the 'absent' father, who was unable to show affection because he, in his turn, had never been 'loved enough.' But Amy does not have words to explain why his affection should dry up once she started to challenge the feminine stereotype. All she knows is how she feels. 'Aren't I good enough?' She repeats with emphasis 'That's the question – "aren't I good enough?"'. She knows that her efforts to break out of the virginal mould have made her unacceptable. Later she was to describe her sister who,

> picked up on what was going on around her and then behaved – 'nicely' – because she didn't want to upset the . . . balance.

The sister who

> from when she was very little . . . was the brightest of the lot of us children. Brightest. And . . . she sensed . . . she sensed what was going on. And she reverted, you know, to – she's quite cold. She's quite . . . expressionless. . . a lot of the time. She's not very loud. She often stares into . . . the middle distance. She's not a very happy person.

Here Amy both recognises and manifests a particular quality of many young women. Gilligan has said that girls are like 'naturalists'. They have the capacity to name, describe and identify the relational world, in particular what Gilligan calls relationship 'violations' (Brown and Gilligan, 1992, p. 52). Amy uses the language of child psychology to name such a perceived violation within her own home. Her parents' troubles have left her feeling 'neglected'. She demonstrates her need through her rebelliousness:

> I used to creep out and stay out all night. Take drugs and totally run riot because I didn't feel in control of myself. So I went out and tried to make them notice that.

But there had already been a precedent in the family; a previous response to a display of need. The voice of the mother is not focused on at this stage but her action is the 'unsaid' part of the narrative. There is an awareness that her mother 'gave up everything' and that after she *did* decide to show her needs she and her husband 'weren't getting on too well'. Amy has begun to register the fact that displayed needs cause problems or would be disregarded.

In contrast, Amy's sister, the brightest of the lot, sensed what was going on, the volatile relationship of her parents and, in Amy's words, tried not to upset the 'balance'. Amy herself observes her sister, and using the language of psychology she describes a syndrome familiar to many who work with adolescent girls. This is the disassociative process that backs off from voicing feelings, as, in the words of one of Gilligan's girls, they 'mess up relationships' because (and note the same word is used by both girls from two cultures), 'no-one would want to be with me, my voice would be *too loud*'. Amy's sister had a strategy. She would not be too loud, too inquisitive. She would not cause waves within her home by flaunting her knowledge of parental behaviour. She became 'expressionless' and silenced her voice. Amy quite consciously names her own approach as 'rebellion'. In her own terms she describes what it is *not* to be 'nice' but to resist making psychologically damaging disconnections. Feeling neglected she *is* loud 'bull-shitty', voicing a protest against the adult world. But staying in touch with her reality was to prove costly for her as well.

In the terms of Amy's own narrative, exposure to the gender relations in her home has had psychological repercussions that have constrained the developing sexual identity of both the sisters. Both Amy and her sister formulated strategies to negotiate the requirements of the context in which they found themselves. Amy labels her anorexia a 'cry for attention' but it may also have been a tactical method to become an 'acceptable' little girl again. Her sister, working at acting 'nicely' – throws herself into work, becoming emotionally remote and socially passive. But the story does not stop there. For both the young women, the constitution and reconstitution of their sexual identities will also draw on their experiences outside the home as they try and make sense of masculine and feminine identities. Both of the young women have boyfriends. Amy's sister, 'spends quite a lot of time working but she . . . goes out. She socialises a lot. It's men and work! [laughter] But difficulties with men . . .' Amy herself found a boyfriend who was, 'very much like my dad. I picked him out probably because he was like my dad. He looked like my dad'.

But how will Amy handle herself amongst her peers? What is the nature of the discourse that she will meet at school and in her social life? She describes it:

You're definitely not encouraged to do too well in the classroom. You're encouraged to do well enough not to get told off. Well enough not to get noticed. You can do 'quite' well. Just above average. Cos girls *bullied* each other. You pretend nonchalantly [laughs] 'Oh I never did any homework' Ha. Ha. You want to join the group? – you haven't done your homework! I think you can only get away with it if you're [small laugh] six foot tall, skinny [more laughter], pretty! If the boys like you a lot. But generally boys don't like girls to shine. I was a real bull-shitter and they didn't like it very much. [Laughs half triumphantly/ half in resignation] To be accepted by boys [sighs] You have to be pretty. Keep your mouth shut. Oh yes! Men are *scared* shitless – excuse my language – with women who are powerful. I mean some men admire it. Only if they're a bit older. But if the women are close to home they wouldn't admire it. They admire it from a distance. Don't see many cases where men like women to be independent. They feel threatened by that. At school – yeah. School – anywhere. Anywhere.

It is striking that Amy in one short paragraph has been able to touch on nearly all the aspects of girls experience that Lees identified in her research into the constitution of female sexual identity. In fact all that is missing is what Lees terms, 'the vocabulary of abuse' that is common coinage within this age group and which, in this instance I am being spared – 'Excuse my language'. The nature of femininity Amy describes depends on qualities of mediocrity, submissiveness, stereotypically 'model girl' physical attributes, and dependency. She is a sixth-form girl, but even now the discourse of liberalism has faded in the face of the discourse of patriarchy. In addition, her experiences at school have definite resonances with the construction of femininity she has encountered in her home. At school these qualities are not only preferred by boys, but, as Lees has pointed out, 'policed' by other girls often through group pressure.

There is no doubt that the construction of masculinity and femininity connects to relations of power. Amy herself is aware of this, as she talks in terms of power. She is still bravely clinging to the feminist discourse that claims women can be powerful. It is not clear whether she has been 'politicised' by her mother, media coverage, or her own reading but this discourse has given her a small hold on another world. In a later interview she suggests that she has come to terms with the initial confusion that her mother's challenge to the feminine ideal had thrown her into.

Before . . . she was just a very perfect mother sort of thing. But I really admire her now. She's a great person. And I really respect her. She's very strong. But she also has feelings. And admits that now. Which is really good.

Will it be enough? Will she be able to draw on her mother's redefinition of female identity, that allows her to feel free to articulate personal needs and desires, and to show strength? Will the presence of a renewed confiding relationship with her mother give her the psychological nurturance that, research has consistently showed, allows girls to continue to speak their minds? Amy's relationship with her father, reinforced by her peer group, confirms that men will find this threatening; that she will not be acceptable if she does not keep her 'mouth shut'. And again there are echoes of her anorexia – keeping her mouth shut against food – shrinking herself back to daddy's little girl, the sexually unthreatening being who can be given love. And Amy realises that this was not just the situation at home – but also at school and, 'anywhere. Anywhere.'

CONCLUSION

Within these narratives girls use a range of different forms of language that reflect the ideologies and social meanings to which they are exposed. It must be recognised that girls live in the same world as adults and they are not oblivious to the changing meanings of the society they live in. Unfortunately there is also often a great sadness as girls search for meanings in all the interconnected parts of their lives, and attempt to draw them into one coherent narrative that may be a base for their sexual and social identity. As Gilligan has pointed out adolescence is a, 'time of heightened psychological risk for girls' (1992, p. 2). Lees suggests that, 'girls lose confidence because their identity rests to such an extent on their sexual reputation' (1993, p. 29). I should also suggest that their confidence is threatened at an early stage by their relationships with family men, and that the construction of their sexual identity relates as much to dynamics within the home as to peer group influences. But contemporary changes in family processes may have far-reaching repercussions. Even if changes in lifestyle in the home, or recognition of evolving social mores, do not lead to direct challenge or change in inter-familial relationships there can be a subtle shift in atmosphere as the *status quo* is sensed to be assailable. It is to be hoped that the fluid situation concerning gender identity may allow some girls to seize on new behavioural patterns and begin to absorb rewarding images of femininity and masculinity that will inform their own social and sexual identities.

ACKNOWLEDGEMENTS

I should like to thank Madeleine Arnot and Carol Gilligan for all their advice and encouragement. This research was funded by the ESRC.

REFERENCES

Banks, M., Bates, I., Breakwell, G., Bynner, J., Emler, N., Jamieson, L. and Roberts, K. (eds) (1992) *Careers and Identities* (Milton Keynes: Open University Press).
Brown, L. M. and Gilligan, C. (eds) (1992) *Meeting at the Crossroads* (Cambridge, MA: Harvard University Press).
Gaskell, J. (1992) *Gender Matters from School to Work* (Milton Keynes: Open University Press).
Giddens, A. (1992) *The Transformation of Intimacy* (Cambridge: Polity Press).
Lawrence, M. (1984) 'Education and Identity: Thoughts on the Social Origins of Anorexia', in *Women's Studies International Forum*, 7: 4, pp. 201–9.
Lees, S. (1993) *Sugar and Spice* (London: Penguin).
Sharpe, S. (1994) *Fathers and Daughters* (London: Routledge).

Part II
Bodies, Medicalisation and Control

5 Breast Feeding and the Social Construction of Heterosexuality, or 'What Breasts are Really for'

PAM CARTER

Breast feeding has been largely ignored by feminists. Critical analysis of infant feeding is linked to campaigns against the production and marketing of baby milk formula (Chetley, 1986; Lobstein, 1988; Palmer, 1988, 1993; Van Esterik, 1989; War on Want, 1982). Alongside these concerns, and influenced by them, runs considerable mainstream policy attention to declining breast feeding rates both nationally (DHSS, 1974, 1980, 1988) and internationally (WHO, 1974; WHO/UNICEF, 1981, 1990). The absence of sustained feminist analysis of breast feeding has meant a lack of attention to what is being said about women in these debates. Concern about breast feeding constitutes concern about women's behaviour. In particular, differential rates of breast feeding between different groups of women means that attention is focused on working-class women who have lower rates of breast feeding (White *et al.*, 1992). At the heart of the breast feeding 'problem' is a preoccupation with the failure of women to use their breasts in ways which are deemed natural. Black women are viewed as suitably natural when they carry out their breast feeding function in Third World countries, but are subject to anxiety and suspicion when they fail to keep up the same rates of breast feeding in this country (Evans *et al.*, 1976; Costello *et al.*, 1992; Jivani, 1978; Goel *et al.*, 1978; Shahjahan, 1991).

These comments could be read as hostility towards breast feeding on the part of the author. They are not intended to be. Questioning pro-breast-feeding policies may appear gratuitous, since positive links between breast feeding and health are well established if somewhat overstated (UNICEF, 1990). Perhaps the fact that raising questions about such a taken-for-granted good thing looks like a hostile act should alert us to an arena which warrants further scrutiny. My concern in this chapter is not with the question of whether breast feeding is or is

not desirable, but rather with the discourses concerning women's behaviour contained within discussions about breast feeding and with
the practices which are linked to these. In particular, I explore these
discourses as they are articulated in popular breast-feeding manuals
published between 1930 and 1980.

Anxiety about women's inadequacies in breast feeding their babies
pre-dates the widespread availability of manufactured baby milk by
several centuries. For example, Cadogan wrote in his 'Essay on Nursing'
in 1749, 'most mothers of any condition either cannot or will not under-
take the troublesome task of suckling their own child' (quoted in Kessen,
1965, p. 23). He attributes this failing to the unnatural behaviour of
bourgeois women. Poorer women, in his view, are more natural:

> The Mother who has only a few Rags to cover her Child loosely, and
> little more than her own Breast to feed it, sees it healthy and strong,
> and very soon able to shift for itself; while the puny Insect, the Heir
> and Hope of a rich Family lies languishing.   (in Kessen, 1965, p. 13)

Contemporary concerns about women's premature recourse to the bottle
have replaced earlier worries about wet nursing amongst certain groups
of women. There is considerable continuity within these recurring debates, in particular their use of discourses about natural and unnatural
womanliness. Ancient exhortations to breast feed are sometimes cited
in later texts to indicate the natural wisdom of earlier periods. One
example is Truby King's 1937 'mothercraft' manual which contains
an appendix entitled 'Parenthood and Race Culture'. Amongst other
material linking breast feeding, proper motherhood, and the further-
ance of the British 'race' is reference to ancient Rome. A document
written about AD 150 complains about women's inadequacies:

> Are you one of those who think that Nature gave a woman breasts,
> not that she might feed her children, but as pretty little hillocks to
> give her bust a pleasing contour? Many, indeed, of our present-day
> ladies do try to dry up and repress that sacred fount of the body, the
> nourisher of the human race, even at the risk they run from turning
> back and corrupting their milk, lest it should take off from the charm
> of their beauty.   (quoted in Truby King, 1937, p. 226)

This passage highlights another layer of continuity with regard to breast
feeding. This concerns the apparent contradiction between breasts for
feeding babies and breasts as symbols of sexuality. While some at-

tribute this conflict to 'Hollywood' or 'modern civilisation' it is clear that it has earlier manifestations within Western culture. This does not, however, mean that precise expectations regarding the sexuality of breasts have remained constant. Expectations regarding shape, size, and display of breasts do change, often over very short periods of time and with considerable local variation. Sexy breasts of the 1950s were not the same as sexy breasts of the 1970s or the 1990s.

NATURAL FUNCTIONS

What appears to have remained constant is the need for women to try to resolve the tensions concerning different perceived functions of the breast. Considerable limitations on how these are resolved arise from the discourses within which breasts themselves and breast feeding are constructed. Exploring the discursive construction of breasts utilises feminist readings of Foucault's work (e.g. Weedon, 1987; Scott, 1988; Fuss, 1990; McNay, 1992). These feminist perspectives add to Foucault's recognition of the links between power and discourses of sexuality (Foucault, 1981) an awareness of gender itself as a fundamental element in the social construction of sexed bodies. Possessing breasts signals femaleness. Only women have the capacity to breast feed. Bodily practices concerning breasts and breast feeding can be usefully explored using Foucault's recognition of the links between the body and disciplinary regimes: what is said; who looks; who prescribes and defines correct practice. But reading the breasts also demands a specifically gendered analysis. Despite the preoccupation in the breast-feeding literature with the inadequate behaviour of women, there is almost no recognition that breast feeding is constructed within gendered social relations. Women are always present within discussions about breast feeding but are presented as unproblematic natural beings. In that respect women are strangely invisible. The assumption within critical discussions about breast feeding, including those few which draw on feminist perspectives (Kitzinger, 1987; Van Esterik, 1989; Palmer, 1993), is that women have been robbed of something natural and fundamental. There is an assumption that breast feeding is always in women's interests, that in itself it is a form of resistance to patriarchy. But there is little attempt to look at breast feeding from the point of view of women themselves nor at the impact of the powerful linkages which are made between good mothering and breast feeding. There are limited opportunities for women to articulate a different perspective. One of the few writers who questions these assumptions notes that the medical profession, which is rather belatedly so articulate in support of breast feeding, 'remains, on the whole, remarkably innocent of what breast feeding entails' (Maher, 1992, p. 3).

There is considerable difficulty in escaping from the dichotomies within which naturalness is framed. Natural is opposed to unnatural with all of its normative, moral, and pathologising connotations. Only unnatural mothers fail to breast feed. Naturalness is also constructed in opposition to science or other symbols of modernity, the machine for example. In relation to breast feeding, these polarities are also important. Although medicine has had an ambivalent role in relation to breast feeding, often undermining confidence in women's breast feeding abilities (Apple, 1987), doctors have also long been prominent in reminding women of the naturalness of breast feeding. William Cadogan, whose 1749 essay is cited above, was a physician and many others have followed in his path. So the naturalness of breast feeding is endorsed by science and controlled by medicine through various surveillance techniques. The opposition between nature and the machine metaphor is also more complex than it first appears. Practices which were fashionable for several decades during the present century, rigid feeding schedules where babies are fed by the clock, test weighing where they are weighed after every feed, depend on baby and mother taking on machine-like qualities. As one baby-care manual published in 1939 expressed it:

> In his first few weeks the baby is almost a machine. His sole business is to take nourishment, digest it and grow, and the day's routine is correspondingly simple. At the appointed times he is fed; once a day he is bathed; between these events he should sleep almost continuously. (Batten, 1939)

Here the machine and nature are virtually one. Biology, which determines the baby's existence, is conceived in mechanical terms. The baby's clockwork character stems from 'his' physiology. The oft-repeated comment that almost all women are able to breast-feed again depicts women either as cow-like or as breast-feeding machines. As one very popular breast-feeding book says in a chapter directed at fathers, 'a woman has to become cow-like when feeding her baby' (Stanway and Stanway, 1978, p. 174). An earlier version of this idea specifies the kinds of women who are most likely to fall into this category:

The ideal nursing mothers are the cow among animals and the peasant-mother among our own kind, who do not think about it all, but get on with the job, and in this matter an ounce of faith is worth a ton or more of science and book-lore.   (Batten, 1938)

This discourse of the natural has only limited possibilities for women in relation to breasts and breast feeding. It provides only a functional language based on biologically framed discourses of femininity and sexuality. Breast feeding is identified as in itself an expression of woman's true sexuality. For example, La Leche League literature addresses the breast-feeding mother as being 'never more aware of your womanliness' (La Leche League, 1963, p. 1) and this sentiment is echoed many times over within other texts. On the other hand, breasts are defined as erogenous zones, essential aspects of women's (hetero)sexuality, both visually and in terms of their tactile sensuality. That both of these positions are linked via their supposed naturalness means that resistance to the latter is most often framed in the language of the former.

FEELING, SEEING, AND LIVING THE BODY

Breast feeding is a bodily activity. This is meant both in the 'body as discourse' sense and in the 'body as lived experience' sense. Breasts and breast feeding are heavily constructed through a wide range of language, practice, and representation. But at the same time, breasts swell, leak, tingle, and sometimes appear to have a life of their own. Within an arena such as breast feeding, where demands and expectations are so contradictory, the material effects of changes in the breasts themselves may have to be accounted for. Recent thinking and writing about the sociology of the body has attempted to see the body as both material and social, the one inseparable from the other (Turner, 1992; Morgan and Scott, 1993). Arising from their work on young women's experiences of heterosexuality Holland *et al.* explore

the ways in which the disembodiment of feminine sexuality regulates women's bodies and reproduces conventional gender relations, while at the same time the materiality of bodies can disrupt these relations. This possibility of disruption can offer some space for women's resistance to men's sexual power.   (Holland *et al.*, 1994)

Leaking breasts can perhaps provide the basis of resistance to the romanticized Madonna image which lurks within writing about breast feeding. At the beginning of one text on childbirth the following poem is quoted in praise of Mary as a symbol of divine motherhood:

> But Mary walked to the choir stalls
> And took a seat, her hair dark intermingled
> With the dusky leaf-work of the carven chair
> Her azure dress fell open in front
> And a light flush stole over
> The half-bowed, high white brow.
> Then suckled she the child.
>
> (Van De Velde, 1935)

While this is an almost delightfully extreme version, it remains a familiar and important symbol of a rather ethereal, very unmaterial motherhood.

It is hardly surprising that women find breast feeding complex. Being a breast-feeding mother demands that women use their bodies in ways which are very different from their previous experience. They may have to negotiate new feelings, changed breast size and shape, different ways of being looked at, undesirable effects on their clothing and altered relationships with others. Breast feeding requires that women tackle all of these potentially demanding experiences. Despite this, mainstream research and policy tends to treat difficulties associated with them as a product of women's irrational attitudes or as the effect of the vague category 'society', rather than as arising from the fact that women's bodies are treated as inherently problematic in a patriarchal world (DHSS, 1974, 1980, 1988).

Government-funded research has time and time again shown that problems associated with bodily practices and experiences are important influences on whether women choose to breast feed in the first place and whether they continue to do so. In Britain only 25 per cent of mothers breast feed for four months or longer, a recommendation which has been official policy since 1974. Only 50 per cent breast feed for two weeks (White *et al.*, 1992). Of those mothers who plan from the start to bottle feed around 30 per cent in several studies say they intend to do this because they 'do not like the idea of breast feeding' (White *et al.*, 1992). Qualitative studies suggest that social contexts involving lack of privacy, loss of confidence, poor material resources in terms of adequate housing and money, feeling restricted, little support with child care, and other responsibilities all play a part

(Blaxter and Patterson, 1982; McIntosh, 1985; Hewart and Ellis, 1986; Carter, 1992; Carter, 1995). These difficulties not only apply to women who bottle feed. In one study all the women interviewed, even those who breast fed, expressed ambivalence and a 'loss of self' (Hewart and Ellis, 1986). That breast feeding is seen as natural disguises this complexity. The involvement of women's bodies in demanding and difficult activities and negotiations is obscured.

Although, as we will see below, fathers are increasingly targeted within breast-feeding literature and policy, broader phallocentric and heterosexual definitions of women's bodies are ignored. Women's attitudes rather than men's are seen as the problem. One recent counterbalance to this was a survey by the Royal College of Midwives which found that half the men they interviewed were opposed to breast feeding in public describing it as 'embarrassing, unnecessary, exhibitionism, disgusting' (Royal College of Midwives, 1993). Such male-defined understandings of sexuality should indicate the need for caution in simply seeing men as allies to women in relation to breast feeding.

DECENT DADS

During the 1930s, breast-feeding rates in Britain declined, later helped along by the introduction of subsidised milk powder, National Dried, in 1940. This was a period when the medical profession was behaving in a particularly contradictory fashion, advocating breast feeding for all women but at the same time prescribing rigid routines which undermined it. Some of the most prominent figures in the child care world talked glowingly of breast feeding but produced their own breast-milk substitutes. Accompanied by a picture of the breast-feeding Madonna, Truby King writes in his classic text:

> A woman's milk is not her own. It is created for the baby, and the first duty of the mother is to ensure, by foresight, a proper supply of the only perfect food – the baby's birthright. (Truby King, 1937, p. 13)

Nevertheless, he had been marketing breast-milk substitutes since the 1920s. Despite the allusions to nature, rigid by-the-clock feeding is recommended, complete with an illustration of an appropriately marked clock face. Apart from the Madonna, all the other women pictured are wearing what looks like nurses' uniform. Mothers are discouraged from playing with their babies. Fathers are not addressed or referred to at all. No mention is made of sexuality in any shape or form. This text represents a rather high-flown discourse of nature and advocates practices which now look anything but natural. From the perspective of the 1990s, breast feeding and baby care as presented here represents 'unnatural' practice – rigid, mechanical, and emotionally and physically distant.

Perhaps in part as a reaction against Truby King and others such as Watson (Hardyment, 1983) who advocated a similar approach, both fathers and sexuality began to appear in texts which followed this period. They were not at first necessarily linked to each other. For example, Gibbens (1955), a London physician, included a chapter for husbands and fathers in his baby-care manual. Pregnancy and lactation, according to Gibbens, mean that women behave in particularly irrational ways. Husbands should humour their wives but also 'apply the brake gently to her activities' (p. 19). Women need extra love from their husbands:

> Reason and argument are useless at such a time, for her difficulties are emotional, not to be solved by the cold light of logic. It is best to humour her whims, to get her out of her mood with extra love and sympathy. A bunch of flowers, a small present, a quiet dinner, tickets for the theatre or cinema – any of these may make her happy. (p. 19)

Sex is a different matter. A husband is expected to show 'delicacy and forbearance' and to be 'content to bide his time' after the birth (p. 21). The notion that men need regular sexual intercourse is questioned:

> Sometimes it is urged that a man's health will suffer if he is denied his wife for many months, but there is little evidence that this is so; on the contrary he will be all the better for a little self-control. (p. 21)

This is in marked contrast to later views on male sexuality, as we will see below. Despite this rap over the knuckles for men and apparent concern for women, mothers who do not breast feed meet with strong disapproval from Gibbens:

> Some refuse out of pure selfishness: the baby means little to them, they are determined to go on having 'a good time', and breast feeding

is a tie. Others refuse in the fear that it will ruin their figures, others because they wish to be with their husbands as much as possible, or they think that the social obligations of being a hostess outweigh the duty of being a mother. (p. 47)

Gibbens makes it clear that none of these reasons are acceptable since 'breast feeding is the baby's birthright, it is one of the finest emotional experiences in a woman's life' (p. 45). The decent father is accompanied by the selfless mother who dutifully breast feeds, experiencing disembodied pleasure as she does so.

Dick-Read, a prominent figure in the development of so-called natural childbirth also described the significance of breast feeding in somewhat non-corporeal ways. He 'severely condemned' bottle feeding because a woman 'feeds her baby with her mind through her breast' (Dick-Read, 1950, p. 43). This was not, however, a conscious process, instead it was again the product of Nature. In fact a peculiarly passive kind of mentality was required:

We must not overlook the importance of the day-dreams of the nursing mother. Not infrequently a new outlook on life is developed, which brings a serenity of mind, enhancing for all time the patience and self-control so necessary in the up-bringing and training of children. (Dick-Read, 1950, p. 44).

WOMANLY ARTS

An important strand within the discourses of sexuality grew out of this sublime and unworldly linkage between the naturalness of breast feeding and its specialness for women. As discourses of sexuality began, in the 1960s, to be more explicit in naming bodily parts and specifying feelings, breast feeding itself began to be talked about in terms of sensuality. Breast feeding was seen as an expression of women's special sexuality.

An important precursor to this is contained in material published by La Leche League, an international breast-feeding organisation which was begun by a group of mothers in Illinois in the late 1950s. Their main text, 'The Womanly Art of Breast Feeding' is certainly more sensual than earlier books although most emphasis is placed on the baby's sensuous feelings rather than those of the mother. For example:

He turns and nuzzles your breast. Quickly you form the nipple with your fingers, a small help for one so little. His tiny mouth grasps and he sucks. Together you relax. What a kind, knowing Nature to demand so little now. Your tired body is not taxed. After the supreme effort of giving birth, this is sweet reward.   (La Leche League, 1963)

This budding sensuality for women is firmly placed within a hetero-sexual nuclear family model. La Leche League's chapter for fathers is concerned to reinforce 'manly men' as well as 'womanly women', to 'keep these father and mother images clear!' (La Leche League, 1963, p. 115). His role is to be one of protector, defending her against inter-fering family and neighbours and old wives tales.

He must also protect her from her own irrationality with his 'clear thinking' about breast feeding (p. 112). After all:

Most husbands are enthusiastic about the idea from the start: they know without much thinking about it that it is not only the best way but the *womanly* way to feed a baby; and womanliness is the trait they most value in a wife.   (p. 19; emphasis in original)

Unlike later texts which link positive images of breast feeding both with female sensuality and heterosexuality, this book has no chapter devoted to sex: sexual intercourse is not addressed directly. No de-manding husbands or decent dads here. But breast feeding has been firmly located with the heterosexual couple in the nuclear family.

'LET YOUR HUSBAND PLAY WITH YOUR BREASTS'

The 1930s, 1940s and 1950s witnessed growing emphasis on the de-sirability of fulfilment through marriage (Clark, 1993). In the 1960s these expectations became increasingly sexualised. Clark writes of the work of marriage guidance as one mechanism through which this dis-course was produced:

sexual regulation within marriage is performed through exhortations to pleasure, rather than denial or abstinence.   (Clark, 1993, p. 31)

It is possible to trace this same path within books on breast feeding. Two popular texts give vivid pictures of new demands on the breast-feeding mother. Her role as lover had to be fitted in to her role as mother: self control for men had disappeared. These two books, Marvin Eiger and Sally Olds' *The Complete Book of Breastfeeding*, American and published in 1972, and Penny and Andrew Stanway's *Breast is Best*, British and published in 1978, are remarkably similar to each other. Both have a chapter for fathers, 'so they don't feel left out', followed by a chapter on breast feeding and sex. Distinct models of male and female sexuality appear in both of these:

> the human male has but one string to his bow – his interest in and performance of sexual intercourse. It is largely around this one activity that male sexuality is defined. A man is generally considered a fulfilled sexual being if he is able to attain orgasmic satisfaction through intercourse.   (Eiger and Olds, 1972, p. 130)

Women's more complex sexuality is 'controlled to a large measure by the interaction of many of the hormones released inside a woman's body' (Eiger and Olds, 1972, p. 130). The Stanways' views are very similar:

> To a man, sex means intercourse. If he is making love to the woman he loves and who is the mother to his children – so much the better. But often men will say how readily they can enjoy intercourse with a woman who means little or nothing to them. Men are relatively simple in their sexual demands and relatively easily pleased.   (Stanway and Stanway, 1978, p. 179)

Although 'primitive women are ruled by their hormones', modern women apparently resist this to their cost:

> Modern society has tried to make women the same as men when their whole physiological make-up is different, and whether we like it or not we are still ruled by the basic laws of Nature.   (ibid., p. 180)

Amongst other things the action of these hormones makes breast feeding sexual. Both these books draw close parallels between the hormones, pleasures, and emotions involved in women's experience of sexual intercourse and of these other aspects of their sexuality. The sexiness of breast feeding and, indeed, that of these other dimensions of female sexuality, is, according to these texts, the same sexiness as that of heterosexual intercourse. Although women's sexuality is multi-faceted it is, nevertheless, a reflection of male sexuality. One way in which this is expressed is through comparisons between lactation and sexual intercourse, 'lactation also provides a woman with some of the same sensations as coitus: contractions of the uterus, erection of the nipples, and a rise in body temperature' (Eiger and Olds, 1972, p. 133). Sexual intercourse as a metaphor for breast feeding has a long history (Ellis, 1903; Freud, 1905).

Breast feeding is thus firmly placed within a sexual hierarchy dom-inated by a narrowly constructed, male oriented, physiologically driven, discourse of sexuality. A further significant link has been made be-tween lactation and sexual intercourse through the work of Masters and Johnson (1966), at least in the ways that their research has been represented within books on breast feeding, as in this extract from Eiger and Olds (1972):

> According to the Masters and Johnson findings, nursing mothers are more eager to resume sexual relations after childbirth than are women who do not breastfeed. . . . In fact, the nursing mothers generally reported that they had even more erotic feelings now than they had had before they became pregnant. (p. 136)

The Stanways assert these views even more strongly, but without making specific use of Masters and Johnson's authority. They also build on the parallels which they have drawn between breast feeding and sexu-al intercourse to explain this:

> Many women say that they find breast feeding so sexually pleasing that they feel more sexy towards their husbands. In fact, it is well known that women who are nursing return to sexual intercourse sooner after birth than do their bottle feeding sisters. Certainly the breast feeding woman returns to normal more quickly physically but it's also more likely that the repeated feelings of sexual arousal (how-ever minimal they are) also make her more receptive to sex. Some studies show that a substantial number of women are more sexually active when breast feeding than at any other time. This is good news for fathers who often feel left out at that time! (Stanway and Stanway, 1978, p. 182)

Here we have a model of breast feeding being used in the service of heterosexual intercourse. Rather than a conflict between breasts for feeding babies and erotic breasts, here biologically driven sexual pleasure serves both. Both of these books give precise instructions about how to combine the two, making sure that sexual intercourse is given its rightful place. Women's bodies in general, and breasts in particular, have to meet the needs of both babies and husbands. The Stanways give a precise ruling in italics on this matter, '*share your breasts with him and the baby*' (p. 185).

Their list of 'hints' on this include,

If feeding makes you feel sexy . . . tell him so and encourage him to make the most of it.

Wear a good nursing bra and remind him that you're doing it for his benefit so that he'll have your breasts looking good years from now.

Keep up your previous 'mistress' image as much as possible. (p. 186)

Most important of all is that it is not only babies who get to touch and suck breasts. Women must make sure that husbands do too:

Show your husband that you still love and want him. Don't let him feel that because the baby's feeding that's all you see your breasts as doing. Let your husband play with your breasts as he did before. He can even drink your milk if he wants to; he won't be robbing the baby of anything.   (p. 183)

Eiger and Olds quote medical authority on this:

Dr Robert A. Bradley, a Denver obstetrician, recommends oral and manual manipulation by the husband of his wife's breasts during both pregnancy and lactation, since he feels that frequent handling of the breasts helps to prevent sore nipples. So you can relax and enjoy yourself as you follow doctor's orders.   (Eiger and Olds, 1972, p. 140)

These texts produce discursive linkages between breast feeding and heterosexuality, particularly sexual intercourse, in a number of ways. The first is that they are portrayed as similar in terms of the hormones which shape them and therefore the physical and emotional feelings which these induce. The second is that the similarities between them mean that the breast-feeding mother feels sexier as a result of being aroused on numerous occasions throughout the day and night and therefore is more eager for sexual intercourse with her husband. Thirdly, husbands playing with, and sucking, their wives breasts are performing a useful service for wife and baby as nipples are toughened up and milk supply maintained. Potential contradictions between the two supposed 'functions' of breasts are ironed out through drawing both into a particular model of female (hetero)sexuality. In fact, rather strangely for such passionate defenders of breast feeding, the Stanways give heterosexual intercourse priority:

> We get rather tired of the 'experts' who keep telling us that breasts are functional organs for feeding babies. Of course they are but not exclusively so and for the forty-odd years of the average couple's married life their erotic role is vastly more important. (Stanway and Stanway, 1978, p. 175)

One way in which this linkage between these two 'functions' is created is through opposition between the natural and the unnatural. Natural women like both intercourse and breast feeding: unnatural, that is, neurotic women like neither. Eiger and Olds (1972) describe nursing mothers as falling into two camps: those who are more sensuous and those who are less. The more sensuous woman is 'more comfortable with her own body than the average woman' (p. 137) and is likely to welcome breast feeding so that she can enjoy a new sensuous experience – this will also mean that she wants more sexual intercourse. The second group of less sensuous women is described as 'compliant about sexual intercourse rather than eager' (p. 138). This obedient, but less sensual, woman is made to sound an altogether less attractive personage than the relaxed woman who can't get enough bodily fulfilment. These natural, relaxed, 'primitive', sensual women as opposed to those who are false, bourgeois, neurotic and selfish are familiar in the breast-feeding literature. According to Dick-Read these two women produce different kinds of milk:

> I asked a woman of the Norfolk marshes, who had brought up fifteen splendid children, how she did it, knowing well the poverty of the marshland folk. She answered, 'I fed them on love milk.' Many years later I realised the truth of this unforgettable remark. There are two milks. Love milk, which prevents or overcomes all difficulties

when breast feeding, and fear milk, which makes difficulties and magnifies them. (Dick-Read, 1950, p. 46)

By the 1970s, it appears, husbands had to have their share of this cheap but powerful 'love milk'.

BREAST FEEDING, FEMININITY AND ROMANCE

There is a real difficulty in affirming breast feeding as potentially a dimension of autonomous female sexuality given its embeddedness within these heterosexual discourses. Even Sheila Kitzinger, a writer and childbirth activist associated with strong images of women's own sexuality, found it hard to make a vigorous challenge to this in her work on breast feeding. Although a note at the beginning of her book on breast feeding acknowledges that mothers may have lesbian partners it is men and male partners who are explicitly addressed on the first page of her book. Throughout the book the gender-neutral 'partner' frequently becomes a man. Hence when she describe the baby as 'born into a system of interaction already flowing between the couple, rather like a duet' the couple appears as inevitably heterosexual (Kitzinger, 1987, p. 14). She begins by describing breast feeding as a psychosexual experience like sexual intercourse. Where she differs from the Stanways, for example, is in describing a sexuality, associated with breast feeding, which is not goal-directed in the sense of geared to orgasm through heterosexual intercourse. However, her challenge to this model is made within the language of the natural, hence summoning all of the linkages, oppositions and assumptions that we have seen elsewhere. For example:

> The point is that lactation is a spontaneous physiological process and breastfeeding a natural act. And yet it is undeniable that many women in modern post-industrial society face problem after problem when breastfeeding. There is an analogy with sex here too, of course. Orgasm is a spontaneous physiological process and comes quite naturally without people having to take lessons in it or learn special techniques. Yet many men and women in Western society face difficulties with it. (Kitzinger, 1987, p. 16)

This familiar opposition between 'civilisation' and the natural 'Other' limits rather than expands understanding.

Kitzinger's chapter on sex and breast feeding begins with a critical appraisal of the uses made of Masters and Johnson's references to breast feeding. From her own experience she suggests that women have all kinds of different reactions to breast feeding, particularly whether or not it made them feel sexy. In response to this recognition of difference and variety, she questions the male-defined models of sexuality which inform sex education and other publications about sex. Having argued that breast-feeding women should not feel obliged to meet sexual goals, however, she then goes on to give detailed instructions about the 'special skills of love making' while breast feeding (Kitzinger, 1987, p. 175). Although these are sensitively written with regard to women's feelings of exhaustion and preoccupation with the baby, in other ways they seem familiar:

> She cannot suddenly be transformed into an exciting sexual creature when she has been walking around with a baby plugged in to her ever since six o'clock. Her partner can run her a bath, make her a drink, tidy up the bedroom, perhaps wash the dishes while she is recovering, then fetch the candles and music. (Kitzinger, 1987, p. 176)

If he bides his time (and even washes up) he gets his dues in the end! Somehow breast feeding here seems a mundane barrier to sexual intercourse which appears as the highest form of bodily pleasure: we all know where candles and music are meant to lead. Rejecting romance may seem a rather jaded response. However, the promise of a different way of thinking about women, sexuality and breast feeding seems to have led us back down a familiar road.

SIGNS OF RESISTANCE?

Resistance to patriarchal definitions and appropriations of women's bodies can neither take the form of always endorsing breast feeding nor of advocating bottle feeding. Both involve complex and often stressful negotiations, including disapproval and disgust, given their pivotal location within discourses of motherhood and sexuality. To simply endorse the pro-breast-feeding lobby without a careful analysis of breast feeding within women's lives seems insufficient. But breast feeding may well be important for women, and for children, and therefore to leave it within its various normative frameworks is to miss opportunities for women to occasionally experience their bodies outside of dominant heterosexual frameworks.

The lack of fit between women's experiences of their bodies and the various demands which are made of them can provide the basis for some resistance. For example the magazine of the National Childbirth Trust (*New Generation*, December 1991, March 1992, December, 1993) featured several articles and letters on sex after childbirth. The theme of this correspondence was that women experienced a wide range of problems in conforming to what they believed was expected of a sexy wife. Breast feeding was identified as especially problematic since many women did not want their breasts to be touched sexually even after feeding had finished. Women expressed their feelings in terms of not wanting their bodies 'used':

> On the rare occasions I get my body to myself I want to keep it rather than give it to someone else.

> I just don't want to be touched.

> At the end of the day I want to keep something of me for me. (*New Generation*, March 1992, p. 38).

Sharing such feelings with others provides the possibility of enhancing women's autonomy. However, the debate is still structured within normative and male defined understandings about heterosexuality. One woman writes of being referred for counselling to a community nurse in the mental health department after she admitted to her doctor that her 'sex life had dwindled':

> I worked through my initial resentment about the easy lot men have to achieve the title of 'father'. Their bodies do not have to undergo major structural changes ending up with a complete overhaul. I was helped by Kathy (the counsellor) to see things from the masculine point of view and she suggested ways we might find more space for ourselves, particularly the importance of talking together about our feelings. (*New Generation*, December 1991, p. 34)

The framework for discussing breast feeding remains that of a heterosexual companionate marriage, presented in this kind of writing as also relentlessly middle class.

Breast feeding is an overwhelmingly heterosexual subject. I have always felt rather apologetic about my interest in the area: it does not seem a suitable area for a lesbian to research. But lesbianism may be an important standpoint. Lesbian experiences of the body may well be different in this respect, as in others. The discourses which construct the lesbian breast may allow different points of departure. Questions about who touches and who sucks take on different meanings and as such invite subversive thinking. The experiences of lesbian mothers in relation to infant feeding offer but one possibility for exploration and research. Another important thread to follow involves work concerning the notion of the lesbian gaze, a challenge to the ubiquitous male gaze. Waterhouse sees this as having an important place in thinking about bodily experiences:

In reclaiming our bodies and the means to bestow meaning upon them we must also take back the power of the gaze. (Waterhouse, 1993, p. 111)

This has particular resonance in relation to breast feeding. The heterosexuality of both breasts and breast feeding is significantly defined through the visual. Breasts have a central place in male-defined visual sexual pleasure. 'Page three' and the girlie calendar are merely the most obvious examples. These kinds of representation are already being challenged but sometimes in ways which carry the risk of what Elizabeth Wilson describes as 'feminist fundamentalism' (Wilson, 1992). Denying the sexuality of breasts, including visual sexuality seems to close off possibility. Lesbian looking may suggest other ways of thinking about the sexuality of breasts. An important dimension of breast feeding is, as we have seen earlier, the question of whether it is acceptable to do it 'in public'. Opening this up for debate, as the Royal College of Midwives has done, provides another possible source of resistance (Royal College of Midwives, 1993).

CONCLUSION

Discourses surrounding breast feeding are expressed within a number of arenas including: medical knowledge and practice; professional and lay writing about childbirth and infant care; practices surrounding birth; and everyday conversation and action. In this chapter I have focused on those which are found in popular baby-care manuals to reveal the increasing (hetero)sexualisation not just of breasts but of breast feeding itself. Challenges to this discursive construction of breast feeding are likely to arise from many sources. The importance of breast feeding as a feminist issue arises from the fact that it is a key arena within which women are offered meanings about their bodies. For the most part, as we have seen, these currently reinforce male-oriented positions. Resistance arises as women talk about what our breasts mean to us and as we refuse to accept being told what our breasts are 'really for'.

REFERENCES

Apple, R. D. (1987) *Mothers and Medicine: A Social History of Infant Feeding, 1890–1950* (Wisconsin: The University of Wisconsin Press).
Batten, L. W. (1939) *The Single-Handed Mother* (London: George Allen & Unwin).
Blaxter, M. and Paterson, E. (1982) *Mothers and Daughters: A Three-Generational Study of Health Attitudes and Behaviour* (London: Heinemann).
Carter, P. (1992) 'Breast and Bottle Feeding in West Newcastle, 1920–1980: A Study of Women's Experiences', unpublished PhD thesis, University of Northumbria.
Carter, P. (1995) *Feminism, Breasts and Breast-feeding* (Basingstoke: Macmillan).
Chetley, A. (1986) *The Politics of Baby Foods: Successful Challenges to Marketing Strategies* (London: Frances Pinter).
Clark, D. (1993) '"With My Body I Thee Worship": The Social Construction of Marital Sex Problems', in D. Morgan and S. Scott (eds) *Body Matters: Essays on the Sociology of the Body* (London: Falmer Press).
Costello, A., Shahjahan, M. and Wallace, B. (1992) 'Nutrition for Bangladeshi Babies', *Community Outlook*, April, pp. 21–3.
Department of Health and Social Security (DHSS) (1974) *Present Day Practice in Infant Feeding*, Reports on Health and Social Subjects no. 9 (London: HMSO).
DHSS (1980) *Present Day Practice in Infant Feeding: 1980*, Reports on Health and Social Subjects no. 20 (London: HMSO).
DHSS (1988) *Present Day Practice in Infant Feeding: Third Report*, Reports on Health and Social Subjects no. 32 (London: HMSO).
Dick-Read, G. (1950) *Introduction to Motherhood* (London: Heinemann).
Eiger, M. S. and Olds, S. W. (1972) *The Complete Book of Breastfeeding* (New York: Workman).
Ellis, H. (1903) *Studies in the Psychology of Sex*, vol. 111, *Analysis of the Sexual Impulse in Women* (Philadelphia, PA: F.A. Davies).
Evans, N., Walpole, I. R., Queresh, M. O., Moron, H. M. and Evely Jones, H. W. (1976) 'Lack of Breast Feeding and Early Weaning of Infants of

Asian Immigrants to Wolverhampton', *Archives of Disease in Childhood*, **51**: pp. 608–12.

Foucault, M. (1981) *The History of Sexuality*, Volume 1, *An Introduction* (Harmondsworth: Penguin).

Fuss, D. (1990) *Essentially Speaking: Feminism, Nature and Difference* (London: Routledge).

Freud, S. (1905) 'Three Essays on the Theory of Sexuality' in *The Pelican Freud Library on Sexuality* (Harmondsworth: Penguin, 1977).

Gibbens, J. (1955) *The Care of Young Babies* (London: Churchill).

Goel, K. M., House, F. and Shanks, R. A. (1978) 'Infant Feeding Practices among Immigrants in Glasgow', *British Medical Journal*, 2: pp. 1181–3.

Hardyment, C. (1983) *Dream Babies* (Oxford: Oxford University Press).

Hewart, R. J., and Ellis, D. J. (1986) 'Similarities and Differences between Women who Breastfeed for Short and Long Duration', *Midwifery*, 2: pp. 37–43.

Holland, J., Ramazanoglu, C., Sharpe, S. and Thompson, R. (1994) 'Power and Desire: The Embodiment of Female Sexuality', in *Feminist Review*, **46**: Spring, pp. 21–38.

Jivani, S. K. (1978) 'The Practice of Infant Feeding among Asian Immigrants', *Archives of Disease in Childhood*, **53**: pp. 69–73.

Kessen, W. (1965) *The Child* (New York: John Wiley).

Kitzinger, S. (1987) *The Experience of Breastfeeding* (Harmondsworth: Penguin).

La Leche League (1963) *The Womanly Art of Breastfeeding* (London: Souvenir Press).

Lobstein, T. (1988) *Warding off the Bottle* (London: The London Food Commission).

Maher, V. (ed.) (1992) *The Anthropology of Breast-Feeding* (Oxford: Berg).

Masters, W. H. and Johnson, V. E. (1966) *Human Sexual Response* (London: J.A. Churchill).

McIntosh, J. (1985) 'Decisions on Breastfeeding in a Group of First-Time Mothers', *Research and the Midwife Conference Proceedings*, pp. 46–63.

McNay, L. (1992) *Foucault and Feminism* (Cambridge: Polity Press).

Morgan, D. and Scott, S. (eds) (1993) *Body Matters: Essays on the Sociology of the Body* (London: Falmer Press).

New Generation (1991, 1992, 1993) magazine of the National Childbirth Trust.

Palmer, G. (1988) *The Politics of Breastfeeding* (London: Pandora).

Royal College of Midwives (1993) *Breast-feeding Facilities in UK Restaurants* (London: Royal College of Midwives).

Scott, J. W. (1988) 'Deconstructing Equality-versus-Difference: Or, The Uses of Poststructuralist Theory for Feminism', *Feminist Studies*, **14**: 1, Spring, pp. 33–50.

Shahjahan, M. (1991) 'Infant and Toddler Feeding Patterns and Related Issues in the Bangladeshi Community in Newcastle', unpublished MSc dissertation, University of Newcastle upon Tyne.

Stanway, P. and Stanway, A. (1978) *Breast is Best* (London: Pan).

Truby King, F. (1937) *Feeding and Care of Baby* (London: Oxford University Press).

Turner, B. S. (1992) *Regulating Bodies: Essays in Medical Sociology* (London: Routledge).

United Nations Children's Fund (UNICEF) (1990) *The State of the World's Children* (Oxford: Oxford University Press).

Van Esterik, P. (1989) *Motherpower and Infant Feeding* (London: Zed Books).

Van De Velde, T. H. (1935) *Ideal Birth: How to get the Finest Children* (London: Heinemann).

War on Want (1982) *Breast or Bottle? Factors Influencing the Choice of Infant Feeding in the UK* (London: War on Want).

Waterhouse, R. (1993) 'The Inverted Gaze', in D. Morgan and S. Scott (eds) *Body Matters: Essays on the Sociology of the Body* (London: Falmer).

Weedon, C. (1987) *Feminist Practice and Poststructuralist Theory* (Oxford: Basil Blackwell).

White, A., Freeth, S. and O'Brien, M. (1992) *Infant Feeding 1990* (London: HMSO).

Wilson, E. (1992) 'Feminist Fundamentalism', in L. Segal and M. McIntosh (eds) *Sex Exposed: Sexuality and Pornography Debate* (London: Virago).

World Health Organization (WHO) (1974) *Resolution on Infant Feeding* (Geneva: WHO).

World Health Organization/United Nations Children's Fund (1981) *International Code of Breast-Milk Substitutes* (Geneva: WHO).

World Health Organization/United Nations Children's Fund (1990) 'Ten Steps to Successful Breast Feeding', reported in UNICEF *The State of the World's Children* (Oxford: Oxford University Press).

6 Women Hearing Men: The Cervical Smear Test and the Social Construction of Sexuality

LINDA McKIE

INTRODUCTION

> sex, far from being the object to which sexual discourse refers, is a phenomenon constructed within the discourse itself. (Weeks, 1991, p. 163)

Listening to women talk about the cervical smear test might seem a somewhat obscure starting point for a discourse on sex and sexuality, and listening to women recount what they hear men say on cervical screening might appear equally tangential. Yet the origins of this analysis lie in the conduct of a research project which sought to listen to women's views on the cervical smear test and identify the implications of (non) involvement in screening services for various aspects of their lives. As women spoke of the test it was apparent that the views of men, as partners, relatives, and doctors, had an impact upon respondents' views of screening and treatment services. Women spoke of men in familial and professional groups whose representations of masculinity were often expressed in, and reinforced by, negative views of female sexuality. Male–female conversations, and silences, surrounding the cervical smear test acted as vehicles for such reflections. Thus through the taking of the cervical smear test, the private nature of sexual activity joins the 'continent' of public scrutiny; a continent, in this case, inhabited only by women but invariably constructed and scrutinised by an essentially masculine heterosexual ideology.

The chapter opens with a discussion of sexuality and discourses on the body and then with reviews, respectively, of the organisation and financing of cervical screening, and a discussion of the aetiology of cervical cancer and abnormalities. In the subsequent section, the research project from which data were obtained is described. Data are then presented in two sections, entitled:

1. meanings and expectations; and
2. ownership and control.

Following the presentation of the data, the social construction of sexuality is discussed and in the concluding section the role of the screening test and service in both creating and reflecting unequal citizenship for women is noted.

SEXUALITY AND DISCOURSES ON THE BODY

As Weeks (1991, p. 164) points out, we are 'enslaved' in the circle of meanings attributed to all sexualities and public lives are dominated by the institutionalisation of heterosexuality. Heterosexuality has long been the dominant category of sexuality and one which affirms masculinity and the dominance of heterosexual men. Religious teaching and medical knowledge have been and continue to be employed as evidence for the dominance of heterosexual meanings. Rich (1980) contended that the institutionalisation of heterosexuality enforces a means of assuring the male right of physical, economic, and emotional access to women and thus male supremacy. As Sue Lees (1993, p. 301) notes, in her study of sexuality and adolescent girls, gender identities are constituted and reconstituted across the life cycle and through day-to-day activities. But in those adolescent years a pattern of male behaviour towards female sexuality evolves. To develop a masculine identity young men need to dissociate themselves from all that is feminine:

he needs to denigrate girls in order to dominate them.   (Lees, 1993)

In identifying and exploring such processes, sociologists have often concentrated upon social systems and dimensions of social control in structures, institutions and discourses. The body as an obvious incumbent of both physical matter and social consciousness was, until recently, ignored (Scott and Morgan, 1993). Increasingly the body has received attention in terms of its role in human subjectivity and its constitution by what Lupton (1994, p. 21) defines as 'both elite and popular discourses'. The body is a mixture of both matter and discourses;

thus the social and many physical attributes of the body are made
(Haraway, 1989, p. 10). Turner (1992) proposes that the body acts as
a metaphor for social organisation and social anxieties, and the regulation, surveillance, and monitoring of bodies are, he further contends,
central to the creation and maintenance of society.

With the ascendancy of medicine over religion, as a dominant paradigm for exploring human behaviour, medicine is a major institution
for social control (Rutherford, 1988; Oakley, 1993). An early indication
of the power of both the legal system and medicine to regulate women's
sexual activity was evident in the Contagious Diseases Acts of the
1860s. A more recent example is evident in the unwillingness of various health professions to recognise homosexuality and, in a period of
medical science and care concerned with HIV and AIDS, to challenge
prejudice and address related care issues (Wilton, 1992). As Lupton
(1994, p. 25) notes, the gendered body and sexually active body are
sites for contesting discourses, especially in medicine and public health.
Women's bodies have become symbols of the competing claims of
biomedicine in a society which espouses liberal notions of the freedom of the individual. The very discourses surrounding these competing claims will reflect and create wider social debates on the body.
That discourse will incorporate not only women who may or may not
participate in screening, but younger and older women, and men of all
ages, and all those who speak, listen and observe the discourse.

In Foucault's early work (1979) he proposed that the body had become the ultimate site of political and ideological control. State apparatuses, he contended, have increasingly been directed towards monitoring
behaviours believed conducive to the spread of disease. Much of this
surveillance has been directed towards the family unit through, for
example, child health care and social work services, with the role of
women as mothers and carers surveyed and controlled (Bloor and
McIntosh, 1990). Increasingly, the social obligation to participate in
screening (Howson, 1993) and financial imperative on the part of service
providers to ensure participation have resulted in public health discourses which are concerned with discipline, control, and, ultimately,
the regulation of behaviour. The public health discourse – the elite
discourse – both generates and impacts upon popular discourses of
screening services. Given the intimate nature of the cervical smear test
and the association between cervical cancer and sexual intercourse,
popular discourses are likely to demonstrate meanings attributed to sexual
activity and sexualities.

CERVICAL SCREENING

In the 1990 GP contract (Department of Health, 1989) a financial incentive was linked to the provision and regulation of local cervical screening provision. Women aged between 25 and 64 in England and Wales, and between 20 and 60 in Scotland are to be invited every three to five years for a smear test. To secure full payment, GPs must screen 80 per cent of women in the target group. If 50–79 per cent coverage is achieved, one-third of the payment is made and if less than 50 per cent coverage is achieved no payment is made. A further incentive to achieve targets is evident in 'The Health of the Nation' strategy document in which a target is set for the reduction:

> in the incidence of invasive cervical cancer by at least 20% by the year 2000 (from a 1986 baseline). . . . The Government believes that the priority for this area must be the continued development of good practice in operating the screening programme, and in encouraging women to be screened.   (Department of Health, 1992, p. 69)

The equivalent Scottish strategy does not set a specific target for a reduction in deaths due to cervical cancer but highlights the potentially preventable nature of the disease. Both strategies emphasise the need to encourage participation in the current screening programme (Scottish Office, 1993, p. 31).

Medical research and service organisers cannot agree how often a test should be taken. Suggestions range from an annual test to every five years. Certainly, decreasing the intervals between tests and lowering the age at which screening commences reduces the risk of death but that reduction of potential risk is limited. If a woman is screened every five years from 20 to 64 the risk of developing cancer is reduced by 84 per cent and she will have nine smear tests. Screening on an annual basis will result in 45 tests and an increased reduction of 93 per cent. Women who have never had a test have a higher risk of death from cervical cancer (Wilson and Johnson, 1990). The current policy in most general practices is to screen women every three years, but they are only paid for a test taken every five years. This compromise partly reflects the increased concern and demands from women who have been campaigning for increased services (Lupton, 1994) and concerns over the cost of preventive services.

The cervical screening service is a service provided, at a local level, largely by women – as nurses and doctors – for women. It is a service welcomed by many women as ensuring peace of mind from the development of cervical abnormalities. Yet women's knowledge and experiences of cervical screening and cervical cancer are absent from service planning, service organisation, and treatment. Nevertheless, cervical screening is commonly perceived as a women's health issue; as a service enhancing a woman's control over her body.

The contemporary focus of much health education reflects a pedagogy in which the individual is perceived as having the potential to control their life style and become actively involved in preventive services (Lupton, 1994). Women are not immune to these treatises, whilst still considered to hold a responsibility for the family's health, they are encouraged to participate in preventive services. Howson (1993) argues that in the case of cervical screening, the obligation to participate has become part of a social discourse incorporating wide social networks. The service is now a national one adopting a population approach. Women are encouraged to attend on a regular basis and those who do not are often considered by health care workers to be irresponsible, feckless, and non-compliers. Yet it is unlikely that health care workers will have met non-attenders and are often working with anecdotal evidence in creating a professional discourse on screening (Gregory and McKie, 1990).

As Armstrong (1983, p. 37) notes, prevention strategies are concerned to identify the 'at risk' who may appear 'normal' and yet much of medicine and public health encourages us to participate only when recognisable symptoms are present. Thus cervical screening, and the encouragement given to attend when symptoms are not present, contradicts commonly held perceptions of involvement with GP and clinic services.

THE AETIOLOGY OF CERVICAL CANCER AND CERVICAL ABNORMALITIES

Cervical screening is a form of secondary prevention – an intervention at an early or presymptomatic stage – in order to stop further development of a disease. Much concern has been expressed with continuing levels of mortality. In the UK, approximately 1800 women a year die from cervical cancer with, in 1992, 82 per cent of these deaths occurring in the over-45 age group (Austoker, 1994). At 65 deaths per million women, 1990, the death rate from cervical cancer might seem low in comparison to deaths from lung cancer, which in the same year were 407 per million women and from heart disease – 2508 per million women. Clearly, cervical cancer is not a major killer of women in the UK, although this is reversed in developing countries (Chomet and Chomet, 1989). Yet much concern has been expressed over deaths from cervical cancer as it is a form of cancer in which the early stages are readily detectable through screening – the cervical smear test – and treatable. In fact, the survival rate from cervical cancer is considered high and the potential for reducing mortality through a national screening system great (Chomet and Chomet, 1989; Ibbotson and Wyke, 1994). However, current research suggests that the causes of cervical cancer are likely to be numerous and are certainly not clearly known (Austoker and McPherson, 1993). It is suggested that the Human Papillomavirus (HPV), which may be sexually transmitted, is found in 80–90 per cent of cervical carcinomas (Burger *et al.*, 1993) but not all the causes have been isolated (Ibbotson and Wyke, 1994).

As Posner (1993, p. 55) points out, the potential benefits of screening must be weighed against the potential risks of involvement in an invasive technique, the anxiety caused by the process, and any further treatment (Posner and Vessey, 1988). Perhaps little attention has been devoted to these issues, as the assumption that screening is a highly laudable enterprise has reigned supreme. McCormick (1989, p. 207) contends that cervical screening does not meet the WHO guidance on the principles and practice of screening for a disease. The cumulative costs for screening over a lifetime are high and given the invasive nature of the test its acceptability amongst women is questionable. A number of risks are involved in participation in cervical screening (McCormick, 1989; Posner, 1993). These risks are both physical and psychological and include the risk of cross-infection due to inadequate sterilisation of specula; anxiety and distress caused by the taking of the test and any wait for the results; concern at social sanction on diagnosis of a positive smear; and inaccurate interpretation of smears. Also, on diagnosis of a positive smear further treatment may be distressing and unnecessary given that certain abnormalities do not progress to cancer. As a consequence of the financial imperative to achieve targets it is likely that choice for women will be restricted and anxieties created for women, their friends, families, and service providers. In addition, there are regular reports of inaccurate procedures and diagnosis of test taking and reporting. Such events have brought aspects of the service into mistrust. Thus there exist much publicised potential benefits but rarely debated disadvantages with cervical screening.

THE RESEARCH PROJECT

This research project sought to gain information on the patterns of participation and views and attitudes of working-class women residing in the North East of England. The motivation of the research team was to ensure that the women participating had a voice and that their views, as stated in their own words, would be recorded and relayed to service providers. Initially a series of nine women-only discussion groups was held. An analysis of these data formed the basis for the design of the subsequent stage of the project, the administration of a questionnaire to 302 women. In this chapter data from the discussion groups are presented (McKie, 1993a, b).

Obviously the intimate nature of the subject reinforced the need for an environment in which views could be freely expressed. Existing community groups were asked to place the issue of cervical screening on their agenda for a future women-only meeting. As a result, women were in familiar surroundings and, to varying degrees, knew each other. Participants in discussion groups were asked to debate several topics ranging from definitions of health to the cervical smear test. They were able to follow through stories in an historical sense, relating health and social issues to time and context.

The groups were recruited to elicit as great a variety of women as possible and included church reading groups, senior citizen lunch clubs, mother and toddler groups, and a women's reading group. A total of 72 women, aged from 18 to 73, took part and 95 per cent were living in public-sector rented accommodation in what were defined by local and regional agencies as working-class areas. All but five women had had a smear test and all knew of someone who had had a positive smear and experienced further examination and treatment. The women who did participate identified current or past involvement in heterosexual relationships. In addition, no one spoke of sexual or child abuse. Yet to expect otherwise would be to deny the potential for social sanction in a locality where knowledge of others' private life was commonplace.

The views expressed are those of women reporting and reflecting upon their lives, the role of men as partners and doctors, and male views of the cervical screening service and process. Whether or not these views represent actual events or perceptions of situations is less of a consideration than the fact that these views were freely discussed and related to self-perceptions and sexual identity. In short, these publicly expressed views had a reality for the women which shaped their 'continent' of sexuality.

In this project there was a high degree of similarity in the issues raised across all groups. The discussion of sex and sexuality came towards the end of meetings with women candidly expressing experiences and views. The progression to these discussions was triggered by one of two debates concerning, namely:

1. women who had had an abnormal smear or cervical cancer, where the discussion began with the subject of the lack of understanding of men about the social and treatment consequences of abnormalities; and
2. women's preferred gender of the test-taker and related male concerns with the activity of male doctors in the taking of cervical smear tests.

The discussion group method is not without its limitations; for example, participants are self-selected. However, a project such as the one reported in this chapter provides a mechanism for constructing a body of knowledge on a service which is a component of women's lives and is evident in the creation of discourses on sex and sexuality.

MEANINGS AND EXPECTATIONS

Women had common understandings and expectations which enhanced the flow of conversation, but these sometimes left a host of implicit meanings for the researcher to consider. Some of the conversations recounted were evocative and were clearly told in a manner of trading critical stories between women. However, these were not contradicted either during or after the discussions and were certainly employed as both 'an appeal to action [and] an appeal to inaction' (Stimson and Webb, 1975, p. 111).

The men the women spoke of were predominantly current or former partners or doctors. Men as other relatives or friends were not mentioned, although the views of workplace colleagues were occasionally reported. In recounting men's talk of the cervical smear test women suggested it appeared easy for men to belittle a test for which there is no male equivalent. Even the men identified as sympathetic to women's health issues were said to be at best ambivalent or silent, and at worst dismissive of a test 'which takes only minutes to perform'; for men *bona fide* anxiety was linked to invasive procedures over a period of time thus focusing upon physical illness as opposed to the social and psychological dimensions of preventive care.

Women demonstrated little awareness of the nature of the test and its role in preventive medicine, but were more concerned with avoiding cancer and perceived sanctions associated with the diagnosis of a positive smear. The research team were alerted to the contentious nature of the smear test and, in particular, the diagnosis of a positive smear, at one of the first discussion groups conducted with a mothers and toddlers group based at a Roman Catholic church. After a two-hour discussion on various aspects of the health and screening services, one woman approached the researcher after the tape machine had been switched off. She wanted to tell the researcher that she had had a positive smear test but had not dared to disclose this in front of friends or neighbours 'as they will think either my husband or myself have been sleeping around'. The woman was adamant that neither herself nor her husband had participated in sexual intercourse outside the marital relationship. What struck the researcher was her fear of sanction from not only friends and neighbours but in particular from her husband. A positive smear had implications for sexual identity which went beyond those posed by the taking of the test and treatment; it suggested sexual activity which was promiscuous (as defined by partners outside the long-term relationship) and most likely to bring attention to the sex life of the woman. This latter point was raised spontaneously by women across the groups.

Discussions of promiscuity took place in a number of groups. All linked the positive smear to public distaste and fear of being labelled as promiscuous. The term 'promiscuity' received a number of definitions: more than one partner; sex at an early age, and 'going at it too much and in unusual ways'. From the discussions it would appear that serial monogamy (i.e. one partner after another) is acceptable to these women and many of the women had moved through a series of relationships across the life cycle. As Elleschild (1994, p. 22) notes, women reinforce the 'respectable/promiscuous' dualism by moral policing of themselves and others. For women in this study the double standard was still evident – they received and expected greater sanctions if they had sex outside a relationship – and this was perceived by many as an acceptable statement of possession *and* a form of caring.

An interesting contradiction was posed by a number of women who lived with partners who might be described as verbally abusive with the potential for physical violence. This might be illustrated by the comments of one woman in response to a debate concerning pain and the taking of a test by a male doctor. Having expressed her fear of the test, her husband added:

> don't worry love. If that doctor hurts you I'll kill him.

The taking of the test did hurt, but the woman commented that she did not say anything as she did not want to start any trouble. Yet she concluded it was nice to know her husband 'cared enough to want to tackle the doctor'.

However, many women were less happy about the views of their male partners:

A: Some men think you're going to get a thrill out of it [the smear test].

B: 'I've heard men make those remarks. It's a sexual thing; they think you're going to be turned on.

C: 'They just think 'oh you'll be all right, you'll get a feel' and that type of thing.

In all nine discussion groups women made comments recounting views of men and, in particular, male partners which reflected a perception by men of the test as having the potential for sexual thrills. Women laughed both in embarrassment and frustration. 'What do you do with them?', commented one woman. The choices might appear stark: go for a smear test and be accused of seeking a sexual thrill with the threat of a positive smear, or don't go for a test and experience failure to meet a public obligation, and fear of developing cancer.

It was noted by the majority of women that the role of men in the development of cervical abnormalities was rarely recognised – certainly not by the men they knew or by many of the women themselves – and that this reinforced the link between the smear test, female sexual identity, and the regulation of female sexual activity. As a result women could be labelled good or bad and their sexual histories recorded, with the screening service actively involved in this process.

OWNERSHIP AND CONTROL

The notion of male partners expressing jealousy with those who undertook internal examinations received resounding support:

D: It's jealousy isn't it; that someone else is violating what they con-
      sider to be theirs.

E: They [male partners] feel jealous. Nobody should touch you but
      them.

F: It all comes down to sex. It's your sexual organs but some think
      they own them. You just try making those sorts of comments to
      them! What a laugh; they wouldn't put up with it.

Concepts of ownership and control pervaded conversations; of men
owning women through relationships and of men surveying women
through the cervical screening service.

In one group, a women's reading group, the concepts of power and
body image were explored in some detail. In reporting this debate I
am noting a dissimilarity across the discussion groups resultant from,
I would contend, these women's mutual experience of considering in
some depth the situation of women in society. One woman opened
this discussion group with a sweeping statement,

> I think generally all women feel the same. Fellas don't understand
> women's health problems. (Respondent G)

This definition of 'fellas' also included doctors:

H: After all they are men. Male doctors are no different to other men.

I: They all look at page three girls ... they have an ideal woman ...
      and then they look at you. I feel really bad. You think they're
      men, what must they think of my body.

J: Yeah, and we have those images pushed at us as well.

It probably seems an obvious comment to make; male doctors are men
subject to and part of the debates concerning masculinity yet the wearing
of a white coat is deemed to give an asexuality to the wearer. But the
often sexual nature of relationships between men and women reflect a
further imbalance in power when that man is a doctor:

K: I found this lump in my breast. But I put off going to the doctor's
      for two months because he always has this smirk on his face. I
      always feel that he's looking at my body.

L: What do you do? They might not touch you but it's in their eyes.

Several women expressed great unease at examinations and consultations with male doctors. So were male partners right to be concerned with the potential behaviour and thoughts of male doctors? As one woman noted 'men will be men whatever their job or the relationship'.

As similar to many other studies, women in this study expressed a preference for a female nurse to take a test. But the gender of the doctor did cause comment by male partners:

M: When I said I was going for a smear test he said, 'I wouldn't mind a job like that. They [male doctors] enjoy taking those tests'.
N: When my friend was going for laser treatment her husband said 'Oh they'll give you a good feel; that's what they do that for'.

However, the majority of women stated that the gender of the health professional would not act as a barrier to participation.

DISCUSSION

There is no denying that a link exists between sexual intercourse and the development of the abnormalities of cells in the cervical region. However, the views of the women and those of the men reported in this chapter demonstrate a sexual definition and context to the internal examination and diagnosis of cervical cell abnormalities. Women transcend a private–public dichotomy through screening and find their sexual lives discussed and scrutinised in a manner alien to men (excepting, perhaps, those men involved in infertility treatment or treatment for testicular cancer). Yet the cervix is, as Thomas (1992) notes, the gateway to life (and thus commencement of celebration) as well as the potential site for the development of cancer and, as a consequence, possible death. Results of this study demonstrated that fear of cancer was a strong motivating factor for participation in screening; for overcoming or ignoring male views, male activities, and other social sanctions surrounding the examination, test, and treatment.

Howson (1993, p. 2) has discussed the manner in which the cervix 'has been socially constructed as an object of knowledge across a range of arenas: medical, lay, public and private' and notes the manner in which surveillance – screening services – has grown to incorporate doctors, other primary health care workers, women as mothers, and women as friends. Yet the apparent focus upon health education and health status have cloaked the distaste of many women for the diagnosis of a positive smear test, as illustrated in these data, as such a diagnosis has been linked in folklore and medical circles to promiscuous female sexual activity. Certainly, the more partners a person has the more likely they are to contract or spread the viruses linked to cervical cancer. But this process involves both men and women; although women are more at risk both psychologically and biologically from sexual activity than men. The current service focus is commonly upon women both as transmitters and contractors of relevant viruses; further evidenced by the focus in the media on prostitutes as bringers of AIDS to heterosexuals and, historically, as bringers of sexually transmitted diseases. Women become those whose cervixes are surveyed and, as a consequence, whose sexual activity comes under surveillance.

This commodification of the cervix will have a range of implications for female sexuality and women's use of health services. Heterosexuality is reinforced as the norm and male discourses present images of ownership and control of women's bodies which reflect traditional aspects of patriarchy. In the discourses reported here the men talking or remaining silent pose a threat to women which women do recognise and employ in moral policing of themselves (Elleschild, 1994). Thus the cervical screening service creates and reinforces negative views of women and female sexuality.

Increasingly, women are obligated to attend by primary health care teams keen to attain targets for financial incentives; by others who propose that cervical screening is predominantly beneficial to their health, and by women who consider participation in screening is a critical issue for women seeking to control their sexual lives. It must be added that many women do want the peace of mind that a negative test can bring. Participation in screening and the attainment of a negative smear can mitigate blame for past sexual activities and reduce fear for future activities. But given the constant controversy surrounding inaccuracies and the mismanagement of cervical screening services how realistic is that peace of mind?

CONCLUSIONS

Data presented demonstrates the role of cervical screening in social control evidenced through popular discourses. Both the service in intent and action, and male working-class responses to the test, reflect an ownership of women's bodies in both public and private domains which denies the self of the woman.

Many of the male partners and male doctors represented views to women which were denigrating; which created and reinforced feelings of inadequacy and vulnerability. That the screening process involves the public scrutiny of private activities buttresses the situation of women as unequal citizens who find their private lives riddled with inequalities which public services support (Edwards and McKie, 1995). So women find themselves shouldering the potential consequences of sexual activity in a manner which appears to dictate aspects of their sexual identity.

But how might the voices of the women and the discourses they hear impact upon service organisation and delivery, thus breaking the circle of meanings attributed to elite and popular discourses on screening? As an interim measure it is imperative that a realistic concept of choice is inherent in services. At the moment, participation is considered in the screening protocol to be purely a matter of informed choice. However, this is not the case. Women are unsure as to the reasons for screening. Women are rarely informed of the risks of screening. Women are pressured into participating and it is often women, as practice nurses, who are 'persuading' women to participate. Popular discourses and, in particular, male discourses are a further dimension in the decision to participate; a dimension ignored in the aetiology, delivery, and social construction of the service. Yet it is also men who, in the current internal market of the NHS, control and organise a service promoted as apparently crucial to women's health and their freedom to enjoy good health.

ACKNOWLEDGEMENTS

I would like to acknowledge the invaluable input and support of: the women of Cleveland; Sue Gregory, University of Surrey; Tony Garrett, North Tees Community Health Council; Irene Bellerby, South Tees District Health Authority; the staff of North Tees Community Health Council; the cytology service staff of both North and South Tees District Health Authorities, and the many colleagues and members of the GP Qualitative Research Group who commented on earlier versions of this paper.

This research project was supported by the ESRC, grant number R000231171. Thanks also to the editors of this volume for their advice and support.

REFERENCES

Armstrong, D. (1983) *Political Anatomy of the Body: Medical Knowledge in Britain in the Twentieth Century* (Cambridge: Cambridge University Press).

Austoker, J. (1994) *Cervical Cancer*, Cancer Research Campaign, Fact Sheet 14 (London: Cancer Research Campaign).

Austoker, J. and McPherson, A. (1993) *Cervical Screening. Practical Guides for General Practice*, 14 (Oxford: Oxford University Press).

Bloor, M. and McIntosh, J. (1990) 'Surveillance and Concealment: A Comparison of Techniques of Client Resistance in Therapeutic Communities and Health Visiting', in S. Cunningham-Burley and N. McKeganey (eds) *Readings in Medical Sociology* (London: Routledge), pp. 159–81.

Burger, M. *et al.* (1993) 'Cigarette Smoking and Human Papillomavirus in Patients with Reported Cervical Cytological Abnormality', *British Medical Journal*, **306**: pp. 749–52.

Chomet, J. and Chomet, J. (1989) *Cervical Cancer* (Wellingborough: Grapevine).

Department of Health (1989) *General Practice in the NHS: A New Contract* (London: Department of Health).

Department of Health (1992) *The Health of the Nation: A Strategy for Action* (London: HMSO).

Edwards, J. and McKie, L. (1995) 'The Potential for Feminist Political Practice to Empower the Unrepresented Consumer', *Journal of Consumer Policy*, Special Issue, 'Gendering Consumer Policy', **18**: 135–56.

Elleschild, L, (1994) 'Bad Girls and Excessive Women: The Social Construction of "Promiscuity"', paper presented at BSA annual conference, *Sexualities in Social Context*.

Foucault, M. (1979) *The History of Sexuality*, Volume 1: *An Introduction* (London: Penguin).

Gregory, S. and McKie, L. (1990) 'Researching Cervical Cancer: Compromises, Practices and Beliefs', *Journal of Advances in Health and Nursing Care*, **2**: 1, pp. 73–84.

Haraway, D. (1989) 'The Biopolitics of Postmodern Bodies: Determinations of Self in Immune System Discourse', *Differences*, **1**: 1, pp. 3–44.

Howson, A. (1993) 'Social Constructions of the Cervix: Fragmentation, Surveillance and the Embodiment of Obligation', paper presented to BSA Medical Sociology Group Annual Conference, Pitlochry.

Ibbotson, T. and Wyke, S. (1994) 'Cervical Cancer and Cervical Screening: A Review', working paper, Department of General Practice, University of Edinburgh.

Lees, S. (1993) *Sugar and Spice. Sexuality and Adolescent Girls* (London: Penguin).

Lupton, D. (1994) *Medicine as Culture: Illness, Disease and the Body in Western Societies* (London: Sage).

McCormick, J. (1989) 'Cervical Smears: A Questionable Practice?', *The Lancet*, 22 July, pp. 207–9.

McKie, L. (1993a) 'Women's Views of the Cervical Smear Test: Implications for Nursing Practice – Women who have not had a Smear Test', *Journal of Advanced Nursing*, **18**: 7, pp. 972–9.

McKie, L. (1993b) 'Women's Views of the Cervical Smear Test: Implications for Nursing Practice – Women who have had a Smear Test', *Journal of Advanced Nursing*, **18**: 9, pp. 1228–34.

Oakley, A. (1993) *Essays on Women, Medicine and Health* (Edinburgh: Edinburgh University Press).

Posner, T. (1993) 'Ethical Issues and the Individual Woman in Cancer Screening Programmes', *Journal of Advances in Health Care*, **2**: 3, pp. 55–70.

Posner, T. and Vessey, M. (1988) *Prevention of Cervical Cancer: the Patient's View* (London: King Edward's Hospital Fund for London).

Rich, A. (1980) 'Compulsory Heterosexuality and Lesbian Existence', *Signs*, **5**: 4, pp. 631–60.

Rutherford, J. (1988) 'Who's that Man', in C. Chapman and J. Rutherford (eds) *Unwrapping Masculinity* (London: Lawrence & Wishart), pp. 21–67.

Scott, S. and Morgan, D. (1993) *Body Matters: Essays on the Sociology of the Body* (London: Falmer Press).

Scottish Office (1993) *Scotland's Health: A Challenge To Us All* (Edinburgh: HMSO).

Stimson, G. and Webb, B. (1975) *Going to See the Doctor: The Consultation Process in General Practice* (London: Routledge & Kegan Paul).

Thomas, H. (1992) 'Time and the Cervix', in R. Frankenburg (ed.) *Time, Health and Medicine* (London: Sage).

Turner, B. (1992) *Regulating Bodies: Essays in Medical Sociology* (London: Routledge).

Weeks, J. (1991) *Against Nature: Essays on History, Sexuality and Identity* (London: Rivers Oram Press).

Wilson, S. and Johnson, J. (1990) 'Abnormalities Detected in Unscreened Women Invited for Cervical Cancer Screening', *Health Trends*, **22**: pp. 76–7.

Wilton, T. (1992) *Antibody Politic: Aids and Society* (Cheltenham: New Clarion Press).

7 Discourses on the Menopause and Female Sexual Identity

GAIL DARKE

MAKING SENSE OF THE MENOPAUSE

Over the last century, discourses in the West have variously regarded the menopause in negative terms. Feminist historical research on medico-moral discourses that focus on the female body, for example, has shown it to be a sign of sin, to evidence of madness and hysteria, through to an evolutionary process and, more recently, a deficiency disease (Kaufert, 1982; McCrea, 1983; Jacobus et al., 1990; Greer, 1991; Vines, 1993). Medical intervention in the menopause has corresponded to changes in these meanings, thus changing the way it is medically experienced. Such responses have ranged from locking women up as mad, to operating on them, through to today's attempts to eliminate the menopause through hormone replacement therapy (HRT) (Greer, 1991).

In contrast, cross-cultural accounts of the menopause indicate it is more positively conceptualised and responded to outside the youth-oriented West (Kaufert, 1982; Greer, 1991; Vines, 1993). Many middle-aged women who have performed reproductive and parenting tasks, for example, find themselves accorded a higher social and political status. Anthropological studies also indicate that symptoms experienced as menopausal are culturally specific, although as Kaufert says, 'whether symptoms are experienced is a separate issue from whether they are defined as menopausal' (Kaufert, 1982, p. 144). Indeed, there are up to 40 menopausal symptoms reported in Western medical research, but as Kaufert argues, most of these could be attributed to other multiple causes. This ambiguity in the signs and symptoms render the menopause open to alternative socio-cultural interpretations and practices.

Clearly this shows the menopause to be more than a bodily process. It has symbolic values and meanings that transcend its physiological, psychological, and somatic effects on women's bodies. Michel Foucault's work on the body and the self has, in a sense, recognised this by illustrating how our public and private lives meet in the body. It is from work with similar Foucauldian concerns that I will seek an understanding of the menopause and its relation to female sexual identity.

DISCOURSE THEORY: THE MENOPAUSE AND FEMALE SEXUALITY

Drawing on Foucault's theory of discourse, I will argue that the menopause, like female sexuality, has been put into discourse in a number of ways that have consequences for the ways in which women experience the menopause and themselves.[1] In particular, the menopause and HRT is the subject of dominant medico-moral discourses that are manifest in the institutions and practices of medicine, self-help manuals, and other popular texts, although these are challenged by alternative feminist discourses. I will argue that these discourses draw from a wider context of dominant constructions of gender and female sexuality that operate through what McNay (1992) calls a regulatory notion of a 'natural' reproductive heterosexuality.

Medico-moral discourses have their roots in the nineteenth century medicalisation of the body, illness, and sexuality, as Foucault and others have shown. Further evidence is found in feminist historical research on scientific discourses that focus on the female body and its secretions (Kaufert, 1982; McCrea, 1983; Martin, 1990; Shuttleworth, 1990). Shuttleworth's study of Victorian medical discourses and popular advertising finds gender distinctions being made in the way that male and female 'biological' and 'physiological' functions were conceptualised, which contributed to the gendered public/private divide. The Victorian concern to regulate and control female secretions, especially menstruation, not only contributed to the construction of femininity but was also used to legitimate and restrict women to the domestic sphere through the 'value' attached to women's reproductive role as 'natural' (Shuttleworth, 1990, p. 52).

The medicalised meaning of the menopause today is *still* in terms of it being the end of women's 'reproductive function'. My interviews with a doctor and practice nurse confirms as typical a recent medical textbook definition of the 'menopause' and 'climacteric' as:

Menopause is the stage of female life when there is physiological cessation of the menses along with progressive ovarian failure.

Climacteric is the transition period during which the woman's reproductive function gradually diminishes and disappears. (Sholtis Brunner and Smith Suddarth, 1989)

The value placed on women's reproductive capacity in our society, then, must by definition diminish when they reach the end of fertility. The historical message, traceable in Victorian medical texts relating to menstrual flow stopping, suggests that

womanhood itself was at an end, since medical texts insistently told their readers that women were attractive to men (and thus truly female) only during the period of activity of their reproductive organs. (Shuttleworth, 1990, p. 62).

The assumption that a woman's worth is measured in terms of her fertility and physical attractiveness to men thus entered into Victorian medical definitions of the menopause. They thereby conflated female sexuality with 'womanhood'. A sexuality, moreover, that was constructed around the 'norm' of heterosexual relations. Similar constructions of female sexuality can be traced in nineteenth century medico-moral discourses on women and hysteria (Foucault, 1978; Bird, 1989; Weeks, 1989). Hysteria was thought then to be the result of women being sexually highly charged and marriage was seen as the morally and socially acceptable means of controlling this sexuality. Consequently unmarried women were seen as being both 'biologically and emotionally predisposed to madness, [hysteria and illness]' (Bird, 1989, p. 93).

Similar heterosexual constructions can be found in the later work of sexologists like Havelock Ellis and other contemporary sex reformers (see Havelock Ellis, 1933; Jackson, 1987). Jackson highlights how these early sexologists tied female sexuality to the service of men by defining it as passive: 'it had no independent existence of its own' (Jackson, 1987, p. 70). She illustrates how the 'facts of life' based on this model of heterosexuality as 'natural' was popularised, promoted, and taught to generations in the guise of sexual liberation by the medical profession and through marriage manuals and sex education literature. The explicit rationale of these discourses being the 'prevention and cure of sexual maladjustment', which caused marital disruptions and threatened not only the institution of marriage itself but also the social order (Jackson, 1987, pp. 59–60).

The Victorian notion of the menopause as the death of 'womanhood' underpins the 1960s medical redefinition of the menopause as a hormone deficiency 'disease' (McCrea, 1983). Robert Wilson, an in-fluential American gynaecologist, in his book *Feminine Forever* (1966), claimed that the menopause is a defect that threatens the 'feminine essence'. As a leading advocate of oestrogen replacement he argued it would save menopausal women from being 'condemned to witness the death of their womanhood' (Wilson, quoted in McCrea, 1983, p. 113). This influential and widely read book, much quoted in women's jour-nals and magazines, is just one of the many manifestations of an on-going Western culture which values youth and sexual attractiveness above all.

HRT has even been offered to women on the grounds that it is ben-eficial to the woman's sexual relationship (McCrea, 1983; Greer, 1991): a relationship that is still assumed to be heterosexual and contained within marriage. Indeed, Wilson and others claimed that HRT can have the effect of returning a woman to her 'wifely duties'. He also saw the potential for social control in the prescribing of HRT, believing it would make women within a family situation 'adaptable, even-tempered and generally easy to live with' (Wilson, quoted in McCrea, 1983, p. 113).

Despite distancing themselves from Wilson's ideas, particularly those on 'womanhood', today's medical advocates of HRT are still involved in constructing and institutionalising female sexuality around the un-questioned 'norm' of heterosexuality. This is evident in didactic litera-ture on the menopause and HRT, (often produced by drug companies), distributed to women through medical institutions such as the maga-zine, *Living with the Menopause*. It says of vaginal atrophy, a symp-tom associated with the menopause,

> vaginal dryness and soreness can cause a lot of anxiety in a sexual relationship, particularly if the man does not understand that the prob-lem is physical. He may think it means that his wife does not love him, not realising that it is the pain of intercourse that is putting her off sex. (Bell, 1990, p. 8)

Moreover, even popular discourses in the form of magazine and news-paper articles and self-help books on the menopause and HRT, largely written by women for women, still assume that women in sexual relation-ships are in a heterosexual relationship, whether inside or outside marriage (see Leeson and Gray, 1978; Shuttle and Redgrove, 1978; Anderson, 1983; Shreeve, 1986; Cooper, 1990; Dalton, 1990).

The crucial point is that both popular and dominant medico-moral discourses on the menopause and HRT that construct female sexuality in the gendered terms of a 'womanhood' that is heterosexual and often confined within marriage, deny lesbian possibilities, individual needs, sexual desires, and other sexual identities that fall outside institutionalised heterosexuality. Many feminist discourses on the menopause and HRT also make heterosexual assumptions, even though they challenge the sexist and ageist images that tie female sexuality to reproduction (see, for example, Shuttleworth, 1990; Martin, 1990; Greer, 1991).

In summary, the menopause has clearly been constructed and inserted into medical discourses and practices which draw from and overlap historically changing constructions of gender and female sexuality in the wider socio-cultural context, whose powerful influence can often have painful consequences for women. This is not to suggest that all women believe or do what their doctors tell them, they do not, but even if they wanted to, some may not have the economic means to do so. Women's resistance to medical discourse and practice is, however, difficult to analyse in terms of Foucault's model of power.

As a number of writers have argued, the problem resides in Foucault's idea of positive power being everywhere, inciting, instilling and producing effects in the body, whilst simultaneously producing resistance at the point where power relations are exercised (see Weeks, 1985, 1989; Callinicos, 1989; Burkitt, 1991; McNay, 1992). That is, the body is both the site of the operations of power and of resistance to power. If, however, the body is the effect of an omnipresent power, where does its capacity for resistance come from? Bio-power in effect produces a 'docile' body, thus Foucault has difficulty explaining individuality: the way individuals actively organise, experience and interpret their everyday lives. Foucault's concentration on bio-power is further criticised for ignoring other competing forms of power, such as the state, which also play a role in shaping choices about sexual activity and identity.

Foucault's later work, however, makes a theoretical shift from bodies to technologies, or 'practices of the self', to argue that they

> permit individuals to effect by their own means or with the help of others a certain number of operations on their own bodies and souls, thoughts, conduct, and a way of being, so as to transform themselves. (Foucault, 1988, p. 18).

This shift allows for what McNay calls a 'more dynamic understanding of how individuals interpret their experiences' (1992, p. 50). It leads her to suggest that the concept of 'practices of the self' offers feminists a way of analysing the differences excluded by 'universalisms', thus avoiding rigid conceptions of patriarchy that see women as power-less, or the essentialism of some theories of gender difference. Following this suggestion, my aim is to explore the fruitfulness of this concept as a way of trying to understand the different experiences that women have of the menopause and themselves through my interview data.

PRACTICES OF THE SELF AND GENDER IDENTITY

Rather than discarding his admitted over-insistence on the technologies of domination and power in his earlier work, Foucault shifts his atten-tion to 'games of truth in the relationship of self with self and the forming of oneself as a subject' (Foucault, 1985, p. 6). He does this through 'practices of the self', which are practices and techniques through which individuals actively participate in a process of (ethical) self-fashioning (Foucault, 1984). They are not, however, a self-invention, but practices defined in the wider socio-cultural context which condi-tion and constrain the individual (Foucault, quoted in McNay, 1992, p. 61). Here what Foucault, like Giddens (1991), is proposing is a dy-namic rather than direct causal relationship between social structure and agency, or self. The point to remember, as McNay insists, is that whilst entailing a degree of autonomy, practices of the self are ulti-mately determined by, although not reducible to, wider cultural con-straints (McNay, 1992, p. 61).

There are many problems in Foucault's work for feminist research (not least the concept of 'practices of the self') which are discussed by a number of feminist writers (some good examples are in Ramazanoglu, 1993). Here I want to pick up on the lack of a socially interactive context in the formation of the self identified by McNay. I aim to address this issue through the insights in Giddens' (1991) work on the reflexivity of modernity and self-identity, where social interaction plays a part both in the formation of self-identity and management of the body.

THE REFLEXIVE PROJECT OF THE SELF

Rather like Foucault, Giddens (1991, p. 2) links structure and agency through his idea of institutional reflexivity – knowledge created in 'expert systems' like medical science are not simply '"about" social processes, but materials which in some part constitute them' – *interacting* with the reflexivity of the self. For Giddens self-identity becomes a reflexively organised project

> which consists in the sustaining of coherent, yet continuously revised, biographical narratives, [that] takes place in the context of multiple choices [offered by high modernity but without any moral guidance over choices selected]. (Giddens, 1991, p. 5).

The self as a reflexive project is linked to the body through the notion of lifestyles, which include particular bodily regimes such as health and fitness programmes which individuals adopt. Medical science is central to the increasing concern to construct and control the body. Of particular interest to my thesis is Giddens' idea of 'socialising biological mechanisms and processes' through medical interventions that open up the body as a site of choices and options (Giddens, 1991, p. 8). I will apply this to the use of HRT as a project of self and explore through my interview data how social interaction plays a part in the women's decision to take HRT.

I will argue, however, that the use of HRT and the risks associated with it are as gendered as medical discourses on the menopause. Hormonal changes in men, for example, are regarded as natural and unproblematic by a (predominantly male) medical profession which largely rejects the idea of using HRT for men but does not do so for women, even though some research suggests it might be beneficial to men (Vines, 1993).

In all, I shall empirically investigate the potential usefulness of discourse theory, and the concepts of practices of the self and a reflexive project of the self through my interviews with women experiencing the menopause. This is an on-going research project and so the findings can be no more than tentative at this stage

METHODOLOGICAL APPROACH

A snowballing technique, beginning with personal friends, constitutes the sample of menopausal women interviewed. The women come from a variety of social-class backgrounds and are all white and heterosexual, with the exception of a self-defined lesbian. This initial study is

further limited to the menopause as it affects women in western culture.
The interviews were semi-structured and organised around central
themes concerning the women's perceptions and knowledgeability of
the menopause and HRT, the source of their knowledge, and what their
lived experience of the menopause and HRT means for them in terms
of their sexual identities, their families and their work.

A reflexive approach to interviewing was adopted: that is, the narrative accounts the women gave of themselves and their experiences
were understood as being reflexively constructed through a self-monitoring process that entailed negotiating, interpreting and responding to
the interview process of open-ended questions and answers. Following
Celia Kitzinger's (1987) methodological arguments, the elicitation of
accounts were not conducted with the intention of discovering 'the
truth' about the menopause and menopausal identities. Rather the aim
was to explore how the women constructed their experience of the
menopause and their self-identities in relation to dominant discourses
on the menopause.

In exploring the complex inter-relationship between structure and
agency in relation to the menopausal experience, I interviewed six self
defined 'menopausal' women, whose anonymity has been preserved
through false names. They were:

Angela: 49, heterosexual, divorced, four children, cook;
Helen: 57, heterosexual, married, two children, retired executive man-
    ager for a nutrition company, had a hysterectomy at 36;
Evelyn: 48, heterosexual, married, three children, hairdresser, had a
    hysterectomy at 31;
Lynn: 50, married, heterosexual, two children, self-employed con-
    ference organiser, had a hysterectomy at 35;
Rose: 50, heterosexual, married, two children, personal assistant to
    bank executives, had a hysterectomy at 42;
Joan: 59, heterosexual, married, two children, retired library assist-
    ant, had a hysterectomy at 50;
Moira: 51, lesbian, divorced, two children, full-time student in higher
    education, a former dental hygienist.

I also interviewed two medical professionals:

Dr Owen: runs various clinics in local GP surgeries and two hospi-
    tals, including Well Woman, Family Planning, Gynaecological and
    Menopause clinics;

Nurse Devon: a practice nurse and practice-nurse trainer runs various health promotion activities, such as Well Woman and Chronic
Disease Management clinics, in a GP practice.

The following section begins by investigating the role played by
discourse in the women's accounts of their experiences, perceptions
and understandings of the menopause. It then explores the relationship
between agency and structure by looking at the way the women interpreted their experiences of the menopause and actively participated in
the process of self-formation as a 'practice of the self'. This is then
extended to a more tentative two-pronged examination; first, of 'practices of the self' as a set of principles by which to live based on the
care of the body; and second, of a 'reflexive project of the self' which
emphasises the medical intervention in the health of the body as a
source of self-identity. Throughout this analysis I will also aim to illustrate how both concepts are ultimately constrained by the larger
cultural constructions of gender and female sexuality.

THE ROLE PLAYED BY DISCOURSE IN WOMEN'S
ACCOUNTS OF THE MENOPAUSE

The Medicalised Language of the Menopause

From my interviews it was clear that medical discourses provide the
language of hormones that most of the women use in their descriptions of what the menopause and HRT is. For example, Angela on the
menopause says, 'well it means when you stop producing children.
When you stop producing oestrogen.' Helen describes HRT as 'the
oestrogen that you would normally produce before you are menopausal
and that is what you lack when you go through the menopause'.

This use of medicalised language in relation to HRT is not surprising given it is a medical invention. Explaining the women's association of the menopause with hormones, however, is not so simple given
the reported lack of medical explanations of the menopause and HRT
the women received from their doctors.

Although all the women used the language of hormones, five of the
women associated the end of their menses with having hysterectomies
rather than the menopause. Four of them were medically informed their
ovaries had not been removed, but either they were not told or did not

realise, that this meant they would still go on producing oestrogen and experience the menopause. Both Lynn and Evelyn were told they might experience the menopause but only Evelyn was told why. On experiencing hot flushes, Lynn associated this with a natural process of ageing, 'because I am of that age', rather than her hormones (Lynn). After their hysterectomies Rose and Joan received no medical explanations about their ovaries and did not expect to have a menopause at all.

The lack of information from doctors was a striking feature of the women's consultations with their GPs about HRT, its risks and side-effects. Instead they were advised to attend regular medical check-ups. Evelyn, for example, says 'I wasn't really warned. They just told me to keep being checked.' Only Joan said her GP had told her regular breast checks are needed 'because there might be a risk' of cancer. Confirming this practice, Dr Owen, worried by the long-term effects of HRT on breast cancer, argues that she informs patients of this risk but does not have sufficient time to discuss this in depth.

The women's knowledge about how their bodies work and what happens when medical intervention takes place was, therefore, partial. Once menopausal, however, some of the women sought further medical knowledge through, for example, talks on the menopause, osteoporosis and HRT organised by the Women's Institute, or medical literature provided by their doctors or passed on by friends.

The Mediation of Medical Knowledge through other Women and the Mass Media

The women's medical knowledge is *mediated* and *assessed* through popular discourses on the menopause and HRT. All of the women talked about the menopause to other women, although many still found it a source of embarrassment and did not talk about it to male partners or sons. Talking to other women did not mean that feminist viewpoints challenging medico-moral discourses on the menopause and HRT were heard or expressed. The only exception was Moira who made reference to her rejection of the Goddess syndrome[2] which sees 'HRT as a cop out'. Indeed some of the women said they were not feminists and did not believe in feminism. It is also clear from what many of the women say that the menopause is not something they discussed or were told about by their mothers or other older women in their families. Indeed, Joan suggested 'that generation, they don't talk about things like we do now'. The menopause appears, then, to be becoming less and less of a taboo subject for today's menopausal women.

There also appears to be a kind of 'common-sense' knowledge, or expectation of reaching the menopause at a certain age, among the women, as in Lynn's account, whereas Moira called this a 'women's tradition'. The problem with these ideas is that it does not tell us why the women's knowledge of the menopause should still be in the medicalised discourse of hormones, particularly as this was not fully developed by medical science until the 1960s.

It is about the late 1960s and 1970s that many feminists began to challenge medico-moral discourses on menstruation, childbirth, abortion, and the menopause. Many of these feminist views are expressed, although not always explicitly, in women's magazines, newspaper articles, television, and radio programmes. It is primarily through these cultural forms that all the women claim their knowledge has been raised. The practice nurse and the doctor interviewed also confirmed the mass media as the prime source of women's knowledge of the menopause and HRT.

The popular media, despite the plurality of discourses available, are the primary source of *medical* knowledge because they draw on, and give weight to the authority of medical expertise. For example, Joan says 'Of course you get a lot of discussion by doctors on the television now on the morning programmes and phone-ins'. Helen thought the 'lady doctor on television . . . was very sensible and practical', while Evelyn says 'women's magazines . . . have got a Health Page and women write in to the doctors on these health pages'. Adding,

> the magazines ask the questions for you [on HRT]. They say, does it cause cancer of the womb, if you've still got a womb? Does it cause cancer of the cervix? Does it cause cancer of the breast? And they have no evidence to prove that it does or doesn't and so you will always have to have check ups. (Evelyn)

This would seem to explain the prevalence of the medicalised language of hormones used by the women in their descriptions of HRT and the menopause. The productive power of medical discourses can also be detected in the women's accounts of their experiences of the menopause.

The Productive Power of Discourses in Constructing Women's Bodily Experiences as Menopausal

There is evidence from all of the women to suggest that the different bodily feelings they were experiencing were shaped by the medically informed popular discourses on menopausal signs and symptoms they had read, seen and heard. Evelyn, for instance, said:

you don't really put it down to anything until you sit down and perhaps read an article in the paper on the menopause. Are you having hot flushes? Are you having headaches? Are you doing this, are you changing and all this, and you think, that's how I feel.

Similar sentiments were expressed by Joan, 'I knew [I was experiencing the menopause] just by reading articles in magazines and things and on television', and Helen:

[I knew] from a television programme because somebody else described the same sort of feeling. You could identify yourself with a lot of the ladies and I think . . . thank goodness I'm not the only one. Its not just me or me being silly and other people can cope with it.

And Angela said:

I read a book and . . . I admit I didn't know the bit about the aching bones, but it was nice to read that bit because at first I thought there was something drastically wrong with my bones.

What all these accounts clearly suggest is the productive power of the naming processes in medical/medically informed popular discourses. The women labelled a range of symptoms and *themselves* as 'menopausal' through these texts. The menopause can therefore actively be seen as socially constructed and reconstructed by the women themselves. Control over menopausal women, and the 'truth' claims made by competing discourses on the menopause and HRT, make it a site of struggle between different groups.

POWER AND RESISTANCE: THE DOCTOR–PATIENT RELATIONSHIP

The lack of information given directly to patients by doctors may be a case of the medical practitioners trying to preserve their power relationship through controlling their knowledge base. The medical profession's exercise of control over patient information, about the menopause and HRT in particular, makes possible other subject positions through the resistance it evokes.

For example, diagnosing herself as menopausal, Helen went to her doctor desperate to relieve symptoms, which at their worst left her feeling she was going to die. Confused about conflicting reports in the media linking HRT and breast cancer, Helen believed her doctor would tell her 'what was right and what was wrong'. Confirming her diagnosis, he suggested that Helen went on HRT, but instead of explaining the risks to her he said, 'well you either trust me and you go on it, or you put up with the way you are'. Helen chose not go on HRT.

Conversely, the medical profession resists women's own discourses on the menopause and HRT, especially popular discourses in the media. Even within the medical profession itself intervention by female medical staff is resisted. Dr Owen, for example, claimed that local doctors would resist her setting up menopause clinics because they would want to keep control of it themselves. Well Women clinics run by female experts, such as Dr Owen and Nurse Devon, mean women can by-pass their own (usually male and often unsympathetic) doctors. Yet, they still control the information available to patients, as Nurse Devon reveals when she says,

> you have to tailor the information you give to the type of person and the professional person will need to know about literature they can read and check for themselves.

Dr Owen also confirms the medical profession's resistance to the data sheets: the list of warnings and precautions about HRT that drug companies are legally obliged to enclose with their preparations. These are often passed around to their friends by women using HRT. This hostility to data sheets expresses the critical role information control plays in doctor–patient power relationship. Dr Owen complained, for example, of a patient whom she had changed from one form of HRT to another who refused to take the new form because of the warnings on the data sheet.

Clearly women are not 'docile' patients where HRT is concerned and are often non-compliant. Rose, for instance, experiments with HRT by taking it on and off at different times, or by taking it every other day instead of every day. Moira also experiments. She stopped taking HRT for a while when she experienced water retention and Evelyn says she will stop wearing the HRT patch if it causes her any problems.

Discourses which challenge medico-moral constructions of the menopause and HRT that women encounter in popular texts can be seen as a Foucauldian form of resistance, although it is antithetically tied to the discourse it is resisting. This renders the individual's identity open to change through a range of other possible meanings. So whilst all of the women used the medicalised language of hormones in describing the menopause, none of them saw it as the 'illness', or 'disease' that is implicit in the use of HRT. This is not to deny, however, that the women experience ill effects from menopausal symptoms.

Resistance to the 'disease' perception of the menopause could also be seen as a 'practice of the self', whereby the women interpret their own experiences and actively participate in the formation of the self. This can be explored more fully through the women's accounts of their identities and the strategies they adopt for coping with menopausal changes.

FEMALE SEXUAL IDENTITY AS A PRACTICE OF THE SELF

Fertility is seen as the essence of femininity in medico-moral discourses; its loss either through the menopause or hysterectomy, however, has not changed the feminine self-image of any of the women. They have not become asexual as the logic of this discourse suggests. Evelyn, for example, says

I don't feel any less a woman now I can't have babies, and I can't say I feel any less a woman because I'm going into the menopause.

However, Rose was reluctant to admit to her hysterectomy for fear people would think she 'was no longer feminine'.

Paradoxically, seeing the end of fertility as a normal process of ageing was another strategy for rejecting the stereotypical stigma and lowering of sexual status attached to the menopause. Angela, for example, did not feel it changed her feminine identity at all, seeing it as 'natural, its just a way of life, you can't change it so you get on with it'. According to Dr Owen and Nurse Devon, most patients were glad to get rid of fertility and did not see it as detracting from their femininity and some were even mistakenly worried that HRT might make them fertile again.

All but one of the women interviewed chose 'femininity' and 'woman' as a concept of sexual identity. Given multiple ways of acting, both Angela and Helen, for example, have 'chosen' feminine sexual identities:

> I'm very very feminine. I don't believe in all this women's lib, but I don't believe women should be down trodden either. I am definitely a feminine woman. I like to be looked after. I mean I can look after myself, and I do look after myself more often than not, but I do like to be looked after by a man. I like to have a man with me, I don't like going out on my own and I don't like going out with a bunch of women.   (Angela)

> I'm very feminine, I really do like to be a feminine woman, I mean that is something I am proud of. I'm old fashioned, I'm not the burning bra's type, I want men to open doors for me. I want to be gentle and elegant rather than glamorous and sexy. I want to be feminine in my job, not to be hard or aggressive as other women were.   (Helen)

Wider cultural representations of gender and female sexuality clearly provides the framework which shapes the 'femininity' chosen by these women. Physical attractiveness to men, for example, is fundamental to their perception of femininity. This is evident in the concern, even depression, at feeling less attractive because of the weight that most of the women had gained at menopause. Rose, Angela, and Evelyn, for example, all felt their weight gain affected their sexuality. Angela, who hates being fat, feels less attractive because 'you just can't wear the same clothes and you waddle about'. While Rose says 'I can't believe that anybody would find me at all attractive and I personally cannot feel attractive. Its quite depressing really.' For Evelyn putting on weight means

> if your dresses don't fit you like they used to, you get that feeling 'oh I'm a frump'. I think a lot of people think that if you have got a good figure, you look good, you're a woman.

The practice of trying to maintain physical attractiveness to men may give the impression that these women are placing themselves in a subordinate position to male desires, yet both Helen and Angela clearly gain personal rewards for their investment in a feminine sexual identity.

Association of the menopause with ageing, in a society which values youth as well as a slim, attractive body, also plays a negative part in the women's self-image. Self-denial of the menopause was common among most of the women, often because they did not want to admit they were that age or because it made them feel older.

Crucially, the heterosexuality of all but Moira, a self-identified lesbian, was so taken-for-granted that it did not enter into the self-definitions of the women's sexual identities, yet when they talked of sex and sexuality it was always in relation to their male partners. This unquestioned heterosexuality was highlighted in the way the women constructed their sexual identities in the gendered terms of 'woman' and 'feminine woman': in other words, they conflated their sexuality with their gender identity. The active participation of the women in the formation of the self would appear to be constrained by, although not reducible to, the construction of female sexuality in the gendered terms of a heterosexual 'womanhood', as found in dominant discourses.

CARE OF THE BODY AS A PRACTICE OF THE SELF

Care of the body as an ethical guide, or principle to live by, can be detected in the account of Angela and to some extent those of others not taking HRT. Angela, like Lynn, believes the menopause is a natural process, it is

> something your body is doing and there is nothing you can do to alter it apart from doing something that isn't natural. Your body should be able to cope with the menopause if you eat the right sorts of foods and things. (Angela)

She also does not believe in taking HRT because

> I never ever mess around with nature, I've never even been on the pill. I'll try anything that's herby and I'll try all the natural things, but anything other than those I'm not interested in.

Angela was not alone in saying that the menopause and its symptoms was something that you 'just get on with', adding 'don't dwell on it, get on with your life and think, this too will pass' (Angela). Similarly, Helen says 'I think you have just got to put up with it, and you'll get over it, it's not an illness . . . so I try and work it off', while for Lynn: 'it's just something you have to go through'.

This practice of 'getting on with it' might be seen as a kind of Foucauldian type 'mastery' of the self, but on closer inspection it seems to be a gender expectation that women silently get on with menopausal problems, particularly in relation to work. Rose, for example, expects little sympathy,

> I wouldn't dream of mentioning it at work, I wouldn't want anyone to think there was any crack or weakness there. It would be put down to the menopause, like PMT, by the men and I resent that.

This expectation may be more about maintaining gendered social hierarchies than an aesthetic practice of the self. Moira seems to confirm this when she says that through socialisation women

> are designed to service, we are designed to keep the stiff upper lip, we are designed to keep the ship afloat no matter what and we can't go blaming little ups and downs on the menopause.   (Moira)

> The menopause comes at a time of life when all sorts of other things are happening to you anyway, like the children have gone or are going, and its just another cross to bear.   (Rose)

Care of the body as individual action, or practice of the self, can also be seen as collective action. While both Angela and Helen are seemingly resisting the medical discourse that advocates HRT, they are in a sense acting on the basis of collective beliefs and values about not interfering in nature. What individual action in the formation of the self lacks, however, is any understanding of the social interaction within which it takes place.

TAKING HRT AS A REFLEXIVE PROJECT OF THE SELF

Women taking HRT as 'a reflexive project of the self' offers a social interactive context for the formation of the self. In this theory, who we are is linked to the times we live in, just as control over the body is fundamental not just to the maintenance of self-identity but also to the continuity of identity. Taking HRT seems to offer some of the women the possibility of control over the menopausal body and continuity of self-identity. Most of the women felt they had lost control over their bodies either through weight gains which threatened their sexual and self-identities, or when they experienced symptoms like hot flushes and night/day sweats. HRT claims to offer control over these bodily processes. For example, Evelyn found that menopausal mood-swings make

> you become a Jekyll and Hyde because you are so nice to people around you and when you go home to your family you go aghrrrrrr.

Asked about taking HRT she said,

> I think if it is going to help me be a better person in myself. If you have all those symptoms dealt with, then life begins again.

Seeing the body as a project of the self is evident in Moira's concern to keep her body fit by taking a lot of exercise, but also by taking HRT in the belief it will solve the problem of osteoporosis. Menopausal symptoms have also meant that

> I felt a different person partly because I was reacting in ways I would normally never have reacted, ways that I had no control over.

Taking HRT

> restored my feelings of being in charge of myself again. It is a way of getting through the menopause without actually having any of the nasties that are associated with it.   (Moira)

The reflexive formation of the self is also recognizable in Moira's account of her identity when she says

> I discovered there is no essential self to dig down into because we are making it up as we go along the whole time. It is an on-going construction.

There is also evidence for the gendered nature of the reflexive project of the self. Dr Owen reported that whilst most women were glad about the end of fertility, many women do see the menopause as having a negative impact on their femininity. 'That is why they want to go on HRT', she says, believing this is influenced by mass-media representations of femininity and the publicity given to HRT. Rose confirms this when she says her husband read about film stars where 'no longer did life start at 40, it was starting at 50 and 60 almost and it was all down to HRT'. This resulted in him telling her to go on HRT: 'because of them staying young longer', although he also 'didn't want to have to wheel me around in a wheel chair' because of osteoporosis (Rose).

HRT as a project of the self is also subject to class and occupational differences as Giddens (1991) suggests and as Dr Owen testifies. There are differences in the level of information and experience of menopausal symptoms in the women she sees. For her, 'lower class women' tend to put the menopause down to nature and do not want to interfere with it. Working women doing jobs like part-time cleaning are more likely to put up with menopausal symptoms, whereas 'middle class' women with more professional jobs or jobs that bring them into contact with the public are more likely to seek medical help in order to cope with the job. The double prescription charges for the combined HRT, plus the cost of any other medication, also make the financial situation of women a factor in whether or not they take up medical treatment for the menopause.

Giddens emphasises a concept of 'trust' in 'expert systems' which plays a reflexive role in the self as a project, but trust in the doctor as an 'expert system' is rather ambivalent in the data. Joan has little faith in male doctors for 'female problems' like the menopause and insists on seeing a woman doctor, whom she thinks will be more understanding. She seems, however, to have total trust in HRT on the basis of 'things I've read and heard the doctors talking about, they seem to think they are so good' (Joan). She is therefore reluctant to come off HRT, claiming it has returned her to 'normal', even if there were any possible side-effects. Rose, because her symptoms are not improving, says 'it has crossed my mind that my doctor is crafty enough that that's a placebo and he hasn't actually given me HRT at all', yet she is still prepared to go on taking HRT. What all this suggests is that the current analyses of the reflexive project of the self lacks a notion of power.

In summary, the application of discourse theory, practices of the self, and the reflexive project of the self would seem to offer themselves as analytical tools with which to understand the menopause in the West today, but, as my concluding comments show, each of these theories are limited.

CONCLUSION

The menopause is more than a bodily process. As this preliminary study has shown, it carries symbolic values and meanings which transcend the effects on the individual woman's body.

Drawing on some examples from a review of relevant medico-moral discourses it can be seen how the 'biological' and 'physiological' meanings of the menopause and female sexuality are historically, socially, and culturally constructed. These discourses are challenged by alternative feminist and popular texts. It can also be seen how these competing and often contradictory discourses overlap and draw from dominant constructions of gender and female sexuality in the wider social sphere. Here the feminist texts which challenge the underlying gender constructions of medico-moral discourses, which conflate female sexuality with gender in a heterosexual 'womanhood', still largely ignore lesbian possibilities.

From my interviews with menopausal women it is possible to see how these discourses provide a framework through which women respond to and experience the menopause and themselves, but not in any straightforward causal way. On the one hand, contemporary medical discourses provide the language, but not necessarily the meaning, through which women perceive the menopause. It should be noted here that having a hysterectomy may have an impact upon these perceptions. Medically informed popular discourses also seem to shape the way the women perceive their bodily experiences of menopausal symptoms. On the other hand, the different ways women perceive themselves and the multiple ways they respond to discourses and practices on the menopause point to the limits of discourse theory. Whilst Foucault's notion of 'resistance' is under theorised it cannot be ruled out as the women's resistance to medical discourses and practices indicates.

Practices of the self seems a fruitful but limited approach to analysing women's active participation in the formation of the self, as McNay suggests. As accounts of their sexual identity indicate, women may choose a feminine self-identity, but one that is constrained within the bounds of wider social and cultural constructions of 'femininity' and female sexuality as a gendered heterosexual 'womanhood'. This concept seems inadequate, however, for understanding women's motivations, either emotional or affective, for investing in a femininity that places them in a seemingly subordinate position to men. Care of the body as an ethical practice of the self is also useful but limited. Self-mastery of the menopause in the form of 'getting on with it' seems to be more about preserving a male-oriented, heterosexual social order.

Seeing medical intervention in the body through the use of HRT as a reflexive project of the self allows for a social interaction context in which the formation of the self takes place. It facilitates an understanding of the way women want to control changes in the body and the role this plays in maintaining both self-identity and continuity of self-identity, as well as changes in self-identity through self-monitoring. The idea seems to lack any satisfactory explanation of the role played by power relations in the interactive formation of the self. The concept of 'trust', which proved ambiguous in the data on women's relations with their doctor, could be seen as an inadequate ahistorical replacement of the notion of power. Like practices of the self, the reflexive project of the self is also tied to wider social constructions of gender and female sexuality, as well as social-class differences.

In conclusion, it seems clear from the data that discourses on the menopause, practices of the self, and the reflexive project of the self are gendered phenomena. Through gendered discourses, women's relationship to institutionalized structures and the organisation of gender and heterosexuality is not on a par with that of men. Dominant constructions of 'femininity' and 'masculinity' are differentially constitutive, thus agency is more restrictive for women, although a comparative study of what a practice of the self would mean for men is a question for further research. The views of partners of menopausal women and the role they play in the women's perceptions of the menopause and themselves also warrant further study.

The relationship between structure in the form of constitutive discourses (and 'expert systems') and agency would seem less of an equal one for women than it is for men. McNay's (1992) suggestion that practices of the self have potential as a feminist analytic tool does seem useful, but such analysis would need to look further into why women like Helen and Angela somehow feel 'rewarded' for putting themselves in a seemingly subordinate position through choosing a heterosexual feminine sexual identity.

Finally, the materiality of the body that is evident in the way the body resists and limits attempts to reconstruct it, such as unsuccessful attempts to lose weight gained through menopause, is missing from both notions of practices of the self and the self as reflexive project. Both, however, support Shilling's (1993) argument for an 'unfinished' biological body that is transformed by the social. The bodily effects of the menopause and the way it is experienced are manifest in the way women often feel they have lost control over their bodies; either through weight gains or through hot flushes and night/day sweats. Attempts to control or reconstruct the body, particularly through medical intervention such as HRT, is limited and may even be harmful. HRT neither delays nor prevents menopause taking place and for some women like Rose it does not control menopausal symptoms and, as Dr Owen points out, our bodies age, decay, and die regardless of HRT. In all, this suggests that further study of the relationship between the biological and social is needed.

NOTES

1. 'Discourses' being historically and culturally variable systems of knowledge in which power is constituted, such as concepts, values, and truth claims that operate through institutions and social practices. What constitutes madness, for example, is defined by medical science and utilised in clinical medicine.
2. Goddess syndrome sees the earth as a mother and women as extremely special, believing they should go through the menopause process naturally. Believers argue women are manipulated by men via doctors and the medical profession into taking HRT (Gunew, 1991).

REFERENCES

Anderson, M. (1983) *The Menopause* (London: Faber & Faber).

Bird, J. F. (1989) 'Foucault: Power and Politics', in P. Lassmann (ed.) *Politics and Social Theory* (London: Routledge).

Bell, N. (ed.) (1990) *Living with the Menopause* (Oxford: The Medicine Group).

Burkitt, I. (1991) 'Social Selves: Theories of the Social Formation of Personality', *Current Sociology*, **39**: 3.

Callinicos, A. (1989) *Against Postmodernism: A Marxist Critique* (Cambridge: Polity Press).

Cooper, W. (1990) *No Change*, 4th edn (London: Arrow).

Dalton, K. (1990) *Once a Month: The Original Premenstrual Syndrome Handbook*, 4th edn (USA: Hunter House).

Foucault, M. (1978) *The History of Sexuality*, vol. 1 (London: Penguin).

Foucault, M. (1984) in P. Rabinow (ed.) *The Foucault Reader* (London: Penguin).

Foucault, M. (1985) *The Uses of Pleasure: The History of Sexuality*, vol. 2 (London: Penguin).

Foucault, M. (1988) 'Technologies of the Self', in L. H. Martin, H. Gutman and P. H. Hutton (eds) *Technologies of the Self: A Seminar with Michel Foucault* (London: Tavistock).

Giddens, A. (1991) *Modernity and Self-Identity* (Cambridge: Polity Press).

Good Housekeeping (1991) 'Are you one of the Guinea Pig Generation?', March.

Greer, G. (1991) *The Change: Women, Ageing and the Menopause* (London: Hamish Hamilton).

Gunew, S. (ed.) (1991) *A Reader in Feminist Knowledge* (London: Routledge).

Havelock Ellis, H. (1933) *Psychology of Sex* (London: Pan).

Jacobus, M., Fox Keller. E, and Shuttleworth, S. (eds) (1990) *Body/Politics: Women and the Discourses of Science* (London: Routledge).

Jackson, M. (1987) '"Facts of Life" or the Eroticization of Women's Oppression? Sexology and the Social Construction of Heterosexuality', in P. Caplan (ed.) *The Cultural Construction of Sexuality* (London: Routledge).

Kaufert, P. A. (1982) 'Myth and the Menopause', *Sociology of Health and Illness*, **4**: 2, July, pp. 141–66.

Kitzinger, C. (1987) *The Social Construction of Lesbianism* (London: Sage).

Leeson, J. and Gray, J. (1978) *Women and Medicine* (London: Tavistock).

McCrea, F. B. (1983) 'The Politics of Menopause: The "Discovery" of a Deficiency Disease', *Social Problems*, **31**:1 (October).

McNay, L. (1992) *Foucault and Feminism: Power, Gender and the Self* (Cambridge: Polity Press).

Martin, E. (1990) 'Science and Women's Bodies: Forms of Anthropological Knowledge', in E. Jacobus *et al.* (eds) *Body/Politics: Women and the Discourses of Science* (London: Routledge).

Prima (1992) 'Hormones: Are you in Control or are they?', January.

Ramazanoglu, C. (ed.), (1993) *Up against Foucault: Explorations of Some Tensions between Foucault and Feminism* (London: Routledge).

Shilling, C. (1993) *The Body and Social Theory* (London: Sage).

Sholtis Brunner, L. and Smith Suddarth, D. (1989) *The Lippincott Manual of Medical and Surgical Nursing*, 2nd edn (New York: Harper & Row).

Shreeve, C. M. (1986) *Overcoming the Menopause Naturally* (London: Arrow).

Shuttle, P. and Redgrove, P. (1978) *The Wise Wound: Menstruation and Everywoman* (London: Paladin Grafton).

Shuttleworth, S. (1990) 'Female Circulation: Medical Discourse and Popular Advertising in the Mid-Victorian Era', in M. Jacobus *et al.* (eds) *Body/Politics: Women and the Discourses of Science* (London: Routledge).

Vines, G. (1993) *Raging Hormones: Do They Rule Our Lives?* (London: Virago).

Weeks, J. (1985) *Sexuality and its Discontents: Meanings, Myths and Modern Sexualities* (London: Routledge).

Weeks, J. (1989) *Sex, Politics and Society*, 2nd edn (London: Longman).

Part III
The Construction of Heterosexuality

8 Contradictions in Discourse: Gender, Sexuality and HIV/AIDS

DIANE RICHARDSON

INTRODUCTION

Although the first cases of AIDS in women were reported in 1981, in the United States, there was very little written about women and AIDS until the late 1980s. Prior to then, researchers paid scant attention to issues relating to women and HIV/AIDS. The year 1987 was particularly important in terms of public recognition of AIDS as a women's health issue. In the United States, the Centers for Disease Control produced its first published report on women and AIDS and a number of books and articles were published which drew attention to the need to address AIDS-related issues which affected women. In the main, these were concerned with providing women with information about AIDS and advice on prevention of HIV infection (for example, Kaplan, 1987; Norwood, 1987). However, a number of writers were also concerned to acknowledge the social and political context of AIDS prevention, diagnosis and treatment (for example, Patton and Kelly, 1987; Richardson, 1989).

Since then, and especially in the last couple of years, concern about women and HIV/AIDS has grown. This is reflected in the increase in the number of books and articles published on the subject, in papers presented at conferences, in the development of new research initiatives, as well as the establishment of organisations specifically concerned with women and HIV/AIDS in various parts of the world. Despite these shifts, issues of significance to women continue to be marginalised and there remains a need for research which addresses women's needs in relation to HIV/AIDS, especially qualitative work. It is also the case that discussion of HIV and AIDS from a feminist perspective has so far been relatively limited in the UK, although there are some notable exceptions to this (see, for example, the collection edited by Doyal *et al.*, 1994). This apparent lack of interest among British feminists in women's experience and needs in relation to HIV/AIDS is interesting for a number of reasons. The development of feminist theory and practice in the area of health has been a major aspect of Western feminism since the early 1970s. As with health, feminists have long been concerned with the links between sexuality and women's oppression, in particular the power dynamics embedded in heterosexual relationships. Consequently, many of the issues raised by HIV and AIDS such as, for example, control over sexuality, access to health care, and reproductive rights, are ones that feminists are familiar with and have addressed in other contexts.

In addition to considering why HIV/AIDS appears to have received relatively little attention in feminist accounts – in the UK at least – it is also important to think about the possible effects of this on the ways in which AIDS is conceptualised. Cultural constructions of AIDS and HIV infection influence the formation of HIV policy and education, research paradigms, media accounts as well as individual understandings of risk and safety. More specifically, they invoke and constitute particular ideas about gender and sexuality which inform representations of women in the AIDS discourse and HIV policy and education. This chapter will examine constructions of gender in the context of HIV/AIDS and, related to this, consider how (hetero)sexuality is conceptualised and constructed within AIDS policy making. In so doing I hope to draw attention to some of the many contradictions existing in the representation of women, men and heterosexuality in AIDS discourse. Finally, it will make links between feminism and women's experience of HIV/AIDS and risk of infection, and examine some of the possible explanations for why, until recently, there has been relatively little written about women and HIV/AIDS from a feminist perspective.

GENDERING AIDS

The relatively small number of women diagnosed with AIDS in Britain may seem an obvious explanation for the initial lack of feminist activism around AIDS. (Up to the end of October 1988 there were 61 cases of women with AIDS reported in the UK, including ten girls, out of total of 1862 recorded cases, DHSS figures.) However, this account overlooks the fact that whilst numbers of people affected may have been low, from 1987 onwards the increasing recognition of AIDS as a public health issue prompted a great deal of public debate on sexuality. The failure of feminists to make a substantial contribution to this debate is more difficult to explain. Commenting on this, Sara Scott remarks that 'Our silence seems bizarre because the issues raised by AIDS are very much on our political patch' (Scott, 1987, p. 13).

Understandings of responses to HIV and AIDS, feminist or otherwise, are much more complex than the question of whether the number of reported cases reaches a level that is deemed to be statistically significant. As I have suggested above, they demand an examination of ways in which HIV/AIDS is constructed and more especially how notions of gender and (hetero)sexuality, as well as race, have been employed in AIDS discourse.

From 1981, when the first cases of AIDS were reported in the United States, AIDS was firmly constructed in the West as a disease affecting male bodies; more specifically the bodies of (white) gay men.[1] The initial association of AIDS and gay men was reified in the original naming of the new disease Gay Related Immune Deficiency (GRID), reflecting the mistaken assumption on the part of medical researchers that this was a disease that was associated with being gay, either as a defect of the body or as a consequence of the lifestyles and behaviours of gay men. The media also played a significant role in constructing this view, frequently referring to AIDS as the 'gay disease' or the 'gay plague' (Watney, 1988).

These early accounts, now discredited, have nevertheless had a significant and long-standing effect on shaping responses to HIV/AIDS: individually, socially, and politically. Most obviously, the initial gendering of the body affected by AIDS as male decreased the likelihood of HIV infection been perceived as significant to women. This was compounded by the association of AIDS with 'homosexuality', a social category also usually gendered as male.[2] This 'male-ing' of AIDS not only influenced individual women's perceptions of HIV risk, but has also shaped women's experiences of living with HIV/AIDS. For example, in terms of the development of 'male' models of service provision, available treatments being tested on male only samples, and possible delays in diagnosis because doctors often fail to think of HIV/AIDS as affecting female bodies. A situation compounded by the fact that until recently diagnostic categories of AIDS/HIV-related illness were constructed through studies of the effects of HIV infection on male bodies.[3]

THE DEVIANT OTHER: SEXUALITY, CLASS AND 'RACE' IN AIDS DISCOURSE

A further consequence of the initial 'gaying of AIDS' was that HIV/ AIDS was linked with sexual 'deviance'. The association of risk of HIV infection and 'deviance', which emerges as a strong theme in AIDS discourse, has been highly significant in constructing ways of thinking about women and HIV/AIDS. Both AIDS education and media reports of HIV/AIDS have frequently relied on traditional construc- tions of 'woman' as white, heterosexual and middle-class (Kitzinger, 1994). More specifically, the term 'woman' represents the 'ordinary', innocent, and heterosexual 'victim' against which other 'women at risk' are constructed as 'deviations' who appear as a danger to others, as bodies which are a risk to men and to children.

In this sense, Cindy Patton is right to challenge the 'often circulated idea that women were "invisible" in the first decade of the epidemic'. (Patton, 1994, p. 2). Whilst it is true to say that until very recently researchers, policy-makers, and governments have largely ignored how HIV/AIDS affects women specifically, certain groups of women are clearly visible in AIDS discourse. In the early stages of the epidemic, women at risk were usually represented as women sex workers, black African women, women who injected drugs, and 'promiscuous' women. Interestingly, lesbians were sometimes included as 'homosexuals', but were gradually rendered invisible not as 'ordinary women' but as a deviant group defined by their sexuality yet whose deviance, paradoxi- cally, is not to engage in 'real' sex.

This division between visible and invisible women in AIDS dis- course is characterised by Kitzinger (1994) as a form of the good woman/ bad woman dichotomy, which is a common feature of representations of women. However, it is not simply a case of the figure of 'Bad- Woman' being depicted, in all her various forms, within AIDS dis- courses, whilst the figure of 'Good-Woman' fails to materialise. Within AIDS education aimed at promoting safer sex among 'heterosexuals' the focus has been upon the need for women to take control in sexual encounters, in particular through encouraging condom use. This is one of the main ways in which 'woman' is visible in AIDS discourse as a symbol of normality, as distinct from 'woman' as deviant other.

Other representations of women which appear in AIDS discourse are 'woman' as carer and 'woman' as mother. Whilst much of the early literature on women and AIDS concentrated on women as poss- ible sources of HIV infection, especially upon female prostitutes, attention was also given to women as carers of people with AIDS. Although it is women who provide much of the day-to-day care of the sick in public health care settings, the focus was primarily upon care within domestic settings by women as wives of men perceived as 'victims' of the disease (most commonly men who had received HIV-infected blood or blood products) or as mothers, usually of gay men. In both of these contexts traditional notions of 'woman' as wife and mother, providing care within the home for male partners and siblings, are invoked.

In contrast to this, the other dominant image of mother depicted in AIDS discourse is that of the woman who has failed her duties as a mother, either by rejecting a child who has AIDS or by passing on the HIV virus to her infant. Information on the risks of pregnancy and childbearing initially advised women who were HIV infected, or who thought they may be at risk of infection, to defer having a child until more was known about HIV/AIDS. However, as the numbers of women reported to be HIV positive steadily increased, so did public concern over perinatal transmission. The implicit message in most AIDS prevention campaigns has been one of preventing women from transmitting HIV to a child during pregnancy or the process of birth. This represents a different version of the female body as a source of possible infection and danger; it is women's reproductive potential which is perceived as a risk factor as distinct from women as bodies which personify sexual danger. Risk-reduction is once again sought largely through the control of the female body, rendering it incapable of reproduction either temporarily, through contraceptive use or a termination, or permanently, through sterilisation (Richardson, 1993).[4]

The representation of certain groups of women as at risk has largely been in terms of the danger they pose to others, it is through them that HIV may be transmitted to men and their 'heterosexual partners', and to children. Such understandings also draw attention to the ways in which constructions of woman as sexually risky/safe are interpreted through the interacting categories of class and race. Historically, the sexuality of working-class women (and men) has often been represented as more lascivious, free, and liberated than that of middle-class women (and men), representing a threat of both immorality and disease (Hall, 1991; Smart, 1992). The image of the woman labelled a 'slut' is predominantly working class: as is suggested by the use of the term 'high-class tart', a class distinguished from the rest.

Similarly, racist stereotypes of black women and men as highly sexed, promiscuous, and immoral may help explain the focus on black Africans as the original source of HIV infection. However, the interconnections between 'race' and gender mean that the racialisation of sexual ideologies has different implications for black women than black men. Discussing representations of black female sexuality, bell hooks (1992) highlights how the association of black women with a heightened (hetero)sexuality leads to an association between black female sexuality and sexual deviancy – in particular an association between black female sexuality and prostitution. These constructions of black female sexuality have important implications for how black women's bodies are perceived as potentially dangerous to the (white) male other and, interestingly, his (white) wife/girlfriend.[5] This is also a good example of how the bodies of (white) heterosexual men come to be represented/ ignored in AIDS discourse as safe. It is through the body of a deviant woman (or man) who acts on their male partner that heterosexual women are put at risk.

In the case of women defined as being in 'ordinary heterosexual relationships' this has encouraged a belief in their invulnerability and safety. A view which is also influenced by the social construction of female sexually as passive, so that in AIDS discourse heterosexual women are generally understood to be sexual partners of men rather than as sexual agents in their own right. Indeed, if women are sexually assertive in heterosexual encounters they run the risk of losing heterosexual respectability and becoming labelled as deviant/at risk.

The construction of the heterosexual man in AIDS discourse as primarily someone who is at risk from others, in particular from certain categories of women who may tempt him or from gay or bisexual men, raises a number of interesting contradictions. For example, between traditional notions of male sexual agency and the situating of the (white) heterosexual male as a body which is acted on, a 'passive victim' to the sexual power of the other who seeks to tempt or seduce him. There is also clearly a tension here between the perception of heterosexual men as 'victims' of strong sexual urges which may lead them into dangerous liaisons with deviant women/men and the invisibility of heterosexual men as a possible source of HIV infection and a danger to others. In this respect one might want to argue that the emphasis within AIDS prevention campaigns on encouraging condom use not only suggests the possibility of 'normal' so-called heterosexual intercourse being unsafe but also the male body, in so far as it is men who wear condoms on their penises and women who are being targeted at encouraging their use.

THE DISAPPEARING HETEROSEXUAL MALE

One of the consequences of the concentration on women as a source of HIV infection within much of the published work on HIV/AIDS is that it helps to render invisible the dangers of HIV infection to women themselves. This has allowed educators and policy-makers to marginalise the issues relating to how and why women become infected. The underlying concern would seem to be how to protect the health of men and children, rather than addressing women's health needs.

As I have already indicated, much of the health education aimed at heterosexuals, both in Britain and elsewhere, is targeted at women (Richardson, 1990). The expectation is that women should persuade their male partners to use a condom if they have intercourse. Such campaigns have reinforced the idea that it is women who are primarily responsible for safer sex and, by implication, heterosexual transmission of HIV, and have colluded with dominant discourses of sexuality which assume that men are 'naturally' less able to exercise self-control in sexual encounters than are women (Scott, 1987). Having said this, there is a contradictory message in expecting girls and young women who are constructed as sexually 'passive' both to carry condoms and encourage their use. Such contradictions are clearly felt by women themselves. In Holland *et al.*'s (1990, 1994a) study of young women, concern over the negative implications of being seen as sexually assertive was an important factor in inhibiting women from carrying condoms or insisting on their use. Research on heterosexual men suggests that women's fears of being labelled by their male partners in negative ways are well founded (e.g. Holland *et al.*, 1994b; Kitzinger, 1994).

A parallel can be drawn here with the concerns expressed by politicians and policy-makers in recent months over the so-called problem of teenage pregnancy. The construction of pregnancy as a deliberate and wilful act by young single girls in order to jump housing queues and quality for welfare benefits totally ignores the problems young women often face in negotiating sexual encounters with their male partners which a number of studies have highlighted (see, for example, Holland *et al.*, 1990, 1994a; Ingham *et al.*, 1992; Lees, 1993). Furthermore, as is the norm in AIDS discourse, the heterosexual male is largely invisible in such accounts, with the emphasis on controlling female bodies. Even the labelling of the 'problem' as teenage pregnancy rather than teenage conception reveals the way in which it is female bodies and behaviour, rather than men's, which are under public scrutiny; it is almost as if women became pregnant through parthenogenesis.

The relative lack of discussion of men's contribution to reproduction in accounts of the 'problem' of 'teenage pregnancy' is ironic given that it is men's behaviour which frequently puts women at risk in sexual encounters and limits women's ability to prevent both unwanted pregnancy and the transmission of sexually transmitted infections like HIV. It could also be seen as somewhat contradictory given the British government's apparent concern with male responsibility in sexual and reproductive matters in introducing the 1991 Child Support Act. The Act, implemented from 1993, represents an attempt to reduce the amount paid to single mothers in welfare benefits by making men financially liable for any children they biologically father. However, the primary focus has been on how to ensure payment rather than how to ensure men's involvement in avoiding an unplanned pregnancy.

Similar issues are raised in the context of HIV and AIDS. For instance, although the World Health Organization (WHO) has identified (heterosexual) men's reluctance to make changes in their sexual behaviour as an important factor in the global transmission of HIV, the 'highest priority' is given to encouraging 'woman controlled' methods to prevent HIV transmission including research into vaginal viricides (WHO, 1993). Whilst the development of such products can be seen, like the female condom, as offering women greater control (although this is controversial) such proposed 'solutions' are nevertheless focused upon the manipulation of female bodies, leaving male risk behaviours seemingly unchallenged.

HETERONORMATIVITY

The omission of critiques of heterosexuality in debates about teenage pregnancy and in health education campaigns aimed at HIV/AIDS prevention, not only fails to acknowledge heterosexuality as a powerful dynamic in the social control of women, but also constructs heterosexuality as exempt from the need to change. This is perhaps unsurprising; social policy is socially constructed on the basis of normative assumptions about sexuality and central to this is the notion of heterosexuality as normal, appropriate, and acceptable behaviour (Carabine, 1992). Furthermore, the association of risk for HIV infection and social 'deviance', to which I have already referred, makes it difficult to see those involved in relationships defined as socially acceptable and normal as 'at risk'.

In keeping with dominant constructions of risk and AIDS, heterosexuality is only likely to be perceived as risky when it is 'deviant
heterosexuality' (some might prefer the term 'queer heterosexuality').
This can be interpreted in a number of different ways, for instance as
'promiscuous' sex, as sex whose assumed heterosexuality is challenged
in the context of the identity of one or more of the partners, or as
specific forms of sexual practice. The first two are gendered understandings, it is the promiscuous heterosexual woman who is deemed
to be deviant/at risk and as the 'active' partner it is the labelling of
the man as sexual other (bisexual or gay) which may lead to the perception of heterosexual women being at risk as his partner. The association of AIDS with certain kinds of sexual practice, anal sex in
particular, relates to the way AIDS is still linked with gay men and
the stereotyping of 'gay sex' as anal or, as it is sometimes referred to,
homosexual intercourse (i.e. penile penetration of the rectum). Deviant
heterosexuality, in this sense, can include the practice of what are
commonly constructed as 'homosexual' acts, but more especially anal
intercourse.

Attempts to understand the occurrence of AIDS among heterosexuals
have appealed to such understandings of deviant heterosexuality. For
instance, in the 1980s many writers sought to explain the wider occurrence of AIDS among heterosexuals in Africa by suggesting that anal
intercourse was more commonly practised in Africa than in the West,
mainly as a cheap method of birth control (see, for example, Leibowitch,
1985).

In situating particular acts (anal intercourse) and individuals (promiscuous women/bisexual men) as deviant/risky the normative boundaries of heterosexual inclusion are firmly constructed and, by implication,
those of safe/normal sex. That is to say, the construction of heterosexuality within AIDS discourse reinforces the idea of heterosexuality
being associated with certain specific practices. A more interesting
question perhaps is whether it also increases the likelihood of a heterosexual identification?

Recent attempts to theorise heterosexuality have included discussion
of the (de)construction of heterosexual identities (see, for example,
Jackson, 1996; and Smart, Chapter 11 in this volume) and greater speci-
fication of the social and political meanings attached to heterosexuality as an identity (Richardson, 1996). Some writers have also queried
the contexts under which such hegemonic ways of being and behaving
are disrupted. For example, (some) feminist gatherings may be one
context where (some) heterosexual women may feel 'part of a marginal

fringe as heterosexuals' (Lips and Freedman, 1993). The question I am
raising here is how far responses to HIV/AIDS in the media, through
policy and education, can be regarded as a context in which the 'heterosexual person' is in the process of being produced. Certainly, the initial conflation of AIDS with 'gay man' both gendered and sexualised
the disease in a way that provided a context where heterosexual men
could declare themselves as not at risk because *they* were heterosexual.
For heterosexual women the potential impact of stereotyping lesbians
as, initially, 'high-risk', and then subsequently as women who are
unaffected by AIDS, is diminished by the relative absence of lesbians
in literature on HIV and AIDS (Richardson, 1994a).

Such constructions rely, at least in part, on the association of risk
with certain social groups which was evident in early AIDS educational strategies that employed the idea of 'risk-groups'. More specifically, the category of risk group has been used to stereotype and categorise
people who are seen as outside the parameters of 'the general population'. Thus, 'heterosexual' has tended to be equated with the general
public,[6] as distinct from other groups categorised as at risk such as,
for example, gay or bisexual men, intravenous (IV) drug users or sex
workers.

By the late 1980s, it was evident that there had been a shift in HIV/
AIDS health education policy in Britain, away from talking about risk
groups to risk behaviours. From this perspective, it is possible to argue that rather than encouraging a new (hetero)sexual categorisation,
AIDS has the potential to disrupt the notion of distinct sexual categories of people – heterosexual, lesbian, gay – through an emphasis on
routes of transmission rather than sexual identities. However, the fact
that this distinction between risk group and risk behaviour is only partial in HIV/AIDS education would seem to counter such possibilities.
Indeed, the (contradictory) emphasis within recent governmental HIV/
AIDS campaigns on partner selection as a risk reduction strategy – the
need to 'Choose Your Partner Carefully' – is one possible reason for
the continued association of risk with particular individuals rather than
specific practices.

This examination of how particular ideas about gender and sexuality
have informed responses to HIV/AIDS, in particular attempts to control the HIV epidemic through the regulation of women's sexual and
reproductive activities, would seem to highlight the significance of HIV/
AIDS for feminism. In addition, HIV/AIDS raises many other issues,
such as access to health care and child-care facilities, which are also
long-term goals of feminism. HIV/AIDS has also, once again, high-

lighted the low priority given to research about women's health needs. However, until recently the links between feminist analysis and HIV/ AIDS have tended to be 'absent from the agenda of both feminism and AIDS activism in Britain' (Wilton, 1994). In the concluding section I will briefly consider some of the possible reasons for this apparent anomaly.

FEMINISM AND HIV/AIDS

The focus on AIDS as a disease affecting (gay) male bodies in early accounts may explain why at first many feminists did not identify HIV/ AIDS as a 'woman's issue', despite the fact that as 'homosexuals' lesbians were initially also often perceived as 'high-risk'. The rapid response of the gay community to HIV and AIDS, both in Europe and the United States, in designing AIDS education and information campaigns, as well as through its involvement in other forms of AIDS activism, may also have encouraged a general perception that AIDS politics = gay politics and a lack of political relevance for women.

Related to this, there is a certain tension between challenging the association of HIV/AIDS with (white) gay men and emphasising women's concerns, and demands from the gay male community that their needs be met. A tension that has led in some cases to political disagreement and divisions between gay men and women asserting their respective need of AIDS resources. Commenting on this, Cindy Patton (1994) remarks that:

> Unfortunately, the increase in attention to women's concerns has sometimes come at the cost of pushing the issues of gay men aside, resulting in both 'de-gaying' and de-funding crucial existing projects. (Patton, 1994, p. 148)

Equally, one could regard the attempts by some gay men to 're-gay' AIDS (see Watney, 1994) as part of an understandable response to the way that gay men have become more and more invisible in the provision of government funded education and services around HIV and AIDS, and as simultaneously a re-maleing of AIDS, and that encourages the marginalisation of women.

Another possible explanation for the relative lack of feminist involvement in AIDS politics, is that HIV/AIDS is perceived as a low priority relative to wider health issues for women. For example, in Britain at present there are many more deaths in women as a result of breast and cervical cancer than are caused by HIV-related disease. Also, the fact that many of the serious health issues affecting women, besides HIV/AIDS, have not received the same level of funding or attention may be seen by some feminists as significant in the assimilation of HIV/AIDS into a broader health agenda (Winnow, 1992). Related to this, observing the ways in which the government, media and medical profession responded to the 'AIDS crisis', in contrast to the attention previously given to women's health/sexual concerns, may also have provoked contradictory responses among some feminists (Coward, 1987).

Elsewhere, I have discussed in more detail these and other possible reasons for, as well as the consequences of, a lack of feminist writing and activism with respect to HIV and AIDS (Richardson, 1994b). Arguably, one of the more important consequences is that the contribution of feminist theory could more effectively inform the policy-making process and influence the development of the provision of services for women. Others have stressed the need for greater feminist engagement with HIV/AIDS because of the way AIDS has become a major focus for public debates about issues which are of central concern for feminists; in particular, sexuality and 'the family' (see, for example, Coward, 1987; Scott, 1987; Richardson, 1989; Holland *et al.*, 1990).

If feminism in Britain has only recently begun to address the implications of HIV and AIDS for feminist theory and practice, then it is also the case that much of the literature on HIV and AIDS, as well as HIV policy and education, has so far failed to acknowledge and/or incorporate feminist theory and research, with potentially far-reaching consequences. As a number of recent studies have amply demonstrated, analysing the gendered power relations embedded in sexual relations helps to explain both how and why women can find the process of negotiating safer sex difficult (Holland *et al.*, 1990, 1994a; Ingham, 1992; Lees, 1993). However, most HIV/AIDS health education material, in emphasising individual choice and personal responsibility, have not addressed dynamics of power in (hetero)sexual relations. In so doing health education reproduces discursive practices which can serve to limit women's possibilities for practising safer sex, thereby potentially increasing the risk of HIV infection.

A further consequence has been the construction of a concept of safer sex which, in largely ignoring feminist analyses of sexuality, has marginalised more traditional feminist concerns about sexual practice (see Cameron, 1992). Feminists, both earlier this century and more recently, have long been concerned with issues of sexual risk and safety in a much broader sense than transmission of HIV; more especially in relation to the prevention of unwanted pregnancy, reducing the health risks associated with certain forms of contraceptive use and abortion, and preventing sexual violence and abuse (DuBois and Gordon, 1984; Jeffreys, 1990).

Feminists have, in the past, also voiced criticisms of heterosexuality as a form of sexual practice (e.g. Koedt, 1974), challenging the centrality of vaginal intercourse in heterosexual relations and legitimising ways of obtaining sexual pleasure through non-penetrative means. This is relevant to the promotion of safer sex, where vaginal and anal intercourse are associated with 'high risk' and alternatives to penetration are safer sexual practices. Indeed, according to Wilton (1994, p. 90) safer sex 'demands that we de-emphasize penetration'. However, it is clear that within mainstream AIDS discourse such possibilities are deeply problematic. Much of the safer sex discourse in relation to HIV and AIDS reaffirms rather than challenges the notion of 'sex' as vaginal intercourse (Campbell, 1987; Scott, 1987). A contradiction that is deepened by the fact that the dominant message in safer-sex promotional materials aimed at gay men has been on the dangers associated with anal intercourse, and the need to avoid such risks by engaging in other less risky non-penetrative sexual practices.

CONCLUSION

In this chapter I have argued that health education in the context of HIV/AIDS, but more especially information and advice about safer sex, has relied on culturally dominant notions of gender and sexuality. However, it is also the case that within AIDS discourse there are numerous contradictions in the representation of women, men and (hetero-)sexuality. In the example given in the previous paragraph, it is the priviliged construction of heterosexuality and heterosexual (vaginal) intercourse as 'safe by nature' (Patton, 1994, p. 118) that gives rise to such contradictions. There are, however, other contradictions within AIDS discourse which threaten to disrupt how gender and sexuality are traditionally conceptualised. For example, as I have already indicated, although AIDS has been firmly constructed as a 'male disease', the heterosexual male is largely invisible in AIDS discourse. The majority of health education campaigns aimed at heterosexuals in the UK have been targeted at women. They have urged women to take control in sexual encounters, whilst at the same time ignoring the processes which make this difficult and, in some cases, dangerous. Thus, whilst the construction of normative female sexuality as 'passive' and male as 'active' is reinforced in certain aspects of AIDS discourse, for example in representing heterosexual women as the sexual 'partners' of men and in the association of female sexual agency with deviancy, it is elsewhere threatened by the allocation of responsibility for negotiating sexual practices to women and the demand that they take active control of the (hetero)sexual encounter. Similarly, the construction of (white) heterosexual men as safe, at risk from dangerous deviant women/men as sexual agents further threatens the active/male, passive/female dichotomy.

Such elaborations are important not only because they highlight how particular ideas about gender and sexuality are represented in HIV/ AIDS policy and education, but also because they help illustrate how gender and (hetero)sexuality are constructed through HIV/AIDS policy-making. Through an examination and exploration of the many contradictions that abound it may also be possible to destabilise the meaning of heterosexuality and the constructions of gender upon which it is organised.

NOTES

1. The racialisation of the body affected by AIDS as white was soon to be challenged. By the mid-1980s, as writers began to focus on 'African AIDS', the disease became increasingly associated with the bodies of black (heterosexual) men and women.
2. The inclusion of lesbians as 'high-risk' in early AIDS discourse highlights how both AIDS and homosexuality were not entirely gendered as male, although the view of lesbians as not-real-women enables the potential disruption to be resisted.
3. In 1993 the Centers for Disease Control altered its criteria for a diagnosis of AIDS and HIV-related illness to include gynaecological symptoms.
4. In countries where abortion is outlawed, such as Ireland, the latter option may be attractive to practitioners and policy-makers who wish to affirm their concern with the future health of children whilst leaving unchallenged the view that abortion is morally wrong whatever the circumstances.
5. Men's fears of women may reflect such racist stereotyping. For example, Jenny Kitzinger (1994) reports that some of the white heterosexual male participants interviewed in the AIDS Media Research Project, conducted

with Peter Beharrell, David Miller, and Kevin Williams, made explicit reference to the dangers of black women.
6. This (hetero)sexualised construction of the concept 'general public' has much wider significance beyond understandings of AIDS education policy. For instance, it has important implications for who is constructed as a citizen and, related to this, as a taxpayer worthy of welfare benefits or other means of government support. This was clearly evident in debates surrounding the introduction of Section 28 of the 1988 Local Government Act when, in support of their argument, proponents of the law stated that taxpayers money was being spent on lesbian and gay projects (Stacey, 1991). By implication, either lesbians and gay men are not perceived to be taxpayers or, if they are, they are deemed to be disenfranchised as worthy citizens by virtue of their sexuality.

REFERENCES

Campbell, B. (1987) 'Taking the Plunge', *Marxism Today*, December, p. 9.
Cameron, D. (1992) 'Old Het?', *Trouble and Strife*, **24**: pp. 41–5.
Carabine, J. (1992) 'Constructing Women: Women, Sexuality and Social Policy', *Critical Social Policy*, **34**: pp. 23–37.
Coward, R. (1987) 'Sex after AIDS', *New Internationalist*, March, pp. 20–1.
Doyal, L., Naidoo, J. and Wilton, T. (eds) (1994) *AIDS: Setting a Feminist Agenda* (London: Taylor & Francis).
DuBois, E. C. and Gordon, L. (1984) 'Seeking Ecstasy on the Battlefield: Danger and Pleasure in Nineteenth-century Feminist Thought', in C. S. Vance (ed.) *Pleasure and Danger: Exploring Female Sexuality* (London: Pandora Press).
Hall, L. A. (1991) *Hidden Anxieties: Male Sexuality, 1900–1950* (London: Polity Press).
Holland, J., Ramazanoglu, C., Scott, S., Sharpe, S. and Thomson, R. (1990) *'Don't Die of Ignorance – I Nearly Died of Embarrassment': Condoms in Context*, WRAP Paper 2 (London: Tufnell Press).
Holland, J., Ramazanoglu, C., Scott, S. and Thomson, R. (1994a) 'Desire, Risk and Control: The Body as a Site of Contestation', in L. Doyal, J. Naidoo and T. Wilton (eds) *AIDS: Setting a Feminist Agenda*, (London: Taylor & Francis).
Holland, J., Ramazanoglu, C., Sharpe, S. and Thomson, R. (1994b) 'Achieving Masculine Sexuality: Young Men's Strategies for Managing Vulnerability', in L. Doyal, J. Naidoo and T. Wilton (eds) *AIDS: Setting a Feminist Agenda* (London: Taylor & Francis).
hooks, b. (1992) *Black Looks: Race and Representation* (Boston, MA: South End Press).
Ingham, R., Woodcock, A. and Stenner, K. (1992) 'The Limitations of Rational Decision-Making as Applied to Young People's Sexual Behaviour', in P. Aggleton, P. Davies and G. Hart (eds) *AIDS: Rights, Risks and Reason* (London: Falmer Press).
Jackson, S. (1996) 'Heterosexuality as a Problem for Feminist Theory', in L.

176   *Sex, Sensibility and the Gendered Body*

Adkins and V. Merchant (eds) *Sexualizing the Social: Power and the Organisation of Sexuality* (London: Macmillan).

Jeffreys, S. (1990) *Anticlimax: A Feminist Perspective on the Sexual Revolution* (London: The Women's Press).

Kaplan, H. S. (1987) *The Real Truth About Women and AIDS: How to Eliminate the Risks without Giving Up Love and Sex* (New York: Simon & Schuster).

Kitzinger, J. (1994) 'Visible and Invisible Women in AIDS Discourses', in L. Doyal, J. Naidoo and T. Wilton (eds) *AIDS: Setting a Feminist Agenda* (London: Taylor & Francis).

Koedt, A. (1974) 'The Myth of the Vaginal Orgasm', in The Radical Therapist Collective (eds) *The Radical Therapist* (London: Penguin).

Lees, S. (1993), *Sugar and Spice: Sexuality and Adolescent Girls* (London: Penguin).

Leibowitch, J. (1985) *A Strange Virus of Unknown Origin*, trans. R. Howard (New York: Ballantine).

Lips, H. and Freedman, S. A. (1993) 'Heterosexual Feminist Identities: Private Boundaries and Shifting Centers', in S. Wilkinson and C. Kitzinger (eds) *Heterosexuality: A Feminism and Psychology Reader* (London: Sage).

Norwood, C. (1987) *Advice for Life: A Woman's Guide to AIDS Risks and Prevention* (New York: Pantheon).

Patton, C. (1994) *Last Served? Gendering the HIV Pandemic* (London: Taylor & Francis).

Patton, C. and Kelly, J. (1987) *Making It: A Woman's Guide to Sex in the Age of AIDS* (Ithaca, NY: Firebrand).

Richardson, D. (1989) *Women and the AIDS Crisis*, 2nd edn (London: Pandora Press).

Richardson, D. (1990) 'AIDS Education and Women: Sexual and Reproductive Issues', in P. Aggleton, P. Davies and G. Hart (eds) *AIDS: Individual, Cultural and Policy Dimensions* (London: Falmer Press).

Richardson, D. (1993) 'AIDS and Reproduction', in P. Aggleton, P. Davies and G. Hart (eds) *AIDS: Facing the Second Decade* (London: Falmer Press).

Richardson, D. (1994a) 'Inclusions and Exclusions: Lesbians, HIV and AIDS', in L. Doyal, J. Naidoo and T. Wilton (eds) *AIDS: Setting a Feminist Agenda* (London, Taylor & Francis).

Richardson, D. (1994b) 'AIDS: Issues for Feminism in the UK', in L. Doyal, J. Naidoo and T. Wilton (eds) *AIDS: Setting a Feminist Agenda* (London: Taylor & Francis).

Richardson, D. (ed.) (1996) *Theorising Heterosexuality: Telling it Straight* (Buckingham: Open University Press).

Scott, S. (1987) 'Sex and Danger: Feminism and AIDS', *Trouble and Strife*, no. 11.

Segal, L. (1990) *Slow Motion: Changing Masculinities Changing Men* (London: Virago).

Smart, C. (1992) 'Disruptive Bodies and Unruly Sex: The Regulation of Reproduction and Sexuality in the Nineteenth Century', in C. Smart (ed.) *Regulating Womanhood: Historical Essays on Marriage, Motherhood and Sexuality* (London: Routledge).

Stacey, J. (1991) 'Promoting Normality: Section 28 and the Regulation of

Sexuality', in S. Franklin, C. Lury and J. Stacey (eds) *Off Centre: Feminism and Cultural Studies* (London: Harper Collins).

Watney, S. (1988) 'The Spectacle of AIDS', in D. Crimp (ed.), *AIDS: Cultural Analysis/Cultural Activism* (Cambridge, MA: MIT Press).

Watney, S. (1994) *Practices of Freedom: Selected Writings on HIV/AIDS* (Durham: Duke University Press).

World Health Organization (WHO) (1993) *Women and AIDS: Research Priorities*, Global Programme on AIDS, ACA (1)/93.8 (Geneva: WHO).

Wilton, T. (1994) 'Silences, Absences and Fragmentation', in L. Doyal, J. Naidoo and T. Wilton (eds) *AIDS: Setting a Feminist Agenda* (London: Taylor & Francis).

Winnow, J. (1992) 'Lesbians Evolving Health Care: Cancer and AIDS', *Feminist Review*, no. 41

9 Gender and Sexuality in the Social Construction of Rape and Consensual Sex: A Study of Process and Outcome in Six Recent Rape Trials

ANNE EDWARDS

Rape has been a central concern of feminism(s), receiving attention equally from both the activist women's movement claiming justice and equal rights for women and from feminist theorists seeking to understand the forms and functions of male dominance and the oppression of women. Rape as a criminal offence has certain 'peculiar' (Berger, 1977), possibly unique characteristics which can largely be attributed to its distinctively gendered nature. Rape until recently has been legally defined and culturally perceived as a crime committed by men against women. This sex and gender specificity has significantly affected the way law enforcement and criminal justice personnel deal with the crime. There is now extensive research showing that, in Western countries, the question of evidence and the role of the complainant, who is also the principal and often the only witness, are handled by police and the courts in cases of rape quite differently from other kinds of assault and serious offences generally. A deep-seated belief that accusations of rape are easily made and often false[1] seems to persist and this then justifies treating the woman (complainant/victim/survivor)[2] as though it were she who were on trial.

In most Western jurisdictions, the criminal offence of rape contains three components:

1. the occurrence of an act of sexual penetration or intercourse (variously defined);
2. the absence of the consent or free agreement of the victim;

3. the intention of the perpetrator to rape (the so-called *mens rea* or mental element).

The fundamental problem, which is not unique to rape, is that whether the act in question (sexual intercourse) should be considered a crime depends on the other elements, both of which are not straightforward matters of fact that can be determined on the basis of observation and physical evidence, but involve interpretation and judgement. Where there is no doubt about the identity of the man, there are two possible lines of defence: the first is to deny that sexual intercourse took place; and the second, where sexual intercourse is admitted, is to claim that it was with the woman's consent or alternatively that the man believed she consented. Since women who bring rape complaints often have medical evidence of sexual intercourse having taken place, it is consent which becomes the central issue and courts find this particularly difficult to determine, especially where there is no visible sign of physical violence having been used.

There have been some changes made to the definition of rape and to rules relating to procedure and evidence in most Western countries over the last twenty years,[3] as a result of sustained lobbying by law reform bodies and women's groups. Consequently, the impression may have been given that the system is now giving more sympathetic treatment to women alleging rape, including non-stranger rape, resulting in an increasing proportion of cases (some studies claim these are now the majority) where the complainant and the alleged offender have had a prior social (and sometimes even sexual) relationship, however brief. However, the general assessment of feminists is that at the fundamental level the system is largely unchanged.[4] Far more importance continues to be placed on 'ensuring that men are not convicted of felonies they could not reasonably have known they were committing' than on 'ensuring that women are not forced to submit to nonconsensual sex' (Wiener, 1983, p. 144).

The purpose of this paper is to build on existing feminist legal and sociological work on rape and the criminal justice system in order to understand why, despite some legal reforms that have been achieved, most research has found that in so-called 'consent' rape trials, even where there would seem to be a strong case made by the prosecution, unless there is also independent evidence of considerable violence, juries are still reluctant to convict. The paper draws also on the findings of a recently completed observation study by Melanie Heenan of six 1990 rape trials in Melbourne Australia (summaries of these cases are given at the end of this paper and a detailed analysis is given in Edwards and Heenan (1994)).

The focus of the paper is on sexuality, gender, and power as these are manifested in rape and in the judicial processing of rape, and more specifically in the rape trial. Rape is essentially about sexual difference and male–female power relations. What makes rape such a critical issue is the fact that it forces society in general, and the criminal justice system in particular, to confront the reality of a fundamental and direct conflict between the desires, interests, and perspectives of men and those of women. For feminists, it is in rape that the fusion of sex(uality), gender, and power takes a particularly overt and dramatic form.

This paper will fall into two main sections. The first describes the specific characteristics of the criminal law and the criminal justice system as these relate to rape, with a particular emphasis on the trial stage. The second looks at social constructions of sexuality and gender and the roles these play in the course of the actual interactions where it is alleged rape may have occurred, in the subsequent accounts of those interactions advanced by the participants, and also in the interpretations and assessments of these reported events that have to be made by the courts and by juries in particular, in the process of arriving at a verdict. The paper ends by posing some questions that emerge from this analysis.

HOW THE LAW AND THE CRIMINAL JUSTICE SYSTEM DEAL WITH RAPE

The category of rape that is increasingly coming to the attention of police and courts and which causes the greatest difficulty for the criminal justice system is where the woman and her alleged rapist are known to each other, where there is little or no sign of violence, and where it is basically her word against his. Although in such cases there are certainly some complex technical legal issues to be determined (*mens rea*, mistaken belief, definition and evidence of threat, fear, and resistance), in determining the critical question of whether or not this was consensual sex, non-legal considerations are often more important. A substantial body of research has shown that the key factors influencing the conduct and outcome of rape trials are the culturally based and masculinist assumptions held by judicial personnel and by jurors about typical, normal or 'reasonable' behaviour for men and women in given situations, and particularly judgements about women's moral character based on their leisure activities and their social and sexual interactions with men (Clark and Lewis, 1977; Scutt, 1979; Edwards, 1981; Adler, 1987; Chambers and Millar, 1987; Estrich, 1987; LaFree, 1989; Naffine, 1992; Lees, 1993; Matoesian, 1993). The six Melbourne cases briefly described at the end of this paper illustrate clearly the various ways in which this masculinist bias operates.

What this means in practice is that women complainants who are not virgins find themselves subjected to relentless personal questioning by defence lawyers as to their moral and social character (including their personal relationships, leisure activities, use of alcohol, etc.) in an attempt to test their credibility as the key witnesses. Even when the accounts the women give are consistent and totally plausible, and no convincing case has been made for why they would choose to undergo the experience of a trial if they were not genuine, their allegations are frequently rejected by the jury (five of the six Melbourne cases provide examples of this). As Lees says:

> Myths about women making false allegations override commonsense explanations of why they should run naked into the street, cry compulsively, spend the night in police stations for fear of retribution for taking the case to court, change their name or even move house. (1993, p. 18)

This is not just a problem of overtly sexist legal practices or practitioners but of the 'power relations that are implicit within the very *structure* of the laws themselves ... [which] reflects the experience and serves the interests, of some and not others' (Tarrant, 1990, p. 574). The basic categories and concepts of the criminal law which are applied to rape are not neutral and objective, but embody the perspectives of men – the dominant group – with regard to women, their bodies and their sexuality (Taylor, 1987). The major problem for women is that prevailing social constructions of masculinity and femininity are highly sexist and are still accompanied by a remarkably persistent double standard of morality.

For those feminists who are lawyers and legal theorists, the starting point for change is that the law must move away from its essentially patriarchal perspective. As long as the protection of men from false accusations by women remains the law's primary objective (justified on the grounds that women are basically untrustworthy in their sexual relations) women will not receive justice. The law must be persuaded to take what women say more seriously and to devise methods of supporting the principle of women's right to self-determination and sexual choice: that is the 'right to choose whether, when and with whom to have sexual intercourse' (Temkin, 1982, p. 401).

In determining consent or nonconsent, courts have traditionally given more weight to indirect indicators such as use of force and signs of resistance than to the credibility of the complainant and of her story of what happened. This has involved applying standards of what constitutes force, fear, and resistance that are not based on women's experience generally or on the actual experience of the particular woman in question, but on what from an unacknowledged male perspective would be considered 'reasonable'. Similarly, in cases where the defendant claims to have believed the woman was consenting and the court has to decide whether or not this was an honest though mistaken belief, 'reasonableness' is measured against male perceptions of female behaviour (Harris, 1976; Wiener, 1983; Adler, 1987; Vandervort, 1987/8; Bumiller, 1990; Lees, 1993; Reekie and Wilson, 1993).

To overcome this problem, feminists have proposed that a different approach should be taken to the question of consent. A clear distinction needs to be made between 'voluntary agreement' and 'acquiescence' or submission as a result of threat or fear (Scutt, 1977, p. 65). Consent should be defined not as an imputed state of mind but as a performative act (Vandervort, 1987/8, pp. 265–9). The obvious first step is that courts should give more importance to what the woman in the interaction actually said and did, and to discovering whether she gave clear assent, rather than taking the opposite view that consent is assumed unless there is strong evidence to the contrary. Where this is not by itself conclusive, the most appropriate information to consider would be details about the sequence of events and the specific circumstances of the interaction where rape is alleged to have occurred and how these might assist in determining whether or not coercion was involved and/or whether in the absence of violence or resistance the subsequent actions of the woman were consistent with her account of the incident (Lees, 1993). Such provisions have recently been introduced in Australia in the Victoria Crimes (Rape) Act 1991. Associated with this general strategy, but not discussed here, are proposed changes to the other key element in determining rape, the intention of the man or men concerned and suggestions as to how to handle the issue of 'mistaken belief' (Vandervort, 1987/8; Faulkner, 1991).

Though there is obvious merit in such proposals, they still leave a number of legal difficulties to be resolved, as Vandervort and other feminist lawyers acknowledge. More importantly, this approach fails to address a fundamental problem that confronts any such attempts at rape law reform wherever the administration of criminal justice is based on the adversarial principle. On one side is the state upholding law and order and attempting to prove that the person accused did commit the criminal offence with which they are charged and on the other side is the alleged offender whose defence rests on denial of the charge and questioning of the prosecution's evidence.

The effect of this is that when a criminal case comes to court, the trial consists of two opposing stories being given about the events in question and the jury has to choose between them. The prosecution and the defence each attempts to present evidence that supports their own side and to cast doubt on the evidence offered by the other side. The jury is offered only two possible verdicts: the accused is either guilty or innocent of the offence as charged. The complainant is either an upright and worthy citizen legitimately seeking legal redress for a wrong, or is dishonest, misguided, ill-intentioned, or ill-advised. One must have been the active party in the encounter, the other the passive (and with agency goes responsibility and blameworthiness).

This puts the woman who is seeking to establish that she has been raped in a totally contradictory position: on the one hand, to be convincing as an injured person she must convey a strong sense of the extreme emotional and psychological distress she was caused both at the time of the event and afterwards; while on the other hand, as the chief witness, she must ensure that in giving her evidence, she is clear, consistent, and coherent and that she controls her feelings even under hostile cross-examination (Bumiller, 1990); the discursive construction of 'victim' in our culture necessarily carries 'paradoxical' normative imputations, as Linda Wood and Heather Rennie (1994) point out. So that,

> like society in general, the rape trial ensnares a woman within a web of shifting gender-structured contradictions: rational and irrational; dependent and independent; trusting and suspicious. (Matoesian, 1993, p. 226)

The same either/or alternatives also apply to the various elements that define rape for the purposes of the criminal law. Sexual intercourse either did or did not occur. It was either consensual or it was not. There was either force, coercion or threat applied or there was not. The woman either did or did not offer resistance. Witnesses are either lying or telling the truth. This, as Carol Smart argues, is the 'legal method' operating in conjunction with the 'binary system of logic' (1989, p. 33). In her words, 'the power of the law' lies in the 'legal process of narrowing the possible interpretations of behaviour [which] is, in turn, linked to law's "claim for truth"' (1989, p. 34).

The effect of this is that with only two outcome options available, complex social phenomena have to be simplified in order to fit within predetermined legal categories and then reduced in the course of a criminal trial to one or other of the two limited alternatives. A criminal justice system which relies on a realist notion of the truth, and utilises an adversarial approach based on binary logic in its adjudication of criminal cases, encounters serious epistemological and practical difficulties when faced with crimes such as rape, where the ontological status of the act is one of the central contested issues and where this cannot usually be independently or objectively determined. Wherever there are multiple meanings of a specific human interaction and no obvious ways of discerning which, for given purposes, can or should be taken as the authoritative one, this poses problems for the criminal justice system and for those who come under its jurisdiction.

THE SOCIAL CONSTRUCTION OF SEX, GENDER, SEXUALITY AND RAPE

> Rape is a 'crime of and about violence' but also 'a crime of and about sex'. (Olsen, 1989, p. 88)

Feminists and sociologists studying rape start from a basically social-constructionist position, taking the view that sex/sexuality is as much culturally determined as is gender. Sexualities are defined and then produced and reproduced through discursive and other social practices. There are a variety of perspectives to draw on, including the relatively determinist social conditioning models favoured by some radical feminists in the 1970s (such as Brownmiller, 1975), Marxist theories of ideology (such as Barrett, 1980), social interactionism (for example, the work on 'sexual scripts' by Gagnon and Simon (1974) and others), and Freudian and Freudian-inspired theories (e.g. Mitchell, 1975; Chodorow, 1978); most recently, the two leading schools seem to be either modified structural theories developed by sociologists like Bob Connell (1987), Jeff Hearn and Wendy Parkin (1987), or Sylvia Walby (1990), or applications of cultural studies and discourse analysis to the study of subjectivity and the body that are influenced by Foucault and post-modernist theories.[5] The focus here is on those writers who have applied these various theoretical ideas to analyses of the inter-relationship between gender, sexualities, and rape.

The dominant view among feminists is that rape is not a psychologically aberrant act that can be explained only in terms of the pathology of the individual rapist. Rather rape should be located within the context of what are considered for any given society to be the 'normal' modes of expression of gender identity and sexuality. 'The attributes of masculinity and femininity, learnt from the beginning of childhood and incorporated into expectations of sexual behaviour, provide the motivational and interactional basis of rape' (Jackson, 1978, p. 30). Any understanding of rape, therefore, requires a careful examination of the social characteristics of masculinity and femininity, and the conventional forms of social and sexual relationships between men and women.

Western feminist writers have identified a number of aspects of gender and sexuality as these are culturally defined that have a powerful influence on the nature of heterosexual relations and on how these are experienced by women. The prevailing conception of masculinity stresses aggression, assertiveness, self-reliance, taking the initiative, and being resourceful in overcoming obstacles, including resistance from others. Femininity has the opposite attributes of passivity, dependency, restraint, and accommodation to others. In the sexual context, where the woman is the object of male desire, masculinity consists in making a conquest and in the process the woman's apparent reluctance is transformed into willing participation. The dominant ideology is one of 'masterful seduction and silent submission as sexual enjoyment' (Pineau, 1989, p. 222).

There are other widely held cultural beliefs about gender and sexuality that also play an important role: the notion that all men have a powerful biological drive that is readily aroused at any time and can become dangerous if not regularly satisfied; a fundamentally contradictory characterisation of women as both sexually restrained, even passive, and actively provocative; and a general attitude towards women that tends to objectify and sexualise them, which seems to reflect if not misogynism, then at least strong feelings of dislike and distrust.

Women are defined from the standpoint of men and in terms that serve male interests. In its extreme form, this results in women and their bodies being used for ends which are contrary to their own; any act of sexual violence 'has the effect of hurting [the woman] or

degrading her and/or . . . takes away her ability to control intimate contact' (Kelly, 1988, p. 41). Even when rape is not accompanied by any
other physical violence, forced sex is an assault on the bodily and
personal integrity of the woman; this is achieved 'by reducing women
to their bodies and refusing to acknowledge the seriousness of the non-
bodily harm inflicted by rape' (Reekie and Wilson, 1993, p. 153). As
MacKinnon (1989, p. 172) observes, 'under law, rape is a sex crime
that is not regarded as a crime when it looks like sex'. 'The problem
is that the injury of rape lies in the meaning of the act to its victim,
but the standard for criminality lies in the meaning of the act to the
assailant' (MacKinnon, 1989, p. 180).

For MacKinnon and others, the fundamental problem is not so much
that the law fails to appreciate that apparently non-violent sexual intercourse can be experienced by women as rape; it is rather that for
women (and maybe for some men), the way femininity, masculinity
and (hetero)sexuality are constructed and gender relations are organised in a male-dominated social order, it is hard to differentiate between coerced and noncoerced forms of social/sexual interaction. Where
there is a pre-existing social relationship or acquaintance, 'women frequently consent [to sex] because they are frightened, because they want
to please men, or because they think it is their duty' (Henderson, 1987/8,
p. 218) and their male partners take this as voluntary assent. The two
parties in such interactions interpret each other's verbal and nonverbal
behaviour in terms of pre-existing gendered understandings of their
meanings. Expecting men and women to be able to communicate
effectively under such circumstances is unrealistic. Communication is
obviously critical to the whole question of consent and the problems
that typically arise are well-documented in the six cases studied by
Heenan and myself.

There are obvious implications for the meanings men and women
attach to the key concepts of coercion and consent and, hence, their
definitions of rape. In a society where the distribution of power and
other resources overwhelmingly favours one group, in this case men,
over another, women, the conditions under which consent in terms of
freely exercised choice can operate may not apply (Pateman, 1980;
Vega, 1988). Although other social variables (such as age, class, race,
culture, and so on) certainly also contribute, it is primarily women's
gender that so severely limits their capacity for self-determination in
their sexual and social relationships.

There is an underlying question here that still divides feminists: whether
the power of patriarchy is such that all (hetero)sexual intercourse even

where the two individuals both believe their relationship is based on mutual respect and free agreement is necessarily exploitative and coercive. The most influential feminist theorist in this area is Catherine MacKinnon. Her thesis, originally expounded in two famous articles in *Signs*, is that sexuality is 'the primary social sphere of male power' (1982, p. 529) and that heterosexuality is the 'eroticisation of dominance and submission' (1983, p. 651), which makes forced sex 'paradigmatic' of the general power of men over women (1983, p. 646).

For Carol Smart, this means that in our culture 'women's sexuality is constructed as separate from women themselves . . . as an essence which can by-pass consciousness or which has a will of its own' (1989, p. 30). Smart (1989, 1990) sees the objectification and sexualisation of women taking a particularly dehumanising form in the rape trial. Here the focus of the court is on woman as sex. The detailed attention to parts of the body, specific sexual acts, and the woman's responses, all of which the woman herself is expected to talk about in open court turns the trial into a 'pornographic spectacle' (1989, pp. 39–40).

Even if one does not take the extreme position on this (and there is argument as to whether MacKinnon herself does – see Olsen (1989) versus Vega (1988), most feminists now share the view that gender and sexuality cannot be separated from power, which includes physical and other forms of coercion. It is not a question of rape being *either* about violence and control *or* about sexual access and gratification, rape contains elements of both. This means that no clearcut qualitative distinction can be made between consensual and forced sex, between (mutual) passion and (one-sided) violence. More useful, suggests Liz Kelly (1988), is the idea of a 'continuum of sexual violence' consisting of a whole range of practices not necessarily distinguishable as separate events, a range which from women's perspective is represented experientially as, at one end, choice through pressure to, at the other, coercion and force. However, men and women are not likely to agree over where on such a hypothetical continuum a particular sexual encounter might fit and (as we have seen) society has traditionally taken the male perspective. So, the critical issue is still how to broaden legal and community conceptions of nonconsensual sex so that many more women's experiences are recognised as rape, both by the women themselves and by society.

A fundamental feature of our way of thinking about sex, gender, (hetero)sexuality, and rape, at least in Western society, is the reliance on a particular logical form, the dichotomy. This involves the simple strategy of reducing whatever one is studying to either one or other of only two mutually defined and often mutually exclusive alternatives; in each pair one carries a positive and the other a negative value. We are all familiar with the particular dualisms with which the male/female dichotomy has been associated in Western culture, culture/nature, public/private, reason/emotion, mind/body, independent/dependent, dominant/submissive, etc. There is also a gender-specific division between 'good' and 'bad' women (the virgin/whore distinction) with only those in the former category deserving male respect and protection. With respect to (hetero)sexuality, there are a number of other dimensions that are culturally recognised as significant and these too are represented as dichotomies: consent/coercion; pleasure/pain; passion/violence.

The distinction between consensual sexual intercourse and rape depends on these and other factors also expressed as either/or alternatives (force/nonforce; injury/noninjury; threat/nonthreat; victim contribution/noncontribution; truth/lie). This rigid structure of binary logic sets the framework within which the law and the criminal justice system operate and allows for only two possible outcomes: the crime was or was not committed, the accused is guilty or innocent (Smart, 1989, Chapter 2). It is what might be termed 'the tyranny of the binary' that is responsible for many of the problems women, the courts and juries in particular encounter in dealing with rape.[6]

Empirical support for this approach to the problem of rape can be found in interview studies with convicted rapists and with women survivors of rape, and in studies of rape trials and juries' decisions, including Heenan's Melbourne study.

RAPE FROM THE PERSPECTIVES OF RAPISTS AND OF RAPE SURVIVORS

The main source of information about rapists' perceptions of rape is the interview study with convicted and incarcerated rapists conducted by Diana Scully in America in the early 1980s (Scully and Marolla, 1984, 1985; Scully, 1988, 1990). These were men mostly aged in their twenties and thirties, who were having regular consensual sex (with other women) around the time of the offence, some of whom admitted the rape, some the sex only, and others neither.

Scully examines in some detail these men's perceptions and attitudes on a number of dimensions, including masculinity, hostility to women, interpersonal violence, rape stereotypes, excuses and justification for rape, rewards of rape, and excuses and conceptions of victims and of how their victims might see them. A common underlying thread was the sexual objectification of women, where women victims (most of whom were strangers to these men) 'had no value outside of the roles they were forced to play in the rape' (Scully, 1988, p. 211). By ignoring the rights or feelings of individual women and/or regarding any woman as a legitimate target, men could avoid recognising themselves as rapists. These men also made it clear that for them the appeal of rape lay in the combination of sex with the exercise of power, though they all played down their use of force, which in some instances had been brutal (Scully and Marolla, 1985). In the accounts given by those who denied rape, the focus was particularly on the sexual component even where the pre-sentence reports indicated a weapon and violence were involved (Scully and Marolla, 1984). As Scully (1990) concludes, though they may appear in a more extreme form, the beliefs and values that men such as these rapists hold derive from the culture of the society in which they and we live.

By contrast, studies which explore women's experience of rape or attempted rape focus particularly on the use of violence by the men. The classic studies by Bart (Bart, 1981; Bart and O'Brien, 1984) of women's experiences concern mainly stranger-rape situations but Liz Kelly (1988) includes domestic violence and nonconsensual sex within established relationships. From her interviews she builds up a picture of heterosexual relations in which a variety of forms of pressure and coercion (some subtle and some direct) are routinely employed by men in order to have sex. Linda Wood and Heather Rennie (1994) look at incidents that could be considered date rape and show how impossible it is for women to work within the usual simple dichotomies of rape/nonrape, victim/nonvictim, coercion/consent. They argue, for instance, that wherever women believed they had been able to exercise some agency in the situation and/or wherever they saw the man as having accommodated in some way to their requests, they were then unable to define the incident as rape or assume the identity of innocent victim. As MacKinnon points out, when the law allows for only one reality and that reality is split, the only answer may be a paradox: that 'the woman [is] raped but not by a rapist' (1989, p. 183).

RAPE TRIALS AND THE ROLE OF THE JURY

There have been a number of studies of rape trials, some already cited
(Adler, 1987; Lees, 1993; Matoesian, 1993), but given the focus here
on non-stranger rapes and the role of jurors in the criminal justice
process, the most useful is the major project undertaken by Gary LaFree
and colleagues on the processing of forcible-sex offences through the
criminal justice system in Indianapolis in the 1970s (LaFree, 1989).
LaFree's work provides strong empirical support for the argument advanced in this paper. The principal finding was that in what were described as 'weak' cases (that is those where 'hard' evidence in the
form of physical injury, a recovered weapon, or an eye-witness is lacking),
subjective assessments of factors such as the victim's moral character
or behaviour at the time of the assault, and the character of the defendant, played a significant role (Reskin and Visher, 1986), and in
cases where the issue was whether sex had occurred and/or whether it
was consensual, the victim's sex-role behaviour was a determining factor
in the outcome (LaFree, *et al.*, 1985).

Other studies of rape trials, including the one conducted by Heenan,
also show how in contested cases the range of procedural, linguistic,
and interactional strategies available to the defence (assisted at times
by questionable interventions by judges and a poorly conducted prosecution), in a society that still does not know how to deal with non-
stranger rape, provides plenty of possible grounds on which, given the
two alternatives, the court can choose to acquit. And yet, the core
evidence given by the complainant is usually quite convincing and if
true would justify a guilty verdict. This means that the role of the jury
is critical. In five out of the six Melbourne cases (Case 1 was the
exception) the jury decided against a rape conviction despite what
appeared to be a much stronger case by the prosecution than by the
defence. The problem then is how to explain the outcome in such cases.

Jurors in particular have to make decisions on which much hangs
for both parties on the basis of their interpretations of the motives and
behaviour of individuals in circumstances which may not fall within
their normal experience and which they may find threatening to their
sense of morality and social order. Extending the concept of rape to
cover the kinds of cases which are increasingly coming before the courts
presents a challenge to prevailing cultural constructions of male and
female sexuality, and the boundaries between consensual sex and rape
that have previously been taken for granted by both men and women.
This may expose women jurors to a particular contradiction, which

perhaps explains why they do not necessarily side with the victim. Most women have personal experience of sexual relationships that includes both dealing with welcome and unwelcome demands from men in the early stages of a relationship and episodes in more established relationships in which they participate in sex as a result of pressure from male partners but which are not perceived as rape.

> Some women may find abandonment of the traditional beliefs represented by rape myths as too threatening to be tolerable insofar as to relinquish these beliefs enhances their awareness of being *personally* vulnerable. (Vandervort, 1987/8, p. 266, footnote 79)

Carol Smart (1989, pp. 42–3) and Lucinda Vandervort (1987/8) both recognise this as a possible influence on women serving on juries in rape trials, while Anne Worrall identifies a similar phenomenon in another part of the criminal justice system: what she calls a 'like-us-yet-not-like-us conundrum' that creates special difficulties for women magistrates when encountering women defendants (1990, p. 90).

What we are talking about are emotional and psychological mechanisms of which the individual is not necessarily aware. We are suggesting that the reasoning by which juries come to the decision to acquit can only be understood as an attempt to preserve their sense of an ordered, predictable, and relatively safe world for themselves and their children, when faced with the frightening alternative prospect that maybe even apparently 'normal' social encounters can turn into dangerous rape situations. Another aspect of this may be a widespread notion that women, perhaps especially young unmarried women, who in the modern world are sexually active, who engage in social and sexual behaviour that in the past would have been heavily condemned, and who later in court are able to give a rational and calm account of the experience, are somehow less affected by these incidents. Jurors may then, in balancing the degree of harm inflicted on the victim from which she appears already to have recovered against the future harm to the accused man of a lengthy prison sentence, decide against conviction.

Jurors are being asked to be key change-agents in this process of societal redefinition of rape, while at the same time their options are severely limited by the relatively unchanged and restrictive framework of the law of rape, underpinned by an inflexible binary logic that governs both the criminal judicial system and cultural understandings of gender and sexuality. Complex patterns of social interaction in which each of the items of behaviour is open to various interpretations, both by the parties at the time and by others such as judges and juries later, simply do not fit into such a rigid structure. Rape incidents involve a sequence of actions and reactions over a period of time, during which the character of the interaction for either or both can change fundamentally, but the definition of rape that has to be applied does not allow for this. According to this definition, if at one stage a woman's participation in social and some level of sexual interaction with a man was consensual or if there was no discernible sign of injury or harm, then this cannot be rape. Both these components are typically found in most non-stranger rape situations and yet courts are being asked to accept that rape may have been committed.

Problems around communication and power in gender relations have been identified as crucial both in the social interaction situations where rape may occur and in the judicial handling of rape allegations. Moving to a concept of consent that places greater emphasis on what the woman actually did or said to convey her active agreement to sexual intercourse and on the presence or absence of coercion, threat, or fear as she perceived this, rather than on circumstantial factors and the man's belief, whether reasonable or not, may help address the problem of the system's current bias in favour of the defendant in contested cases.[7]

However, far more difficult to resolve is the much more fundamental question of how could the law, which must work within the constraints of an imposed binary framework and within a given social structure, ever be expected to deal adequately or fairly with the complex, ambiguous, and disputed area of human sexuality as long as that structure is one based on deep-seated gender divisions and gender inequalities located within a system of male domination.

NOTES

1. The legal authority for this assertion, which has been enormously influential in the history of the criminal law of rape, is the much-quoted Sir Matthew Hale, Lord Chief Justice of the King's Bench in England in the 1670s, who issued a cautionary warning to juries that referred specifically to the status of the testimony of the complainant in a rape case (Berger, 1977, pp. 9–10; Taylor, 1987, pp. 74–81).
2. The terminology here is a problem in itself and any of the terms that denote women who have (or claim to have) been raped have specific

meanings, with the term 'victim' carrying particularly negative connotations. Mostly in this chapter I will simply talk of women in the context of
the rape trial, 'the women', or the more technical designation 'woman
complainant'.
3. The following authors look at changes in Australia, Canada, England, and
the United States: Berger (1977); Scutt (1980); Temkin (1982); Wiener
(1983); Hinch (1985); Snider (1985); Adler (1987); Vendervort (1987/8);
Waye (1992). In Australia, there were major changes made in Victoria in
the Crimes (Sexual Offences) Act 1980 and 1991) (Vic.) and the Crimes
(Rape) Act 1991 (Vic.), the latter following a major report by the Law
Reform Commission of Victoria in 1991; there were official reports also
in New South Wales (Bonney, 1985) and South Australia (Naffine, 1984).
The Victorian legislation broadened the definition of rape, removed the
mandatory corroboration warning, restricted the use of evidence about the
complainant's prior sexual history, and adopted a concept of consent which
emphasises the woman's free agreement and how this should be interpreted
(and even allows for withdrawal of consent during sexual activity).
4. Lynne Henderson (1987/8) in a review of Susan Estrich's (1987) book
Real Rape, however, warns against an overly-generalised feminist critique
of rape law that glosses over the variations and particularities of different
legal provisions and fails to acknowledge any progress in recent times.
5. This has emerged as a very lively and exciting area of inter-disciplinary
feminist writing since the late 1980s (see, for example, de Lauretis, 1987;
Diamond and Quinby, 1988; Jaggar and Bordo, 1989; Butler, 1990; Smith,
1990; Sawicki, 1991; Ramazanoglu, 1993; Elizabeth Grosz, 1994.) Apart
from MacKinnon (1989, Chapter 7) and Smart (1989 Chapter 2; 1990),
and a most original recent article by Terry Threadgold (1993), feminist
work in the area of rape does not seem to have made much direct use of
this literature. For a critical comparison of Michel Foucault, Monique Plaza,
and various American feminists with respect to sexuality and rape, see
Vicki Bell (1991).
6. Though very critical of the use of dualisms with respect to the conceptualisation of gender and gender-associated dimensions of human existence,
feminists themselves make use of the binary form, though more often for
rhetorical effect than as a characterisation of social reality; a dramatic
example would be the posing of the question as to what rape is as a
dichotomy: either violence or sex.
7. A much more radical feminist suggestion is that the law could adopt quite
a different model altogether for regulating behaviour in sexual relationships, one based on trust and responsibility. This would result in men and
women being required to conform to certain standards of 'care' for their
partners within the context of an expectation of mutual trust. Where a
man was alleged to have raped or abused his partner, a necessary part of
his defence would be evidence of how in the course of the interaction he
had exercised due care for the needs and wishes of his partner. See Balos
and Fellows (1991) and Pineau (1989).

APPENDIX: SIX MELBOURNE CASES

Case 1

This involved a relationship that had been established for several weeks between a woman in her early twenties and a forty-one year old man. As the two lived a distance apart, they met only at weekends. On this occasion, the woman had come to Melbourne and after drinks at the defendant's flat, they went out to dinner. When they returned, they engaged in the preliminaries to intercourse, but when the woman requested that a condom be worn on this occasion as on previous ones (and AIDS was mentioned), there was an argument and the man became violent, pushed her into the bed-room and subsequently raped her. It was some time before she managed to escape from the flat, naked and screaming, pursued by the defendant who hit her. The occupants of a neighbouring flat heard noises, opened their door and, on observing the two, took the woman into their flat.

The main points at issue were whether the woman consented, her state of mind in view of her alcohol consumption during the evening, the significance of the condom, and the degree and cause of the violence. The accused maintained that he was not aware that the victim had not been consenting to sex in the bed-room, although he admitted hitting her, grabbing her by the hair, and her still being 'upset' whilst they were in the bedroom. The defence case emphasised the close and loving nature of the relationship, thus questioning the likelihood of the male partner resorting to violence, while at the same time attempting to convince the all-male jury that the admitted physical attack of the defendant was an understandable reaction from a man to the morally offensive imputation that his female partner needed the protection of a condom because of the possibility of AIDS. The defence suggested that the rape complaint was the result of the woman not being able to handle the situation emotionally and 'over-reacting' to a 'lover's tiff':

> She's young, she's from the country, it's been a long day, she'd had too much to drink. . . . These are all factors that led to her over-reaction to the situation.

By contrast, the prosecution represented the action of the young woman in requesting the use of a condom as socially responsible and entirely reasonable and defended her unwillingness to continue their sexual activities when her request was refused, which in turn resulted in the totally unexpected and excessive use of violence against her. This issue was dealt with at length by both the defence and the prosecution in their presentation and in their summing up. However, the extent and visual impact of the injuries incurred were probably the principal reason for a conviction in this case. Photographs were shown of the victim with blackened eyes, swollen face and nose, and missing clumps of hair.

Case 2

The background to this case was that the alleged offender had met the complainant on a Melbourne train station. The victim was down from the country with the intention of finding accommodation in the city. Both were in their twenties. The two spent some time together during the day and had a meal, before the offender offered his flat as a place the victim could stay whilst looking for alternative accommodation. That night the two had consensual sex. The victim agreed to stay at the flat for a couple more days. The following day the two went to a barbecue at the home of friends of the man and the alleged rape occurred after they returned to his flat.

The point at dispute was whether following this social occasion, the defendant had forced the complainant to engage in oral and vaginal sex, using considerable force in the process. It was argued by the defence that drinking too much at the barbecue ('She was never without a beer in her hand') resulted in a 'hysterical' temper tantrum when the defendant later proposed oral sex. The defence denied that the defendant had persisted and explained the injuries as the accidental product of his attempt to calm her down.

Here we have both the credibility and the capacity for self-determination of the complainant being undermined by references to her drinking and emotional volatility. In addition, her willingness to start a sexual relationship after only five hours with a stranger was seen as highly morally questionable, as indicating 'a very low level of inhibition'. The prosecution counterclaimed that the defendant was also drinking at the barbecue and became aggressive later; there was an act of sexual intercourse which the complainant did not want but decided it would be easier not to refuse, but then objected to the requirement that she perform oral sex. This then led to the violence and the alleged rape. The fact that the victim left the accused's flat naked and screaming, and with injuries, did not convince the jury of her story, though he was convicted of threat to kill and causing injury. In both this and the earlier case, a major factor in producing a conviction seemed to be the discrepancy between the injuries incurred and the explanation advanced by the defence. In none of the other four cases was there physical evidence of forced sex or serious other injuries (although some medical evidence was given in Case 5).

Case 3

The complainant, an eighteen-year-old dental nurse, had spent the day at the races, betting and drinking with three friends, two female and one male, the boy-friend of one of the girls. Afterwards they went to a nearby pub. A man, who was there, was an acquaintance of one of the girls and joined the group with his male companion. At the end of the evening, the girl with the boy-friend drove him home, the other girl and one of the men took a taxi in one direction, and the other man who was going in her direction offered a lift to the complainant. He suggested going on to a football club for another drink which she agreed to, but instead he drove to an isolated bush area near the river and allegedly raped her in the front seat of the car. She was screaming (which was heard by a family living nearby) and escaped, to be found by the family. He drove away. His account was that she behaved 'like a hysterical drunk' only after the mutually consented-to sexual intercourse, when she discovered he was married with children and that this was a 'one-night stand'.

Alcohol and risky behaviour by the young woman were advanced by the defence as contributing to events, as indicating a high probability of willing participation in the sexual activity, and as casting doubt generally on the truth of the victim's story. As defence counsel put it: 'She's not the shy little girl she wants you to believe.' Earlier counsel had suggested to her that on leaving the pub: 'You wanted to kick on. . . . You wanted to have a canoodle in the football club car park.'

The medical evidence showed no physical injuries and that she was not drunk. He was acquitted.

Case 4

The complainant was a Vietnamese refugee. She met the accused, a middle-aged single man, while waiting to catch a bus in the afternoon from an inner city area to her friend's house where her children were being looked after. He approached her at the bus stop and asked if she would like a lift. She accepted, having waited a long time for the bus. She claimed he drove to a creek, got out a knife, indecently assaulted her, and then demanded that she get into the back seat. At that moment the victim saw a police car in the distance. She screamed out and managed to get out of the car.

The accused denied having pulled a knife out and threatening the woman with it (though he admitted he had a knife in the car). He stated that he thought she was a prostitute, and that she had agreed to engage in sexual intercourse with him for $50 before getting in the car. According to the defence case, the complainant was about to engage in an act of prostitution with the accused and jumped out of the car crying rape only because she was afraid, on seeing a police car approach, that she would be caught.

However, throughout the trial there was never any evidence produced to substantiate the allegation that the complainant was indeed a prostitute or that at the time the defendant had any grounds for believing this to be so, other than his word. The accused was convicted on the detention charge only.

Case 5

This case was the first of two involving the same man. This man had offered a lift to a young woman and her female friend who were sitting outside a suburban pizza parlour at 10.30 on a Friday night. The man, a thirty-one year old and unmarried, was unknown to them. The two young women both sat in the front seat of the van and the man had a bottle of whisky in the van with him. The victim's friend was driven home first. The victim then alleged that the accused drove to a swimming pool car park where she was repeatedly raped and assaulted. During this, the accused apologised after committing each act. She was then allowed to get out of the car. She went immediately to a nearby house where the lights were on, complained of the rape to the male inhabitant and telephoned her boy-friend who took her to the police station. In the following weeks, the victim discovered she was pregnant and had contracted genital warts.

The accused agreed that he had picked up the two young women on this night, however he denied having touched the alleged victim in any way. The accused later told the police that he would not have committed such a crime since he had genital warts.

In order to determine the truth of the victim's accusation, the relative likelihood of her explanation for her pregnancy and genital warts needed to be weighed against any other possibilities. Both of these conditions could only occur through sexual intercourse and at a particular point in time. The defence successfully sought permission to lead evidence about her prior and subsequent sexual history, and relationship with her boy-friend, in order to challenge her assertion that the accused was the person responsible.

According to the defence, the allegations made by the victim were invented in order to avoid responsibility for promiscuous behaviour. Despite evidence produced by the prosecution that the accused had failed to attend police interviews and had been diagnosed with genital warts, and medical evidence supporting the victim's allegations of an attempted strangulation and other physical assaults, the jury acquitted the accused on all charges.

Case 6

In the second of the two cases involving the same accused, the man met his alleged victim at the house of a mutual male friend. The woman, her seven-year-old son, and her boy-friend were spending a social evening at this house with the owner and his three children on the night in question. During the evening, a fight broke out between the three men and the victim's boy-friend was thrown out of the house by the other two men. The woman remained.

Some time later, the accused offered to drive the woman to her home in order to collect some clothing for her child who was going camping the following day with the other children. Upon arriving at her flat, the boy-friend was discovered asleep in the main bedroom. Once again the accused physically removed the man from the premises.

Once alone, the victim alleged that the accused pushed her into the bedroom, indecently assaulted her and then attempted to rape her. Afterwards, he apologised. He then drove her back with the overnight bag to the friend's house as planned and left her at the house. Failing to awaken the man, the victim told his teenage daughter what had happened and she rang the police.

According to the accused, there was no physical or sexual contact whatsoever. He told the police:

> This whole thing's crazy. She's fat and I've got this lovely-looking girl-friend. . . . Rape is wrong.

In this case too, the accused was acquitted of the charges.

As with the previous case, the task of the defence became one of establishing that the victim had lied, that she was the type of woman who would lie, and that she had motive for lying. The prosecution, on the other hand, had to convince the jury beyond reasonable doubt that the events involving physical/sexual contact that the victim alleged occurred on the night in question had taken place.

In the first of these two cases, the young woman's general sexual behaviour was presented as the crucial evidence relevant to the truth or falsity of her allegation. In the second case, the moral implications of the woman's

behaviour for her role as a mother became a major issue. The defence barrister made much of her being single, and having what he described as a 'nomadic live-in lover'. In both these cases, the defence was apparently able to
convince the jury that women who demonstrated such socially deviant characteristics were either not the sorts of women who needed to be protected
from sexual encounters of this kind, if indeed they had occurred, or were the
sort who have reasons for inventing stories of rape and making false accusations against men who are totally innocent.

REFERENCES

Adler, Z. (1987) *Rape on Trial* (London: Routledge & Kegan Paul).
Balos, B. and Fellows, M. L. (1991) 'Guilty of the Crime of Trust: Non-
  stranger Rape', *Minnesota Law Review*, **75**: pp. 599–618.
Barrett, M. (1980) *Women's Oppression Today* (London: Verso).
Bart, P. (1981) 'A Study of Women who both were Raped and Avoided
  Rape', *Journal of Social Issues*, **37**: 4, pp. 123–37.
Bart, P. and O'Brien, P. H. (1984) 'Stopping Rape: Effective Avoidance Strategies', *Signs*, **10**: 1, pp. 83–101.
Bell, V. (1991) 'Beyond the "Thorny Question": Feminism, Foucault and the
  Desexualisation of Rape', *International Journal of the Sociology of Law*,
  19: 1, pp. 83–100.
Berger, V. (1977) 'Man's Trial, Woman's Tribulation: Rape Cases in the
  Courtroom', *Columbia Law Review*, **77**: 1, pp. 1–103.
Bonney, R. (1985) *Crimes (Sexual Assault) Amendment Act, 1981: Monitoring and Evaluation*, Interim Reports 1, 2 and 3, Department of Attorney
  General, Bureau of Crime Statistics and Research, New South Wales
Brownmiller, S. (1975) *Against Our Will: Men, Women and Rape* (New York:
  Simon & Schuster).
Bumiller, K. (1990) 'Fallen Angels: The Representation of Violence Against
  Women in Legal Culture', *International Journal of the Sociology of Law*,
  18: 2, pp. 125–42.
Butler, J. (1990) *Gender Trouble* (New York: Routledge).
Chambers, G. and Millar, A. (1987) 'Proving Sexual Assault: Prosecuting
  the Offender or Persecuting the Victim?', in P. Carlen and A. Worrall (eds)
  Gender, Crime and Justice (Milton Keynes: Open University Press), pp.
  58–80.
Chodorow, N. (1978) *The Reproduction of Mothering: Psychoanalysis and
  the Sociology of Gender* (Berkeley: University of California Press).
Clark, L. N. G. and Lewis, D. (1977) *Rape: The Price of Coercive Sexuality*
  (Toronto: Women's Press).
Connell, R. W. (1987) *Gender and Power* (Sydney: Allen and Unwin).
De Lauretis, T. (1987) *Technologies of Gender* (Bloomington: Indiana University Press).
Diamond, I. and Quinby, L. (eds) (1988) *Feminism and Foucault: Reflections
  on Resistance* (Boston, MA: Northeastern University Press).

Edwards, S. S. M. (1981) *Female Sexuality and the Law* (Oxford: Martin Robertson).

Edwards, A. and Heenan, M. (1994) 'Rape Trials in Victoria: Gender, Socio-Cultural Factors and Justice', *Australian and New Zealand Journal of Criminology*, 27: pp. 213–36.

Estrich, S. (1987) *Real Rape* (Cambridge, MA: Harvard University Press).

Faulkner, J. (1991) '*Mens Rea* in Rape: Morgan and the Inadequacy of Subjectivism: Or Why No should not mean Yes in the Eyes of the Law', *Melbourne University Law Review*, 18: 1, pp. 60–82.

Gagnon, J. H. and Simon, W. (1974) *Sexual Conduct: The Social Sources of Human Sexuality* (London: Hutchinson).

Grosz, E. (1994) *Volatile Bodies: Toward a Corporeal Feminism* (Bloomington, IN: Indiana University Press).

Harris, L. R. (1976) 'Towards a Consent Standard in the Law of Rape', *University of Chicago Law Review*, 43: pp. 613–45.

Hearn, J. and Parkin, W. (1987) *'Sex' at 'Work': The Power and Paradox of Organisation Sexuality* (Brighton: Wheatsheaf).

Henderson, L. N. (1987/8) 'What Makes Rape a Crime?', *Berkeley Women's Law Journal*, 3: pp. 193–229.

Hinch, R. (1985) 'Canada's Sexual Assault Laws: A Step Forward for Women?', *Contemporary Crises*, 9: 1, pp. 33–44.

Jackson, S. (1978) 'The Social Context of Rape: Sexual Scripts and Motivation', *Women's Studies International Quarterly*, 1: pp. 27–38.

Jaggar, A. M. and Bordo, S. R. (eds) (1989) *Gender/Body/Knowledge: Feminist Reconstructions of Being and Knowing* (New Brunswick, NJ: Rutgers).

Kelly, L. (1988) *Surviving Sexual Violence* (Cambridge: Polity Press).

LaFree, G. (1989) *Rape and Criminal Justice: The Social Construction of Sexual Assault* (Belmont CA.: Wadsworth).

LaFree, G. D., Reskin, B. F. and Visher, C. A. (1985) '"Jurors" Responses to Victims' Behaviour and Legal Issues in Sexual Assault Trials', *Social Problems*, 32: 4, pp. 389–407.

Law Reform Commission of Victoria (1991) *Rape: Reform of Law and Procedure*, Appendices to Interim Report no. 42.

Lees, S. (1993) 'Judicial Rape', *Women's Studies International Forum*, 16: 1, pp. 11–36.

MacKinnon, C. A. (1982) 'Feminism, Marxism, Method and the State: An Agenda for Theory', *Signs*, 7: 3, pp. 515–44.

MacKinnon, C. A. (1983) 'Feminism, Marxism, Method and the State: Towards Feminist Jurisprudence', *Signs*, 8: 4, pp. 635–58.

MacKinnon, C. A. (1989) *Toward a Feminist Theory of the State* (Cambridge, MA: Harvard University Press).

Matoesian, G. M. (1993) *Reproducing Rape: Domination through Talk in the Courtroom* (Cambridge: Polity).

Mitchell, J. (1975) *Psychoanalysis and Feminism* (Harmondsworth: Penguin).

Naffine, N. (1984) *An Inquiry into the Substantive Law of Rape*, Women's Adviser Office, Department of the Premier and Cabinet South Australia.

Naffine, N. (1992) 'Windows on the Legal Mind: the Evocation of Rape in Legal Writing', *Melbourne University Law Review*, 18: pp. 741–67.

Olsen, F. (1989) 'Feminist Theory in Grand Style', *Columbia Law Review*, **89**: pp. 1147–78.
Pateman, C. (1980) 'Women and Consent', *Political Theory*, **8**: pp. 149–68.
Pineau, L. (1989) 'Date Rape: A Feminist Analysis', *Law and Philosophy*, **8**: pp. 217–43.
Ramazanoglu, C. (ed.) (1993) *Up Against Foucault: Explorations of Some Tensions between Foucault and Feminism* (London: Routledge).
Reekie, G. and Wilson, P. (1993) 'Rape, Resistance and Women's Rights of Self-defence', *Australian and New Zealand Journal of Criminology*, **26**: 2, pp. 146–54.
Reskin, B. F. and Visher, C. A. (1986) 'The Impact of Evidence and Extralegal Factors in Jurors' Decisions', *Law and Society Review*, **20**: 3, pp. 423–38.
Sawicki, J. (1991) *Disciplining Foucault: Feminism, Power and the Body* (New York: Routledge).
Scully, D. (1988) 'Convicted Rapists' Perceptions of Self and Victim: Role Taking and Emotions', *Gender and Society*, **2**: 2, pp. 200–13.
Scully, D. (1990) *Understanding Sexual Violence: A Study of Convicted Rapists* (Boston, MA: Unwin Hyman).
Scully, D. and Marolla, J. (1984) 'Convicted Rapists' Vocabularies of Motive: Excuses and Justifications', *Social Problems*, **31**: 5, pp. 530–44.
Scully, D. and Marolla, J. (1985) '"Riding the Bull at Gilley's": Convicted Rapists Describe the Rewards of Rape', *Social Problems*, **32**: 3, pp. 251–63.
Scutt, J. A. (1977) 'Consent versus Submission: Threats and the Element of Fear in Rape', *University of West Australian Law Review*, **13**: 1, pp. 52–76.
Scutt, J. A. (1979) 'Admissibility of Sexual History Evidence and Allegations in Rape Cases', *The Australian Law Journal*, **53**: pp. 817–31.
Scutt, J. A. ed. (1980) *Rape Law Reform: A Collection of Conference Papers* (Canberra, ACT: Australian Institute of Criminology).
Smart, C. (1989) *Feminism and the Power of Law* (London: Routledge & Kegan Paul).
Smart, C. (1990) 'Law's Power, the Sexed Body and Feminist Discourse', *Journal of Law and Society*, **17**: pp. 194–210.
Smith, D. E. (1990) *Texts, Facts, and Femininity* (New York: Routledge).
Snider, L. (1985) 'Legal Reform and Social Control: The Dangers of Abolishing Rape', *International Journal of the Sociology of Law*, **13**: 4, pp. 337–56.
Tarrant, S. (1990) 'Something is Pushing Them to the Side of Their Own Lives: A Feminist Critique of Law and Laws', *University of West Australian Law Review*, **20**: 3, pp. 573–606.
Taylor, J. (1987) 'Rape and Women's Credibility: Problems of Recantations and False Accusations echoed in the Case of Cathleen Crowell Webb and Gary Dotson', *Harvard Women's Law Journal*, **10**: pp. 59–116.
Temkin, J. (1982) 'Towards a Modern Law of Rape', *The Modern Law Review*, **45**: 4, pp. 399–419.
Threadgold, T. (1993) 'Critical Theory, Feminisms, the Judiciary and Rape', *The Australian Feminist Law Journal*, **1**: pp. 7–25.
Vandervort, L. (1987/8) 'Mistake of Law and Sexual Assault: Consent and Mens Rea', *Canadian Journal of Women and the Law*, **2**: 2, pp. 233–309.
Vega, J. (1988) 'Coercion or Consent: Classic Liberal Concepts in Texts on

Sexual Violence', *International Journal of the Sociology of Law*, **16**: pp. 75–89.

Walby, S. (1990) *Theorising Patriarchy* (Oxford: Blackwell).

Waye, V. (1992) 'Rape and the Unconscionable Bargain', *Criminal Law Journal*, **16**: pp. 94–105.

Wiener, R. D. (1983) 'Shifting the Communication Burden: A Meaningful Consent Standard in Rape', *Harvard Women's Law Journal*, **6**: pp. 143–61.

Worrall, A. (1990) *Offending Women: Female Lawbreakers and the Criminal Justice System* (London: Routledge).

Wood, L. A. and Rennie, H. (1994) 'Formulating Rape: the Discursive Construction of Victims and Villains', *Discourse and Society*, **5**: 1, pp. 125–48.

10 Keeping them in their Place: Hetero/sexist Harassment, Gender and the Enforcement of Heterosexuality[1]

DEBBIE EPSTEIN

INTRODUCTION

Since September 1991 I have been engaged in a research project in which we set out to explore the experiences of lesbian and gay students, teachers, and parents in relation to the English system of education.[2] In the course of the project, we have interviewed or held group discussions with some 30 lesbians and gay men, as well as carrying out ethnographic work in four schools and in a lesbian and gay youth group.[3] While the majority of our respondents have been white, we have also spoken with lesbians and gays of African and of South Asian descent.[4] My own contribution to the field work for this project has been that of interviewing many of our lesbian and gay respondents and participant observation in one of the schools. Doing the research, I have been struck forcibly by the various forms of harassment experienced by our female respondents as well as by those men and boys who identified as and/or were perceived as gay or effeminate by their peers and/or teachers. During the same period, and partly because of the research findings, I have found myself reflecting on my own experiences of harassment and those of my students in both the recent and more distant past. This chapter is, in large part, the result of these reflections and of discussions I have had with students, colleagues, and friends about the issues involved.[5]

In this chapter, I will argue that the term 'sexual harassment' is misleading. I do not wish to suggest that the term has not been useful, particularly in the way that it has been used to make women aware of the sexual content of gender inequality. However, I believe that the more or less orthodox feminist view of sexual harassment, which argues that sexism is, by definition, sexual (see, for example, MacKinnon, 1979; Wise and Stanley, 1987), is now due for reconsideration. I will also argue that, within this reconsideration, it is imperative to pay close attention to the harassment of gay men as well as that of women, since both can be understood as a kind of pedagogy of heterosexuality and a key way in which heterosexuality is institutionalised. Indeed, it may seem that this paper is over-weighted towards the consideration of the harassment of gay men. This is deliberate, precisely because I believe that it is an important area of sexist harassment which has not been considered in detail.

Definitions of 'sexual harassment' in policy documents often refer to a range of activities that extend well beyond the obviously 'sexual'. Despite these wide-ranging definitions of what constitutes 'sexual harassment', this term is usually used in more limited ways that appeal to certain commonsense notions of what it is to be 'sexual'. This limiting of the term may, indeed, be a key factor that hinders women from taking formal action against their harassers. I will, therefore, propose that the term 'sexist harassment' may well be more useful to those at its receiving end. I will also suggest that, to develop a fuller understanding of sexist harassment, we need to see it within the context of what Adrienne Rich (1980) calls 'compulsory heterosexuality' – that is, the ways in which heterosexuality is rewarded (for example through social approval, the legal institution of marriage with its manifold material and other benefits) while lesbianism (and gay sexuality) is punished (for example through social stigmatisation, the frequent loss of custody of children, the impossibility of having one's relationship recognised in law). More fruitful for my purposes in this paper is, perhaps, Judith Butler's (1990) notion of the 'heterosexual matrix' which she conceives as including not only the institutionalisation of compulsory heterosexuality, but also the wider discursive field which shapes our understandings of gender in terms of binary opposites tied together through (presumed heterosexual) desire.

DEFINING SEXUAL/SEXIST HARASSMENT

The bulk of my research has taken place in schools or has asked interviewees to reflect on their experiences of school life in relation to sexuality. It seems appropriate, therefore, for me to use the definition

of sexual harassment given by the National Union of Teachers' (NUT)
pamphlet on *Dealing with Sexual Harassment* (1986). It is important
to note that this definition is typical of those employed in institutions
(educational or otherwise) that have policies pertaining to sexual
harassment:

> any uninvited, unreciprocated and unwelcome physical contact, com-
> ment, suggestion, joke or attention which is offensive to the person
> involved, and causes that person to feel threatened, humiliated, pat-
> ronised or embarrassed.   (cited in de Lyon, 1989, p. 122)

De Lyon points out that the wide range of actions covered by such
a definition and the subjective nature of its terms 'can cause certain
difficulties' (p. 122). I would suggest that not least among these difficulties is the fact that it can be difficult to define harassment as 'sexual'
when, in commonsense terms, it is not.

Rebecca,[6] for example, described to me the ways in which a more
senior colleague in her university department, a sociologist who both
taught and wrote about inequality, would frequently invade her space.
But, she explained, his touches could not really be said to be 'sexual'.
She perceived them more as an infantilising process than as 'touching
up'. They would occur if she disagreed with him and he would touch
her in a way that indicated that he found her immature, not to be
taken seriously. Rebecca was neither young nor inexperienced. She
was, however, on a temporary contract and a lesbian, and felt totally
unable to take any official action against her harasser, feeling that this
would:

(a) be countered by William becoming angry and denying any form
    of harassment; and
(b) result in her failure to become a permanent member of staff.

The point, here, is that the wide-ranging definition of 'sexual harassment' in operation in Rebecca's university, which is almost identical
to that quoted from the NUT, did not help her report the harassment
or take official action against William. Her difficulty was, in part, due
to her particularly vulnerable position as a lesbian on a temporary contract.
It also fits into a frequently reported picture of the under-reporting of
sexual harassment (see, for example, de Lyon, 1989). It was, moreover, clearly about the term 'sexual harassment' itself. She felt that in
the course of a disciplinary hearing she would have to agree that the

touches she had endured while being harassed were not specifically 'sexual'. At no time had William made 'sexual advances' to Rebecca. This deterred her from taking action against what she clearly perceived as his sexist actions.

This story is representative of stories which have been told to me over and over again by students and friends. In addition, such stories have come up in relation to the experiences of both lesbian and gay respondents in our research. The point of all these stories is that the very term '*sexual* harassment' constrains the action these people have felt able to take. In this context, the term '*sexist* harassment' may well have been more helpful to them. Language is a powerful force in the making of meanings. Over the years feminists have, for example, argued that the use of the word 'man' to subsume women constitutes an erasure of women. Similarly, the term 'sexual harassment' erases the experience of *sexist* harassment which is not overtly or obviously sexual in content or form. A consequence of this is that it becomes even more difficult for many women to have recourse to official procedures than it might otherwise have been – a recourse which would, in any case, be difficult simply because of the patriarchal hierarchies of educational and other institutions. I would, therefore, suggest that the term 'sexist' rather than 'sexual', harassment, may be more helpful to those who experience this kind of behaviour.

SEXISM, HETEROSEXISM, AND THE HETEROSEXUAL MATRIX

Drawing on the work of Rich (1980) and Wittig (1980, 1981), Judith Butler uses the term *heterosexual matrix* 'to designate that grid of cultural intelligibility through which bodies, genders and desires are naturalized' (1990, p. 151). She argues that gender (and its instabilities) need to be understood in the context of the heterosexual matrix. Butler suggests that gender is a constructed and excluding category which is put in place through its connection, via desire (culturally assumed to be of the opposite sex) to heterosexuality. She is also argues that a great deal of cultural work goes into the maintenance of the oppositional, binary 'gendered possibilities' available to us and that this work rests on the presumption of heterosexuality as both 'normal' and normative (see also Epstein and Johnson, 1994). I will suggest below that sexist harassment constitutes a significant part of this cultural work.

The limits of what is permissible for each gender are framed within the context of compulsory heterosexuality. This is established very early in childhood and is part of the way in which the education of young children is structured. It is clear, for example, that the meanings both of being a 'good girl' and of being a 'real boy' are constituted within a silent heterosexuality, which is made all the more powerful by its very silence.[7] Clarricoates (1987, p. 156), for example, in her much cited work on primary school teachers and children, offers the following quotes from teachers:

> the girls seem to be typically feminine whilst the boys seem to be typically male ... you know more aggressive ... the ideal of what males ought to be.

> I think the boys tend to be a little more aggressive and on thinking about it the male is the same in the animal world ... we are animals basically.

Clarricoates' paper is concerned with the gendered ways in which teachers treat children and the gendered ways that children behave, having learnt their gender-appropriate 'sex roles'. However, nowhere does she point out that these roles are not simply about the genders of the children, but also about the assumed heterosexuality of those genders. Being 'typically feminine', for example, does not make sense except in a heterosexual relationship to its binary opposite, the 'masculine'. Women, for example, are supposed to show their femininity by dressing and behaving in ways which are attractive to men (see also Lees, 1986, 1993). Indeed, it is this (presumed heterosexual) relationship of femininity to the masculine which is often parodied by drag queens, who adopt stereotypically 'ultra-feminine' ways of dressing and behaving.[8] Equally, the notion that 'boys tend to be a little more aggressive' provides a basis for later discourses of the male sex drive (see Hollway, 1984, 1989), which assume that men will take the lead in sexual encounters with women and have strong needs for (instant) gratification of their sex drive.[9] The underlying assumption here is that men are (biologically) programmed to 'pursue' women in more or less aggressive ways while women will wait to be pursued, their most active agency involving putting out signals of availability. Within this discourse, sexual harassment is seen to be simply the expression of men's (biological) needs to pursue potential sexual partners in the search for immediate sexual satisfaction. In this way, feminist discourses of sexual harassment can be appropriated by and incorporated into an inherently anti-feminist framework.

Feminists, have not generally explained sexual/sexist harassment in these biological terms. Rather, most feminists have argued that biology is not destiny and feminist explanations of harassment have, therefore, been in terms of the relative power of men and women and of the ways in which sexual/sexist harassment serves to reinforce and pre-serve this power relationship (see, for example, MacKinnon, 1979; Wise and Stanley, 1987; Hanmer and Maynard, 1987). What I would like to suggest is that this relationship of power is not simply one in which men oppress women, and in which women are marked as Other. Rather, building on Butler (1990), I would suggest that it is one in which:

(a) gendered and sexualised relationships are complexly constructed in relation to other differences, such as those of age, race, eth-nicity, class, and/or disability;
(b) heterosexuality is presumed and deviations from heterosexual norms are punished;
(c) the harassment of gay men (and of men perceived to be gay) is not a separate issue, which is of relatively minor importance in understanding the harassment of women but is, rather, an im-portant aspect of policing culturally produced boundaries of both gender and sexuality; and
(d) sexist harassment can be seen as a pedagogy which schools women and men into normative heterosexuality (but not always suc-cessfully).

The next sections of this paper explore these four points in more detail.

THE COMPLEXITY OF SOCIAL RELATIONS AND SEXIST HARASSMENT

The gendered power relations which are constructed in part through sexist harassment are themselves complex and somewhat fluid. It would, therefore, be a mistake to assume that the sexist harassment of black women, for example, takes exactly the same forms as that of white women, for there are particular racialised constructions of black women's sexuality and their gender-appropriate behaviour which impact upon the forms of sexist harassment which they might experience.[10] There are, therefore, likely to be differences in the forms of (racialised) sex-ist harassment experienced by black women from those experienced by white women, and in the forms of (sexualised) racist harassment experienced by black women from those experienced by black men. The case of Anita Hill and Clarence Thomas provides ample evidence of the complexity of the ways in which sexist harassment becomes racialised in a racist society and, conversely, in which racism becomes sexualised in a sexist society (see Morrison, 1993). Indeed, as Morrison argues, the case could not have happened in the absence of particular racist/sexist tropes which gave rise to the case in the first place (p. xvii).

It is important to note, here, that neither the category 'black' nor the category 'white' should be considered to be monolithic. Within the category 'white' there are different constructions of WASP (White, Anglo-Saxon Protestant) and other heterosexualities, *vide* the stereotypical 'Latin lover'.[11] Equally, there are different versions within Anglo-American popular culture (both white and ethnic minority) of the sexualities of (to adopt American terminology) 'people of colour'. They are, nevertheless, versions of heterosexuality and the experiences of harassment of lesbian and gay people of colour are shaped both by racist and by heterosexist assumptions.[12]

For disabled people, the assumptions about sexuality take a some-what different form. Even more than 'nice girls', disabled people are supposed not to be sexual. However, the presumption is, almost in-variably, that any sexual desire that exists or any sex which takes place will be hetero, as will any loving or romantic relationships. Hence the well-publicised cases of the sterilisation of mentally and physically disabled women (and sometimes men) who, it is feared, might become sexual but fail to take precautions against pregnancy. Moreover, people who become disabled as the result of illness or accident, may find that their relationships with same sex partners are denied by doctors, fam-ilies of origin, and legal institutions.[13] While the denial of sexuality to disabled people might, on the face of it, appear to rule out harassment, this very denial can be experienced as harassing in itself.[14] Further-more, when hetero/sexuality *is* recognised as being part of the lives of disabled people, it may be medicalised, with disabled people being offered physical assistance for mechanical versions of sexual intercourse in which the 'release' of orgasm is assumed to be the only issue and closeness in and through sexuality disappears. Here, hetero/sexist as-sumptions about sex and penetration being identical are writ large. This, too, can be experienced as a form of 'official hetero/sexist harassment'. Finally, an important aspect of the experience of visible disability is being seen as undesirable, ugly, and unsexy. In a society where the necessity of having a 'body beautiful' is stressed, disabled people may be harassed about their appearances in ways which do not constitute sexual approaches (wanted or unwanted) but are most definitely harassing. For those disabled women and men identifying as lesbian or gay, then, the struggle to express themselves sexually is shaped both by constructions of disability as a/anti-sexual and by constructions of sexuality as heterosexual.[15]

In this section I have explored two aspects of the complexity of social relations in and through which sexuality and gender are constructed and within which sexist harassment takes place. However, the argument could be extended to cover other inequalities. The point, here, is that there is not one, univocal form of hetero/sexist harassment but, rather, that the forms of harassment experienced shape and are shaped by the particular social locations of those who are harassed and, indeed, their harassers.

THE PRESUMPTION OF HETEROSEXUALITY AND THE PUNISHMENT OF DEVIANCE

Richard Johnson and I have argued elsewhere that the almost universal presumption of heterosexuality is part of what makes it compulsory (Epstein and Johnson, 1994, p. 198). Furthermore, deviance from normative heterosexuality is regularly punished in a myriad of ways too numerous to be fully documented. Most obvious, are, perhaps, the legislative discrimination against gay men in relation to the age of consent and other sex 'crimes'. Furthermore, as Evans (1993, p. 123) points out, neither European (including British) nor American legislation generally protects lesbians and gay men from discrimination in employment.

Similarly, there is juridical and bureaucratic discrimination against lesbians in relation to issues of child custody, adoption, and fostering (effectively endorsed by the Save the Children Fund when they dropped Sandy Toksvig from speaking at their annual conference after she came out as co-parent to her female partner's children).[16] The prevalence and increase of violence against gay men and lesbians, particularly those on the 'scene', is also indicative of punitive action against those who dare to deviate from the heterosexual path. Other punishments include the bullying of boys and men found to be 'cissy', 'wimpish' and/or gay and the taunting of certain girls as 'lezzie' (see Alistair *et al.*, 1994; Rogers, 1994; Mac an Ghaill, 1994). Throughout our interviews with lesbians and gay men, respondents reported to us a combination of the experience of being harassed because they were perceived as being, in some way, not sufficiently like 'real boys' or were not 'feminine' enough. They also reported the experience of fearing such harassment and taking avoiding action, often through a heightening of their own homophobic behaviours and even heterosexual activities. Thus, for example, Alistair talked about having a 'pretend girlfriend', while several of our lesbian respondents spoke about seeking to have boyfriends in order to avoid both being labelled as lesbian and to avoid other forms of sexual harassment. In other words, heterosexist harassment can be seen as one form of punishment of deviance from the straight and narrow.

THE HARASSMENT OF GAY MEN AND THOSE PERCEIVED AS GAY

Herbert (1992) argues, firstly, that men cannot be sexually harassed because harassment can take place only if the harasser has both institutional and personal power over the person harassed (p. 12). Secondly, she also posits that 'sometimes a gay person sexually harasses a straight person, sometimes a gay person is sexually harassed by a straight person, and sometimes a gay person is sexually harassed by a gay person' (p. 23). What is noteworthy, here, is that her first statement (that men cannot be harassed) must logically, in the light of her second (that gay people can be harassed either by straight people or by other gay people), apply only to heterosexual men (unless, of course, gay men do not count as men). In addition, her suggestion that gay people can harass straight people seems not to make sense within her own terms since, in relation to sexuality at least, gay men and lesbians lack 'institutional and personal power' over straight people.

In fact, most writing about sexist harassment assumes that the harassment of boys and men who appear to be gay or effeminate is different in kind and in effect to the harassment of women. Sometimes, as in the case of Herbert, the heterosexist or homophobic harassment of lesbians and gay men is mentioned in passing. Sometimes, as in the work of Mahony, it may be pointed out that:

When a boy gets 'pushed around' it is not, I would suggest, in virtue of being a boy but because he is not the right sort of boy. Perhaps he is perceived as possessing qualities which run counter to
dominant notions of masculinity. In this case he may also be subject
to verbal abuse, 'poof', 'queer' and 'you've got AIDS'.

For him the lesson to be learnt is how to become a *real* man,
dominant and not subordinate. (1989, pp. 162–3; original emphasis)

However, even Mahony's very clear description of girls' experiences
of sexual harassment, including violence, in mixed schools does not
make explicit the extent to which such harassment is directed towards
the production of *heterosexual* girls and boys, that is, girls and boys
for whom heterosexuality is inherent in their sense of themselves as
gendered. Thus, for Mahony's boy to learn to be a 'real man, dominant and not subordinate', he will also, as is clear from the range of
insults directed towards him, have to constitute himself as heterosexual (and specifically not a 'poof' or a 'queer'). Similarly, Julian Wood's
(1984) quite shocking account of the horrendous sexism of boys' sex
talk (which includes fantasies of violent rape), takes for granted that
this talk will be entirely and aggressively heterosexual. Indeed, reading his article, it is difficult to see how a gay, or even a less aggressively heterosexual, boy could begin to survive (or, at any rate, to thrive)
within this context.

The gay men with whom we spoke during the course of our research project mentioned that they experienced several different kinds
of harassment while they were still at school: firstly, they spoke about
being harassed for being gay and/or effeminate; secondly, they spoke
of harassing other men; and thirdly, they recalled harassing women.
With regard to the first point, the harassment which they endured was
part of school cultures which seemed to be designed to punish those
boys who were not stereotypically masculine, or, indeed, macho. Thus,
Michael recalled a friendship with another boy, Alan:

we became really good friends and I remember one day actually
just completely spontaneously, um, the bell went and we were off. . . .
And we just grabbed each others' hands and ran off, together, holding
hands and all the other people in the class started shouting homo,
homo, yurgh, homo, and I didn't understand what it meant, um, but
I just realised that, you know, they were sort of shouting something
abusive, and it was obviously something to do with Alan and something
to do with us holding hands, so we stopped, and, um, felt quite

guilty about it actually. I didn't really understand why and then a couple of days later there was this joke going around. . . . Um, somebody would come up to you and say, so are you a, and you know this idea of homo somehow had stuck in my head as something bad and then somebody came up to me. . . . and said are you a homo sapien [*sic*] and I didn't know what that meant, but I just heard the word homo and I thought, no no no, I'm not a homo sapien and everyone laughed at me.

In this case, Michael's friendship with Alan was made the subject of verbal harassment in such a way that both of them felt constrained to cool the friendship. Furthermore, the later teasing of Michael by others whose vocabulary allowed them to play on the word 'homo' was an additional punishment for his deviations from the norms of heterosexual masculinity. Michael was, then, made to feel guilty about being 'homo'(sexual) in the first instance and through the later teasing, he was put in a situation whereby the denial of being 'homo' meant that he had also to deny being human. The joke, here, was not only about his naiveté, but about the Catch 22 situation in which he was placed – a situation made more significant because the denial of full humanity to particular groups has, historically, been one of the ways in which a variety of oppressions have been held in place.

Gay men also spoke about their own harassment of other gay men. Such harassment was often entered into in an effort to defend their own masculinity. Thus, Alistair recalls:

I remember, when I was about fifteen or so, people at school who were, kind of, singled out as queer, who, um, I don't know, were just, kind of, a couple of camp men that spring to mind, who, um, I kind of befriended, um, in a detached kind of way. . . .
I mean, I did use, y'know, I did call people queer and that kind of stuff, but I didn't do it to them. I did it to, uh, um, people who probably were, y'know, not people who were maybe unsure, um to, um, kind of protect myself from them, I think. I mean, looking back on it, that wasn't why I did it at the time, so, if somebody was saying something about a bloke, y'know, or something, I'd say queer, y'know, in order to protect myself from them, whereas these, kind of, um, nellies in the woodwork, or whatever, I could be nice to them and keep my masculinity intact.[17]

This story of Alistair's was told in response to a story told by one of
the women taking part in this group discussion. Teresa had talked about
how she and a gang of other girls used to call a boy 'queer' and 'poof'
because, she said, he was different:

> He was, like, really quiet and he was, um, he always used to get his
> homework done, used to have his school uniform on and then, none
> of us had a school uniform. He did. And this sort of thing. So he
> was just different I think, just different.

Alistair's stress, in his response to this, was on keeping his masculinity intact. He recognised that the difference Teresa described was,
specifically, a difference in the form of masculinity which her target
had inhabited. In her story, being clean, quiet, and academic (an 'ear'ole'
in Paul Willis' (1977) terms) was seen as equivalent to being 'queer'.
Alistair was able to avoid this label, despite befriending some 'nelly'
(that is effeminate) boys, primarily by joining in the harassment of
those who were not his friends. Thus, he was able to present himself
as masculine, and *feel* masculine, by virtue of behaving homophobically;
his masculinity, in the school context, was, in part at least, constituted
by and through the expression of homophobia.

The third way in which the gay men we spoke to recalled being
involved in harassment was when they joined in, or were urged to join
in, with the harassment of women or girls. In one group discussion,
for example, David explained how:

> [O]ne day, um, just out walking with the gang of four boys, y'know,
> we decided that it was time for [getting together with a girl]. . . .
> Yeah, they spotted these women, these young women, right, and
> there was a woman . . . and she's really good-looking. I liked her
> because she looked good, right. She carried herself well. Because . . .
> this woman had all the qualities that my sisters had and my mother,
> y'know, and I liked her for that. But it was perceived by the other
> guys as being, y'know, attracted to this woman and of course, it
> was, like, *behaving like men*, y'know, 'Go on, go on, go on, go on'.
> [my emphasis]

Here the pressure on David was not only to be heterosexual, but to be
heterosexual in a particular way ('behaving like men') which involved
the harassment of women. The fact that he thought about the young
woman in terms similar to those in which he thought about his sisters

and mother was, it seems, illegitimate within the heterosexualised homosocial context he describes. The imperative to 'go on' is an urging to objectify and harass thereby constituting himself as a (heterosexual) man. Furthermore, implicit within this statement (and confirmed later in the interview), is David's fear that if he did not take part in harassing this young woman, he would, himself, become the subject of homophobic abuse.

Similarly, Michael recalls how he:

> went to sixth form, where you're supposed to be able to be who you want to be, theoretically, and of course nobody is, they're all trying so hard, desperately hard to prove that they've slept with as many people as, you know, they're always bragging about how many girlfriends they've had and this, that and the other. And I was always the odd one out. . . . They'd all start talking about tits and, look at the jugs on that, and that's not something I've ever been able to do. I find it quite difficult to talk about men in those terms, let alone women. Um, no, I do, but you know in that sort of really derogatory way, which it is when you start talking about, oh, jugs on her, oh what I'd like to do, I've never been like that.

Here, Michael notes that the difference between him and the other young men in his sixth form was as much to do with his failure to enter into abusive and objectifying discussion of women as to do with his being gay. In these situations, masculinity is constituted both by misogyny (and the associated harassment of women) and homophobia.

SEXIST HARASSMENT AS A PEDAGOGY OF HETEROSEXUALITY

I have focused above on the experiences of gay men partly because (as I pointed out above) they are often ignored in discussions of harassment which are, thereby, rendered incomplete. More importantly, however, I have tried to show how the harassment of gay men and of those perceived to be gay or effeminate is one of the ways in which heterosexuality is rendered compulsory through the punishment of deviance from heterosexual norms of masculinity. In this sense, the heterosexist harassment of gay men can be understood as a pedagogy of heterosexuality. Similarly, the harassment of women can be understood as one of the ways in which we are schooled into gender-appro-priate, that is, heterosexual, sexuality. Thus Rebecca's experience of harassment, for example, can be read not just as sexist, but also as heterosexist in that the fact she was a lesbian made her doubly vulner-able to William's harassment. Furthermore, most (if not all) out lesbi-ans will recognise the experience of being sexually harassed precisely as a result of coming out. The 'all you need is a good fuck' phenom-enon is alive and kicking within the experience of the all our lesbian respondents. Moreover, the terms 'lesbian', 'lezzie', and 'dyke' are common forms of abuse in and outside of schools. Indeed, it is a com-mon experience for women and girls who resist sexual/sexist harass-ment to be labelled 'lesbian' (particularly if they associate themselves with feminism), regardless of how they identify themselves. Indeed, the term 'feminist' has, in some quarters, become a synonym for 'lesbian'.[18]

The point here is that the options open to women in response to sexist harassment are limited in ways which tend to reinforce hetero-sexuality. Strategies of resistance are often contradictory and strategies for avoidance are also mixed in their effects. For example, women often comment that shouting back at men who harass them on the street appears to be taken as a form of provocation from which the men seem to derive pleasure. On the other hand, ignoring harassing men, remaining silent and 'well-behaved' can feel like allowing them to trample all over one's sensibilities and as if one has, indeed, col-luded in one's harassment in some important ways.[19] Furthermore, if women adopt styles and behaviours which try to avoid harassment through being quiet and 'well-behaved', this can seem to signify a particular kind of heterosexual femininity in which women are seen to be pass-ive, waiting for men's attentions. Furthermore, as Sue Lees says:

> The danger of avoidance is that you can then get the reputation for being a lesbian or too tight. . . .
> Girls also talk about the need to avoid boys if a girl begins to get a reputation. *Better still, getting engaged is a greater protection.* (1993, pp. 274–5, emphasis added)

The safety achieved through getting engaged (or married or living with a man) is a dubious form of safety at best, given that most sexual violence is carried out by men known to their victims. Sexual harass-ment by other men is, indeed, less likely when a woman is in the company of a man who seems to be her partner, no doubt at least partly because she is seen as belonging, in some sense, to him. Similarly, women are able to feel safer on the streets when they have a man with them. Again, these are double-edged rewards for heterosexuality.

Another possible strategy for dealing with sexist harassment is to try to treat the whole thing as a joke, but this often ends up in the kind of flirtatious banter which characterises much social contact between women and men, particularly in ultra-heterosexual spaces like (straight) clubs, discos, and pubs. Within these contexts it is often expected that men will 'pull' women (and sometimes vice versa). One purpose of going to such events is to find potential sexual partners and those who go simply because they like music or dancing may well be seen to be deviant. In order to keep control of these situations, women may well enter into jokey teasing with underlying hetero/sexual content. Indeed, in my own (long distant) experience of working as a barmaid, it was, effectively, part of the job description to be able to take 'teasing' and joke with male customers in this heterosexual way (though similar banter with other women would, almost certainly, have been a dismissable offence). In this context I was not expected to have sex with male customers, but was certainly expected to behave hetero/sexually with them in order to keep them happy and under control (but still drinking). Judging by recent discussions with students doing this kind of work, there have been few changes in the expectations of barmaids in heterosexual pubs and clubs (see also Adkins, 1995).

Interestingly, in discussions about ways of dealing with harassment, accounts of successful resistance often involve the woman concerned taking up what might be seen as a 'super-feminine' position. Jane, for example, told me about a woodwork teacher at her school who had a reputation for regularly harassing the girls in his class. There were rumours amongst the pupils that he had previously been complained about and been given a verbal warning about his behaviour. However, he continued to invade their space, including touching them up, and the girls had no confidence that any further complaint would make any difference to his behaviour. It was with delight that Jane told me how, in her year, some of the girls had made a pact to wear stiletto heels to school. As she commented:

> Then, if he touched us, we could stamp hard on his feet, which would really hurt, but he couldn't do a thing. It was always 'Sorry, sir, that was an accident'.

The teacher had retreated defeated (at least for the moment), but the solution was not permanent. Furthermore, in order to achieve this respite from constant harassment, these girls had had to adopt a style which signified heterosexuality. Of course, it may well be the case that wearing stiletto heels was particularly satisfying because it was against the school rules. However, this does not negate the use of the device as a form of resistance, and one which rendered the girls hyper-feminine (not to mention hurting their feet and making it difficult for them to stand or walk for long periods and impossible for them to run!).

CONCLUSION

The harassment both of women and of gay and/or 'effeminate' men, then, seems to be related to the enforcement of heterosexuality. It is difficult for women to find responses to harassment which do not reinforce heterosexuality, either directly or by invoking the stigmatisation of lesbianism. For men, both the avoidance of stigmatisation and the production of acceptable masculinities seem to depend, at least in part, on harassing women and other men. It seems, therefore, that harassment is strongly implicated in the production of heterosexual gendered identities and can, therefore, be seen as not simply sexist, but heterosexist, in nature. This indicates the potential for developing new feminist ways of thinking about sexist harassment – ways which I have only begun to open up here.

Earlier feminist analyses of sexual harassment had implications for, and influence on, the development of policy, however unsatisfactory the implementation of such policy has proved to be. Equally, my analysis here calls for a rethinking not just of the ways in which we understand hetero/sexist harassment but for policy development. It is beyond the scope of this paper to develop the policy implications of my argument fully. However, I would like to end with some questions about policy:

- is there a case for policies and codes of practice on sexual harassment to be rewritten so as to take account of hetero/sexist harassment?

- if this were to happen, should the concept of sexual harassment be retained as a specific kind of hetero/sexist harassment, or should it simply be subsumed under the wider terminology?

- if harassment is, indeed, hetero/sexist, what are the implications for practices of, in particular, anti-sexist and girl-friendly schooling?

- finally, and perhaps most importantly, what would anti-hetero/sexist policies and practices actually look like?

Like earlier feminist thinking about sexual harassment, the argument I have presented here, however convincing in theory, will only achieve its objectives when such theorisation is taken on board in policy and practice.

NOTES

1. I would like to thank Joyce Canaan for her detailed comments on an earlier draft of this paper. I would also like to thank Diana Leonard, who chaired the BSA conference session at which I gave this paper and Janet Holland for her editorial comments in relation to this book. Thank you also to Richard Johnson, Deborah Lynn Steinberg, and Gaby Weiner for their comments on earlier drafts of the paper.
2. This project has been carried out in collaboration with Richard Johnson. Part of the project, concerned specifically with sex education, was carried out with Peter Redman. We grateful to the Universities of Birmingham and Central England and to East Birmingham Health Authority for their support for our work. Other people who have been involved in our work are Louise Curry, Mary Kehily, Gurjit Minhas, Anoop Nayak, and Shruti Tanna.
3. Louise Curry was responsible for the work in/with the youth group.
4. Shruti Tanna was responsible for the interviews with all our South Asian respondents. Some of the interviews with African Caribbean respondents were carried out by myself. However, the bulk of the information from them comes from group discussions which they themselves taped, without any of the research team present but using a number of stimulus questions which I suggested.
5. Discussions which have taken place within the meetings of the Politics of Sexuality Group, Department of Cultural Studies, Birmingham University, have particularly influenced my thinking.
6. Names of respondents, and, where necessary, some other details have been altered in order to maintain anonymity. The exception to this is where respondents have specifically requested that their names be used.
7. It is interesting to note, here, that these are the adjectives most often applied by teachers (and other adults) to children's stereotypically gendered behaviours. Furthermore, children constitute themselves as gendered through these discourses. For example, in BBC1's *Panorama* programme 'The Future is Female' (broadcast on 24 October 1994) one little boy com-

mented that if a boy worked hard at his school work this would mean
that he was not a 'real boy' – a point echoed by older, secondary age
boys and their parents later in the programme.
8. See Tyler (1991) for an interesting discussion of the politics of drag.
9. Kerr (1991) points out that gay men often also operate within discourses
of male sex drive.
10. bell hooks (1991, 1992) gives particularly detailed and rich accounts of
the racist sexualisation of Black women. See also, Patricia Hill Collins
(1990). See Bhattacharyya (1994) for a discussion of racist sexualisation
of Asian women in the UK.
11. See also, Cohen (1988) for a discussion of the ways in which Jews have
been sexualised within Anglo-American and West European cultures.
12. See, in particular, the work of Julien and Mercer (1988) and Isaac Julien's
Arena programme broadcast on BBC2 in February 1994 for discussions
of the racist and heterosexist sexualisation of people of African descent.
13. For a discussion of this case and of the position of disabled lesbians
more generally, see Appleby (1994).
14. See Morris (1991) for a discussion of disability and hetero/sexuality and
related issues.
15. I would like to thank David Colley for his help with this paragraph.
16. See the *Pink Paper*, 14 and 21 October 1994.
17. See Alistair *et al.* (1994) for an edited version of the discussion during
which this statement was made.
18. Sue Lees (1993), for example, notes the association made by young women
between lesbianism and feminism.
19. I would like to thank Joyce Canaan for pointing this out to me.

REFERENCES

Adkins, L. (1995) *Gendered Work: Sexuality, Family and the Labour Market*
(Buckingham: Open University Press).
Alistair, Dave, Rachel and Teresa (1994) 'So the Theory was Fine', in D.
Epstein (ed.) *Challenging Lesbian and Gay Inequalities in Education* (Buck-
ingham: Open University Press).
'"Apologise", Save the Children Told', *Pink Paper* (1994b), 21 October, p. 6.
Appleby, Y. (1994) 'Out in the Margins', *Disability and Society*, 9: 1, pp. 19–32.
Bhattacharyya, G. (1994) 'Offence is the Best Defence? – Pornography and
Racial Violence', in C. Brant and Y. L. Too (eds) *Rethinking Sexual Har-
assment* (London: Pluto Press).
Butler, J. (1990) *Gender Trouble: Feminism and the Subversion of Identity*
(London: Routledge).
Clarricoates, K. (1987) 'Dinosaurs in the Classroom – The "Hidden" Curricu-
lum in Primary Schools', in M. Arnot and G. Weiner (eds) *Gender and the
Politics of Schooling* (London: Hutchinson/Open University).
Cohen, P. (1988) 'The Perversions of Inheritance: Studies in the Making of
Multi-Racist Britain', in P. Cohen and H. S. Bains (eds) *Multi-Racist Britain*
(Basingstoke: Macmillan).

Collins, P. H. (1990) *Black Feminist Thought: Knowledge, Consciousness, and the Politics of Empowerment* (London: Harper Collins Academic).

de Lyon, H. (1989) 'Sexual Harassment', in H. de Lyon and F. W. Migniuolo (eds) *Women Teachers: Issues and Experiences* (Milton Keynes: Open University Press).

Epstein, D. and Johnson, R. (1994) 'On the Straight and the Narrow: The Heterosexual Presumption, Homophobias and Schools', in D. Epstein (ed.) *Challenging Lesbian and Gay Inequalities in Education* (Buckingham: Open University Press).

Evans, D. T. (1993) *Sexual Citizenship: The Material Construction of Sexualities* (London: Routledge).

Hanmer, J. and Maynard, M. (eds) (1987) *Women Violence and Social Control* (Basingstoke: Macmillan).

Herbert, C. (1992) *Sexual Harassment in Schools: A Guide for Teachers* (London: David Fulton).

Hollway, W. (1984) 'Gender Difference and the Production of Subjectivity', in J. Henriques, W. Hollway, C. Urwin, C. Venn and V. Walkerdine, *Changing the Subject: Psychology, Social Regulation and Subjectivity* (London: Methuen).

Hollway, W. (1989) *Subjectivity and Method in Psychology: Gender, Meaning and Science* (London: Sage).

hooks, b. (1982) *Ain't I a Woman: Black Women and Feminism* (London: Pluto).

hooks, b. (1989) *Talking Back: Thinking Feminist – Thinking Black* (London: Sheba Feminist Publishers).

hooks, b. (1991) *Yearning: Race, Gender and Cultural Politics* (London: Turnaround).

hooks, b. (1992) *Black Looks: Race and Representation* (London: Turnaround).

Julien, I. and Mercer, K. (1988) 'True Confessions: A Discourse on Images of Black Male Sexuality', in R, Chapman and J. Rutherford (eds) *Male Order: Unwrapping Masculinity* (London: Lawrence & Wishart).

Kerr, E. (1991) 'Perversion and Subversion: A Study of Lesbian and Gay Strategies of Resistance', unpublished MA dissertation, Department of Cultural Studies, University of Birmingham

Lees, S. (1986) *Losing Out: Sexuality and Adolescent Girls* (London: Hutchinson).

Lees, S. (1993) *Sugar and Spice: Sexuality and Adolescent Girls* (London: Penguin).

Mac an Ghaill, M. (1994) '(In)visibility: Sexuality, Race and Masculinity in the School Context', in D. Epstein (ed.) *Challenging Lesbian and Gay Inequalities in Education* (Buckingham: Open University Press).

MacKinnon, C. A. (1979) *Sexual Harassment of Working Women* (New Haven, CT: Yale University Press).

Mahony, P. (1989) 'Sexual Violence and Mixed Schools', in C. Jones and P. Mahony (eds) *Learning Our Lines: Sexuality and Social Control in Education* (London: Women's Press).

Morris, J. (1991) *Pride against Prejudice: Transforming Attitudes to Disability/A Personal Politics of Disability* (London: The Women's Press).

Morrison, T. (1993) 'Introduction: Friday on the Potomac', in T. Morrison (ed.) *Race-ing Justice, En-gendering Power: Essays on Anita Hill, Clarence Thomas and the Construction of Social Reality* (London: Chatto & Windus).

National Union of Teachers (1986) *Dealing with Sexual Harassment* (London: NUT).

Rich, A. (1980) 'Compulsory Heterosexuality and Lesbian Existence', *Signs: Journal of Women in Culture and Society*, 5: 41, pp. 631–60.

Rogers, M. (1994) 'Growing Up Lesbian: The Role of the School', in D. Epstein (ed.) *Challenging Lesbian and Gay Inequalities in Education* (Buckingham: Open University Press).

'Staff Split over Toksvig Row', *Pink Paper* (1994a) 14 October, p. 5.

Tyler, C.-A. (1991) 'Boys Will be Girls: the Politics of Gay Drag', in D. Fuss (ed.) *Inside/Out: Lesbian Theories, Gay Theories* (London: Routledge).

Weeks, J. (1981) *Sex, Politics and Society: The Regulation of Sexuality Since 1800* (London: Longman).

Willis, P. (1977) *Learning to Labour: How Working Class Kids get Working Class Jobs* (London: Saxon House).

Wise, S. and Stanley, L. (1987) *Georgie Porgie: Sexual Harassment in Everyday Life* (London: Pandora Press).

Wittig, M. (1980) 'The Straight Mind', *Feminist Issues*, 1: 1, pp. 103–11.

Wittig, M. (1981) 'One is Not Born a Woman', *Feminist Issues*, 1: 2, pp. 46–54.

Wood, J. (1984) 'Groping Towards Sexism: Boys' Sex Talk', in A. McRobbie and M. Nava (eds) *Gender and Generation* (Basingstoke: Macmillan).

11 Desperately Seeking Post-heterosexual Woman

CAROL SMART

INTRODUCTION

Heterosexuality poses problems for feminism. There is a sense in which it always has. The suffragettes and first-wave feminists were fiercely divided over aspects of heterosexuality. From Josephine Butler's campaigns against the Contagious Diseases Acts in the 1880s to later ideas of free love in the 1920s it was clear that early feminists would rather have ignored women's sexuality as they strove to find a legitimate place for women in civil society. It was relatively easy for these feminists to condemn male heterosexual practices and excesses because these were identified as the cause of so much suffering for women, whether in terms of the trade in prostitution, multiple pregnancies or the spread of venereal diseases to the innocent wife. It was much less easy for early feminists to deal with women's sexuality unless it was either disguised or transposed into discussions about reproduction and aspects of maternity. Thus these feminists could (eventually) publicly debate the benefits or otherwise of contraception, but not the benefits or otherwise of orgasm. Feminist campaigners therefore constructed a lasting mode in which to engage publicly with heterosexuality. This mode cast the woman as either the sexless mother or the fallen victim. Male heterosexuality was framed in terms of excessive desire which required restraint. This meant that campaigns dealt mostly with men's exploitation of female and child sexuality. Although women obviously did enter into discussions about 'free love' as with the Men's and Women's Club, such thinking rarely entered the public domain to become part of the early campaigns (Walkowitz, 1992).

Obviously, since the late 1800s much has changed. Feminism has taken many aspects of heterosexuality, aside from the question of male exploitation, into the public domain. But it does appear to be the case that this exploitation/victimisation model remains the dominant inferential framework for many discussions. Thus there is much published on rape, child sexual abuse, sexual harassment. However, in spite of this immense verbosity, Wilkinson and Kitzinger (1993) are obviously right when they point to a peculiar silence at the heart of this feminist discourse. Heterosexuality is constantly addressed, in feminist and other work, but where is the heterosexual woman or, more specifically, the heterosexual feminist woman? Arguably in feminist sociology she appears only as victim. She is invoked, but she has not become a subject – only an object. She is authentic, but only when she speaks of the harms that heterosexuality has inflicted upon her, when she renounces heterosexuality or when she shifts the focus to motherhood.

So in this chapter I propose to consider why no heterosexual (feminist) subject[1] has appeared on the sociological landscape. I shall attempt to do this by mapping the development of certain discourses, not necessarily feminist, to see how they may have failed in general to produce such a subject. I will then focus on how this failure to produce the heterosexual subject has not meant that heterosexuality is a non-issue, but rather has precluded us transforming or, more importantly perhaps, transgressing conventional (problematic) heterosexuality. If we think, for example, about how the lesbian subject or the gay subject has been transformed and is transforming our understandings of sexuality from notions of homosexual to gay to queer, or from excessive secrecy to an 'in your face' stance on sexuality in public, we can see that we really have not moved very far in terms of reconstructing heterosexuality. Whereas the conceptualisation of heterosexuality takes us back around old themes (especially of normality or of exploitation/victimisation) repetitively, conceptualisations of lesbianism and gay sexuality have transgressed the old boundaries.

It might be useful to draw an analogy at this point. This analogy is based on a dream that a feminist friend told me about. In this dream she went to a feminist party wearing red lipstick. When she got there all the women were extremely angry with her and her friends refused to speak to her. In fact they stood in groups talking about her and ostracising her. She was terribly upset. The problem was that she could not get them to understand that the lipstick she was wearing was 1990s lipstick, not 1950s lipstick. On seeing the lipstick her friends felt that there was only one message that it could convey, namely subservience to a patriarchal ideal or fashion. However, my friend had worn the lipstick as a form of transgression because the political and cultural meaning attached to red lips had changed. This was what she meant by saying that she was wearing lipstick within the political context of the 1990s not the 1950s. The lipstick was not the same because the meaning had changed. By analogy, what I am suggesting is that feminism has no 1990s heterosexuality, if you wear heterosexuality you are inevitably trapped in a discursive formation of the 1950s (or earlier). No one believes that there is a 1990s version because, unlike lipstick, heterosexuality has not been discursively or politically transformed. Heterosexual feminists have not been able (or willing?)[2] to engage in this reconstruction and so the meaning of heterosexuality seems to have become fixed into a framework crafted by the Victorians and only intensified by further concentrations on its abusive forms.

DISCOURSING ON HETEROSEXUALITY

I want to focus on what I regard as two dominant frameworks for the public discussion of heterosexuality. The first is the ideology of sexology, the second is the ideology of guilt.

I have quite deliberately shifted my terminology here. Whilst I think that the core meaning of the Foucaultian term 'discourse' lies in the idea of the production of the subject, and whilst I share his concern that the very term 'ideology' suggests the possibility of an opposite, namely objective or scientific truth, I use ideology here precisely because I want to argue that these writings and narratives have not produced the heterosexual subject. They have remained inside the terrain of ideology, so to speak, because, although they constitute powerful ideas with material consequences, they have not provided a self-conscious identity. They may have produced sub-sets of heterosexual subjectivity such as the pervert or the masturbating schoolboy,[3] but the heterosexual subject is not the combined outcome of all these subjectivities added together. The self-conscious heterosexual subject does not emerge from these fragments. Heterosexuality remains, conceptually speaking, in an *a priori* or pre-cultural state. It does not have to address itself as such; there is no reflection on the state of *being* heterosexual in spite of excessive quantities of literature on how to practice heterosexuality successfully.

One might of course wonder why I would be critical of this fragmentation at a time when the idea of the unified subject is so unfashionable. It might, for example, seem as if I am bemoaning the lack of an identity politics for heterosexuality. But I am quite expressly not trying to invoke some essence of heterosexuality on which an identity politics could be founded. Such a politics would be deeply problematic because of the unreconstructed nature of the concept of heterosexuality. Rather I am exploring why this identity has failed to emerge historically, what consequences this may have had for feminist theories of heterosexuality, and how this absence may ironically relate to the current difficulty of transgressing or transforming heterosexuality.

IDEOLOGIES OF SEXOLOGY

Feminist critics of sexology have often pointed out that sexology has both celebrated heterosexuality and, at the same time, confirmed gender differences in an oppressive way. The heterosexuality that is celebrated is (or at least has until recently been) of a specific kind as well. Typically it has focused on the ideal of penetration and ejaculation *in vaginam*. Thus, within the heterosexual matrix, it has attended to heterosexual male needs and release (as currently constituted) and has identified practices now more closely associated with women's needs, as secondary. The list of examples of this is long.[4] From Havelock Ellis (1967, originally 1933) to Eustace Chesser (1966, originally 1946) it is clear that there is a supposedly natural sequence of sexual acts which leads to an almost rule-like insistence that without the ultimate penetration and ejaculation, sexual behaviour is perversion. Later Alex Comfort's (1977) idea of hors-d'oeuvres or starters, pickles and main courses echoes this idea of the minor and major sex act.

We can see in these works very explicit technologies of gender (de Lauretis, 1987). Here we have, in the sexual sphere, the making of masculinities and femininities. One is, of course, in more recent texts such as Comfort's (1977) *More Joy of Sex* encouraged to become adventurous. But these are forays from a home base which is inevitably a heterosexual coupledom in which a natural order is presupposed. Comfort's insistence that we are simply mammals and that sexual behaviour follows a natural course calls upon, and reinforces, ideas of natural differences between the sexes. It is true that he does not rest all his arguments on nature. He adds a little psychoanalysis to explain that for many women the penis and a baby have the same significance. He also invokes ideas of distorted socialisation as when he states,

> Girls have often been already trained by disillusioned mothers to realise that male love can be hostile. (1977, p. 25)

In this kind of sexology, variations in sexual practices are offered to couples in tightly bound ideological packages and any resistance to the normative ideal of unswerving commitment to penetration is dismissed as pathology. There is much one can say on the content of these texts but my focus is slightly different. I am less interested here in these demonstrations of compulsory heterosexuality than in the discursive effects of such texts. I want to argue that this pervasive ideology is productive of gender difference rather than being productive of the heterosexual subject. These texts are handbooks on the practice of heterosexuality, but they are productive of the gendered subject rather than the heterosexual subject. There are three main elements to this argument. The first is the Foucaultian distinction between practice and subject identity; the second is the significance of cultural awareness of *being* heterosexual; and the third is need to distinguish between the identity of gender and the practice of heterosexuality.

Practice versus Identity/Subjectivity

If we consider Foucault's homosexual subject, he is constituted as a type of life, a category of person who comes to identify, in various ways, with this discursive construction (Foucault, 1981). Quite explicitly, Foucault argues that homosexual acts were practised long before the homosexual entered the social landscape. He therefore stresses the distinction between practices and subjectivities. Walkowitz (1980), following Foucault, performs a similar analysis on prostitution, arguing that the modern prostitute as a type or specific category of woman, comes about as a consequence of the Contagious Diseases Acts of the 1860s, not because of the act or practice of selling sex for money. Similar debates have occurred in relation to lesbianism and whether certain sexual acts (which are transhistorical) define the lesbian, or whether the lesbian comes into being through certain discursive events at a specific moment in history (Faderman, 1985). From such discussions we can see that *doing* (practice) needs to be distinguished from *being* (identity). In as much as this conceptual distinction is valid in relation to many sexual practices and subjectivities, I suggest that it can be applied to heterosexuality also. I want to suggest therefore that boundless numbers of manuals and videos on the practice of heterosexuality or on varieties of heterosexual acts, do not necessarily have the discursive effect of constituting the self-conscious heterosexual subject or a heterosexual identity, even though heterosexuality is clearly expressed as the normative ideal.

The heterosexual has never become a type even though the construction of the homosexual invites this possibility. What I mean by this is that the construction of the homosexual as Other presupposes a category against which he can be assessed and defined. But whilst I suggest that homosexuality patrols the boundaries of heterosexuality and creates a consciousness of being heterosexual, as when heterosexual men abuse gay men or heterosexual women abuse lesbians in order to assert their heterosexuality (Comstock, 1991), this moment of self-consciousness is not (I think) a lasting one nor a self-defining one.

Problematising a Consistent Awareness of being Heterosexual

In relation to a slightly different, but related issue, Denise Riley (1988) has made the important point that one is not always a woman; one is not always gendered. One does not go around constantly aware of being a woman. However, she argues that there are moments when we are reminded of this and these moments can be fairly frequent and regular. Her point is that it is only within the highly politicised, identity politics framework of feminism, that we might feel like women all the time. She relates this point to the way in which feminist discourse has brought the woman as subject into being in a specific way, and in turn links this to her anti-essentialist thesis about what a woman is. The question is whether this kind of analysis is also applicable in the sphere of sexuality. Are we[5] mostly asexual, but become heterosexualised for certain moments or at certain times? Does it work like this for men? Is one always a lesbian or does one become a lesbian at certain times? Is one always gay, or does one become gay at certain times? It seems likely that one can forget being heterosexual more readily than one can forget being gay or lesbian.[6] From this perspective, therefore, heterosexuality can be seen as merely a fleeting subjectivity even though the subject position of heterosexuality is ever-present, even omnipresent and constantly available, even oppressively available (Rich 1980).

The Identity of Gender versus the Practice of Heterosexuality

It is part of my argument to suggest that we should avoid the temptation to collapse these two categories into one and in the light of this I have suggested that sexology has been constitutive of gender difference rather than of heterosexuality as an identity. I have so far suggested that these texts have brought into being refined practices rather than identities, and that even though heterosexuals may be brought into an awareness of *being* heterosexual, that this is often quite fleeting. If we can accept the argument so far, it seems valid to say that in spite of this immense verbosity we do not have a heterosexual identity, it keeps slipping away from one's grasp. Yet it is possible to argue that the subtexts of these extensive writings do contribute towards a technology of gender which is productive of the gendered subject or gender identity. If by technology of gender we mean those practices which repetitively produce orthodox differences between men and women and which rest upon a presumed foundation of natural or biological difference, then the difference which is stressed between the heterosexual male and heterosexual female in sexology texts is a contribution to reaffirming gender difference, rather than part of the constitution of the heterosexual subject.[7] It is precisely in the assertion that heterosex is *natural*, and that in the performance of this act there are *natural* differences (of desire, of fulfilment, of orientation, and so on) between men and women, that one can see a constant reaffirmation of a naturalised gender difference. What is offered are lessons in how to become a natural woman/man who is skilful in the practice of heterosex. It is, I think, important to read these sexology texts alongside other technologies of gender, and not to isolate them from other normalising practices such as those inherent in women's magazines, soap operas, film, and other media. Read in this way we can understand them as contributing to the forming and fixing of gender identity/difference which is actively being constituted elsewhere as well. However, in isolation, they do not appear to have had the effect of producing heterosexual identity. They are not part of a wider set of discourses which produce this effect, largely because heterosexuality remains unspoken and dormant elsewhere. Sexology texts are therefore not part of a wider interpellation of the heterosexual subject and so that subject remains the silent signifier or dominant inferential framework which is yet to be realised.

IDEOLOGIES OF GUILT

I have suggested that sexology has been, for heterosexuals, an ideological practice rather than a mode of discursive constitution. I have suggested that the immense verbosity around heterosexual acts has not produced the heterosexual. I now want to shift my focus to sexual guilt and I want to suggest here that whilst mechanisms of guilt may bring a self-consciousness, within the heterosexual matrix this guilt has not been the trigger of a political consciousness which could produce a specific identity. Rather, it is this guilt (in a variety of different forms) which has operated to prevent this to a large extent.

A Short, Contemporary History of Guilt

We know of course that the Christian tradition has imbued all things sexual with guilt. The Victorians fine tuned this, making it into an exquisite art form for both men and women – although materially this had greater consequences for women. We know even that the guilt itself has become a sexual commodity. One might almost wonder whether for some, sexual arousal is possible without guilt, so closely entwined have they become.

Yet, ironically, it was this guilt that gave women in the Victorian era a means of speaking publicly about sex. Feminist campaigners could speak of men's guilt in their sexual exploitation of women. Working-class women could speak of sex in confessing their own guilt and in embracing their reform, or in speaking of unspeakable acts enacted against them. Sex could be spoken of as long as it was denounced – all else was deemed to be pornography (Smart, 1992).

Early feminism, in its public address, used this denunciatory mode of speaking of sex. However, in its re-emergence in the late 1960s, second-wave feminism did not, at first, utilise this same mode of speaking about heterosex. The early 'second-wavers' did not denounce the pleasures of heterosexuality. Rather they demanded better heterosex, emphasised women's great sexual capacities than men's and spoke much of orgasms and the site of these. This was the era when American feminist poet Erica Jong (1977, originally 1974) wrote about zipless fucks and women were encouraged to enjoy their orgasmic potential and to benefit from the increasingly secure ways of separating sex from reproduction. As feminist sexual politics developed in the 1970s, however, the problem of heterosexuality was redefined in terms of the undesirability of having sex with men at all, rather than in terms of how to demand better sex from/with men. This meant that focus shifted from reconstructing heterosexuality to avoiding heterosex.

Moreover, there is now a kind of feminist received wisdom that interprets this early period as a moment of intensified heterosexual oppression (Campbell, 1980). The idea that having lots of sex with men could possibly have been liberating is now construed as a kind of false consciousness or a sad episode before feminism developed a proper sexual politics. Whilst, of course, to presume this decade represented a simple sexual liberation would be naive, I am not so sure that any analysis based on the oppression/freedom dichotomy is useful any longer. Following Foucault's re-analyses of the 'repressive moment' we have largely ceased to interpret the Victorian era in terms of a struggle between freedom and oppression, yet we still cling to this framework in relation to the late 1960s. The sexual radicals claim that it was a moment of freedom and feminists tend to argue that it was a moment of intensified oppression. We seem to be constantly reliving a kind of Marcusian moment in relation to this period. Our feminist interpretation of history seems to have become stranded in a perspective which is determinist, essentialist, and patronising (i.e. the idea of false consciousness and false needs).

The framework for this approach was provided by Marcuse (1955) who developed a theory of the relationship between capitalism and sexuality which managed to interpret both sexual repression and sexual freedom as forms of manipulation of the working class. He used the idea of repressive sublimation to explain how capitalism repressed natural sexuality in order to discipline the workers into obedient *producers* for the benefit of the owners of capital. Second-wave feminist theory tended to share this view but substituted the concepts of patriarchy and men for capitalism and capitalists. Thus it was assumed that women were denied their natural sexuality all the better to serve men's interests. Then, just as Marcuse gave up the idea of repressive sublimation, feminism too gave up the idea of an enforced repression of women's natural libido. For both Marcuse and feminism it obviously became untenable to suggest that women were no longer allowed to have sex or to be represented as sexual. So Marcuse turned to the idea of repressive *de*sublimation. In this thesis he argued that capitalism creates false sexual needs in order to discipline us into becoming placid *consumers*. Feminist analysis seems to have followed this same formulation, arguing that although once patriarchy repressed our sexuality to meet its needs, its needs changed and thus it created a false sense of heterosexual freedom. Under this new method of manipulation women were made endlessly sexually available and were tricked into imagining that they had gained what they had been demanding for so long (i.e. the ability to have sex without getting pregnant, a choice of sexual partners, the ability to orgasm again). It seems odd to me that having rejected so many of these essentialist and determinist theories of sexuality elsewhere, we still seem content to accept the idea (at least where heterosexuality is concerned) that once it suited patriarchy to make (most of) us frigid, and that it now suits the same patriarchy to make most of us frenzied. This kind of approach constantly reproduces heterosexual women as the dupes of patriarchy.

Notwithstanding the inadequacy of such theorisations, some feminist theories of heterosexuality in the early 1980s did construe heterosexual women as either dupes or collaborators (Leeds Revolutionary Feminists, 1981). Accusations of sleeping with the enemy were powerful, not simply because of a convincing internal logic, but because many White, middle-class women[8] were already saturated with heterosexual guilt. What was being said was substantially the same as their (our) mothers and fathers had always said, albeit this time the sisters were saying it with an even more powerful political gloss. This reassertion of guilt had a powerful effect of closure on the possibilities for feminism of attempting to transform or transgress heterosexuality. One can think of an important parallel to be found in early reactions in the gay movement(s) when AIDS was first discovered and when it was still seen in terms of GRID. Many gays argued that gay men should change their lifestyles and sexual practices, but this anti-sex response to AIDS (as Watney (1987) refers to it) was vigorously rejected in the main – albeit that it caused pain and intense feelings of guilt. Instead of falling silent and absorbing the guilt, gay men insisted that they would not give up a core element of their gay identity. They refused to be pushed back into the closet and instead used the opportunity to become more positive about gay sexuality. On being faced with a similar guilt, heterosexual feminists did not fight against this anti-heterosex argument however, they went quiet. Guilt produced its more usual effect, namely reticence, and heterosexual feminists were all too ready to slip back into silence about sex.[9] There was no sense of counterculture on which to mount an alternative framework and so the moment was lost.

Of course, this does not mean that there was a general silence about heterosex after the 1970s. As we know, it became increasingly a commercial commodity and women's sexual capacities are widely used in the market. But there has been no feminist voice in this clamour over women's sexuality even though second-wave feminism was the catalyst to this re-evaluation of women's sexual pleasure. The idea that women might enjoy heterosex, or that they might want better heterosex, was increasingly taken up in non-feminist and anti-feminist writings. This growing association of pro-heterosex positions with anti-feminism then added to the difficulties of raising a feminist voice on this subject since it was too easily presumed to imply a reactionary politics.

More recently heterosexual feminists have tried to find a voice. In the ongoing debates on pornography, heterosexuals have joined forces with lesbians to begin to talk about forms of erotica and women's sexual fantasies. But more typically, where heterosexual feminists speak publicly on heterosexuality, it is almost inevitably on subjects of rape, sexual harassment, and child sexual abuse. Speech is only about bad heterosex (as it was for Victorian feminists). At the same time the heterosexual woman is always constituted as victim. We focus on the fact that the sexually active teenager is called a slag (Lees, 1993), not on the way she might feel empowered. We still focus on the dangers of sex, with little or nothing on heterosexual pleasure and desire.

In this respect, the recent book by Wilkinson and Kitzinger (1993) is immensely significant. So many of the short pieces written by heterosexual feminists are so candid and unguarded. Yet, in precisely the moment I thought of their courage, I realised how odd it was to think, in these days of explicit videos, sex-advice chat shows, magazines packed with articles on orgasms and so on, that it should be difficult for feminists – who have been so frank on matters to do with bodies – to speak of their heterosexual practices. And yet so many of the contributors seemed apologetic, they seemed to be saying that they recognised the structural problems of heterosexuality, but they were *lucky* because their partners were so sensitive and caring. Many also said that they practised heterosexuality but did not feel heterosexual. They were implicitly criticised by the editors for this, as if this betrayed a kind of dissimulation. I do not see this 'denial' as hypocrisy but as part of the problem of there being no real, let alone radical, heterosexual subjectivity for feminists (or other women?) to adopt. The only specific subjectivities available seem to be (a) as oppressor (of lesbians) or (b) as victim (of men). It is a bit like being caught between a rock and a hard place.

Heterosexual feminists have therefore not escaped the effects of the deployment of guilt, but this has not created a radical alternative, or radical subjectivity.[10] We (with a few notable exceptions) have succumbed to silence because (White, middle-class) women's silence on sexual matters is commonplace and because there is no radical positioning generated by this guilt. Oppressor or victim (as the only available subject positions) really do not seem to mobilise women given the history of women's heterosexuality in Britain. How can we seem to celebrate heterosexuality if this invokes or implies the oppression of other women? How can we use our victim status to mobilise a counterculture if we still sleep with the victimiser?

IS A HETEROSEXUAL SUBJECT EMERGING IN THE LITERATURE?

For all the energy that has been spent on trying to define what a lesbian is or what a gay man is, little has been spent on trying to define what a heterosexual is. Does 'doing' heterosexuality mean that one is heterosexual, that is to say that one has a heterosexual identity? Where would this place married men who cottage and cruise, or married men whose secret passions are for men? If one gives up heterosexual sex, does one cease to be heterosexual? The idea of the lesbian continuum, after all, allows that women may be lesbian without having genital sexual contact with other women, so perhaps one can be heterosexual even if one never has sex with someone of the opposite sex. Perhaps then, heterosexuality is a life-style? This broader definition would obviously embrace a larger category of people, including those for whom genital heterosexuality had never been or had ceased to be feature of their relationships. But what would such a broad definition mean for lesbians married to men for example?

The point is that whilst we can talk about structural systems of heterosexuality, such as marriage, pension schemes, assisted reproduction, age of consent, and so on, it is more difficult to fit individual subjects into these categories unless we simply say that all married persons are heterosexual or even that all people are heterosexual unless they declare otherwise. Whilst we know that, culturally speaking, this is precisely the presumption that most people may make, this is probably not an adequate presupposition for sociological purposes. I would suggest that we need to look much more critically at heterosexual labelling, heterosexual identity, heterosexual subjectivity, and also the processes whereby people position themselves within heterosexuality or heterosexualities.

In their book *Heterosexuality*, Wilkinson and Kitzinger (1993) seem surprised that many feminists were 'offended' at being hailed as heterosexual. In other words, Wilkinson and Kitzinger seemed to presume that there was no problem in assuming that all women are heterosexual unless they declare otherwise. It would seem, therefore, that they did not expect to be challenged on the factual status of heterosexuality. But the issue of being surprised and being offended runs deeper than this. Women living heterosexual life-styles are often seen as benefiting from heterosexist structures and institutions. It is, therefore, from the perspective of lesbianism, a little difficult to accept that such women might be, seemingly, trying to deny their privileges by challenging

their interpellation as heterosexual. This 'denial' of heterosexual identity or subjectivity can also be read as a way of slighting the harms
done to lesbians who have more openly rebelled against the system
and who do not benefit from heterosexism. There is, therefore, a sense
in which some feminists clearly feel that other women identified as
heterosexual ought to stand up and be recognised, and not try to wrig-
gle out of their responsibilities (and guilt). But herein lies the problem. I think it is quite possible to acknowledge some of the benefits
of living the heterosexual life-style and still seek to problematise the
concept and category of heterosexuality. In their refusal of this heterosexual subjectivity many of the women who write in *Heterosexuality*
are, in my view, attempting to transgress heterosexuality, not to deny
heterosexuality. This, I would argue, is precisely what is required, and
should not be confused with an unethical means of trying to avoid
responsibilities.

For feminism the purpose of the exercise of turning our gaze once
again to heterosexuality, should surely not be to create a unifying heterosexual identity, but rather to deconstruct existing heterosexual subject positions and to work towards post-heterosexuality. In any case,
we already know that there could be no unitary heterosexual subjectivity. Our consciousness of difference means we already have to speak
of heterosexuali*ties* at the very least. Clearly, we still need to move
out of the present impasse in which heterosexuality is the omnipresent, silent signifier in feminist and sociological work. But in giving
voice to heterosexualities we have to avoid the apparent deployment
of even more heterosexist power. Heterosex has to come out of the
closet and then be put in its place. But we need to do this without
resorting to essences.

TOWARDS POST-HETEROSEXUALITY

When I invoke the term post-heterosexuality I do not mean to suggest
a regime under which one gives up heterosexual practices or that all
women must become lesbian and men gay. Rather I want to challenge
the idea that there are actual, fixed or pre-given heterosexual practices
and I want to encourage further moves away from the idea of insisting
on a fixed heterosexual subject.

I have suggested that there are three cross-cutting issues embedded
in the notion of heterosexuality. These are:

1. heterosexual life-style,
2. heterosexual identity and subjectivity,
3. heterosexual practices.

Heterosexual Life-styles

Dealing firstly with heterosexual life-styles, we can envision changes to the privileges of these domestic and quasi-public forms. Although a political struggle is entailed, we can see ways in which such privileges can be extended so that the heterosexual couple is no longer given a special status. Thus we can equalise the age of consent, we can extend pension, housing, and inheritance rights to a range of relationships. We can alter the basis of marriage. To some extent, the widespread effects of divorce are already dismantling some of the old privileges of marriage anyway but, none the less, there are still certain advantages which are unavailable to people who are denied the right to marry. These are matters of citizenship which are open to fairly traditional politico-legal interventions.

Heterosexuality Identity and Subjectivity

Turning to heterosexual identity and subjectivity, I have suggested that neither seem to exist in a self-conscious fashion (even though hetero-sexual subject positions clearly do). However, we do not want the ubiquitous heterosexual subject position to remain a kind of invisible, overdetermining presence and so it is this that still needs to be made visible and deconstructed. It would be inexcusable for us to presume that, because the dominant discourse has not produced a heterosexual subjectivity, that a powerful, silent essentialism does not hold sway. Feminist work, I would suggest, needs to take up the challenge offered by Pringle (1992) and Martin (1992) when they argue (separately) that we have been over-concerned with gender, and that this focus has sub-ordinated sexuality to gender. Put simply, Pringle suggests that we have acted as if explanations of the latter automatically explained the former. Thus, how men behave sexually (i.e. proactive, aggressive, instrumental) has been understood to arise from masculinity. Equally, how women behave sexually (i.e. vulnerable, caring, nurturing) has been presumed to arise from femininity. Under this regime of meanings it is implicitly assumed that if we can alter masculinity and femininity we will also be altering heterosexuality. So rather than tackling hetero-sexuality directly we have tackled it indirectly through masculinity and femininity and ideas about gender. But this has meant that we have not really done enough to challenge the presumed naturalness of heterosexuality, any more than, in Judith Butler's (1990) terms, we have denaturalised biological sex.

Heterosexual Practices

My third area concerns the meanings attached to heterosexual practices and new challenges to these meanings. I am not talking here about a new version of pre-figurative life-styles, nor sexual charters or guidelines for correct heterosexual behaviour. Rather I want to consider the de-coding of acts as heterosexual, and the re-coding of acts as ambivalent. I was struck by a remark I recently heard which suggested that penetration is as heterosexual as kissing. This simple statement made me recognise the extent to which I had accepted both the phallic propaganda of the significance of penetration and the radical feminist argument that penetration is an invasion or act of colonisation of *women's* bodies.[11] I discovered that I had always assumed that penetration was the essence of heterosexuality and that feminist work had insisted on this just as much as the canons of sexology. On disengaging these two ideas I discovered that penetration suddenly lost its power to define. It was suddenly apparent, through the growth of writings on sexual practices, that men penetrate men, women penetrate women, and that women can penetrate men. These acts did not turn these actors into heterosexuals. This diversity of practices allows for penetration to have various meanings, not the exclusive meaning of dominance and submission which is endlessly mapped onto the binary of male and female. Wrenching penetration out of a heterosexual matrix of meanings deprives it of its symbolic power. Just as the recognition that a penis is not a phallus is vital to the demystification of men's power, so the recognition that men's bodies are penetrable, and not only by men, is equally significant. (We have, of course, to add to this the effects of a general move against the supremacy of penetration arising from a new focus on safer sex.)

The growth of writing on S/M also challenges a number of presumptions about heterosexual practices. What does it mean if a great many (how many?) men desire to be spanked and beaten by women? Whilst there may be several meanings, I find I am unhappy with those accounts which assert that both women's sexual submission and women's sexual dominance unswervingly and unproblematically serve the interests of patriarchy. I do not necessarily think that S/M is revolutionary, but

I am intrigued by the silence that has surrounded it until recently. As more sex workers speak out, we are beginning to learn how extensive this practice is and how many respectable, heterosexual men pay for this service or now engage in it in the conjugal bedroom. It is, I would argue, potentially disruptive knowledge since it means that heterosexual practice is not solely confined to the (metaphorical) missionary position. Indeed it becomes unclear what is specifically heterosexual about heterosexual practice at all.

We need to resist the tendency to see these acts as mere perversions. (As Dollimore (1991) argues, all of us are perverts who do not have sex simply to reproduce.) If we call such acts perversions we miss their social significance by confining them to the individual psyche. One is reminded of the case of Steven Milligan the Conservative MP for Eastleigh who was found hanged as a consequence of engaging in autoerotic asphyxiation in 1993. The 'official' response to his death was to reconstrue him as a very lonely and unhappy man. Thus his act of masturbation was confined to his disturbed psychology and he was discursively transformed from a 'normal heterosexual' into a 'pervert'. However, his family provided a counter-discourse in which they argued that Milligan had been a very happy and contented man (i.e. not psychologically abnormal). They added, however, that not everyone can hope to have the *balance* of their lives exactly right. In this way, they strove to save him from the category of perversion and instead appealed to a presumed constituency of normal heterosexuals who could acknowledge that what might go on in the privacy of their own sexual fantasies and practices could be far from 'balanced'. It is precisely the meaning of this appeal that we should grasp. If we see heterosexuality as a matter of *balance*, which may be quite unstable, although with the appearance of unchanging stability, we can begin to grasp both the tensions which surround being heterosexual and the extent of the uncertainties which actually surround the supposedly unproblematic meaning of heterosexuality.

The definition of acts such as S/M or autoerotic asphyxiation as perversions, reinstates as dominant a form of heterosexuality which is, in fact, mythical. Thus, whether it is sexual conservatives or radical feminists who make this argument, this kind of discursive categorisation only serves repetitively to normalise and institutionalise a highly simplified notion of heterosexuality. We need to acknowledge the fragility of heterosexuality through such instances, rather than presume that such sexual behaviours are the result of a denial of proper (missionary) heterosex or of a disturbed mind. As authors like Segal and McIntosh

(1992) argue, we are only just beginning to appreciate the complexity of sexuality. Heterosexuality is not simply reducible to masculinity, nor to be understood endlessly as something women endure because of a socialisation into femininity. But it is hard to get to a position of transcending orthodox heterosexuality if instances of destabilised heterosexuality are dismissed as perversions or if women's heterosexual agency is always already interpreted as a product of patriarchy.

CONCLUSION

Segal (1992, 1994), who has written extensively on heterosexuality, has argued that a new focus on women's sexual agency should be another part of the move to destabilise the heterosexual order. She argues for the need to displace the phallic imperative by nurturing this sexual agency. This means that whilst acknowledging and acting against the harms of heterosexuality, we need also to hear what women say about its pleasures and what they say about making it more pleasurable. This requires men to alter their practices as lovers. Feminist have, I fear, given up talking about this even though young women – possibly alienated from a feminism which appears intolerant of their desires – may not have done so. In 1918 Marie Stopes wrote

> The idea that woman is lowered by sex-intercourse is very deeply rooted in our present society.   (1923, p. 56, 1st edn 1918)

It is ironic that some seventy years later, this seems only to hold true in feminist circles where it is still problematic to talk of sexual intercourse unless we redefine it as rape or abuse.

Stopes' book *Married Love* might not find a great deal of support today for the way in which it presents women as subject to tides and moons and thus somewhat helpless in the face of nature. But in the book we can find an argument for women's sexual agency and against the social requirement that, in sexual matters, woman 'mould herself to the shape desired by man' (p. 48). Perhaps we still need more talk of this agency today, but in more feminist terms. Such talk need not bind women into marriage and reproduction as it is argued much of sexology has done. If we combine a discursive assertion of this sexual agency with ideas of ambivalence around sexual desires, acts, and longings (which do not presume an inevitable and fixed form of hetero-

sexuality) we might start to get closer to the post-heterosexual woman
of my title.

NOTES

1. I have put feminist in brackets here because I am really addressing two
   related but separate issues. My thesis suggests that there is no obvious
   and routine heterosexual identity/subjectivity for women-in-general but
   that for feminists this is even more strongly the case. Obviously for some
   women it is possible to assume a highly heterosexualised subjectivity
   and this can be signalled in terms of dress, demeanour, posture, and so
   on. But this is not a mode available to all women and it is certainly not
   attractive to feminists.
2. As I shall suggest later in the chapter, I think there was a time in the
   early 1970s when work was done by heterosexual women on heterosexuality. There was talk of more egalitarian relations in bed and women's
   right to pleasure. However, the solution to the problem of heterosexuality became lesbianism – politically speaking even if this was not a
   personal solution for everyone. Trying to work on heterosexuality, therefore, became seen as futile, as well as rather difficult in its own right. I
   think therefore that many heterosexual women focused their attention on
   related matters such as abortion, child care, and maternity benefits.
3. Even these subsets of heterosexual subjectivity seem unlikely to produce
   an identity.
4. See, for example, Weeks (1985), Jeffreys (1986), Chartham (1969), Ellis
   (1967) and Chesser (1966).
5. 'We' is very problematic of course. But what I mean to do here is restrict myself to hailing heterosexual women.
6. This is for the often-stated reason that the social world is organised around
   heterosexuality and so if one is heterosexual one does not experience an
   incongruence which might bring about a self-consciousness. Gay men
   and lesbians also have to police themselves far more in the sense of
   avoiding touching, avoiding gestures of affection, and so on. This brings
   a self-consciousness to which heterosexuals are oblivious.
7. In saying this I am appreciative of the fact that sexology texts mesh
   heterosex and gender, using one to naturalise the other and vice versa.
   But I suggest that the outcome is, on the one hand, a contribution to
   gendered subjectivity whilst, on the other, a failure to produce heterosexual subjectivity.
8. Undoubtedly many other women who were not middle class, White or
   heterosexual, felt guilty about sexual matters. However, I am invoking
   this group because the Women's Movement at this time was so dominated by such women.
9. I am not trying to blame lesbian feminists/separatists here, nor am I arguing that it is heterosexual women who were most oppressed or anything as trite as that. Rather I am enquiring into why heterosexual women

did not resist the argument against their sexual practice more forcibly.
10. I think that there are indications that some ethnic minority heterosexual women have been more able to use heterosexuality in a politically radical way. I am thinking of Joan Nestle's celebration of her mother's heterosexuality (although she is herself lesbian) and her acknowledgement of heterosexual pleasure as important to her mother's survival (Nestle, 1984).
11. I am, of course, aware of the significance of penetration to gay sexuality but, oddly, this knowledge did not dislodge my assumptions about penetration as quintessentially heterosexual. No doubt, underlying this assumption, has been that orthodox presumption that gay penetration merely mimics the real thing. I find I am embarrassed to admit to such uncritical presumptions.

REFERENCES

Butler, J. (1990) *Gender Trouble* (London: Routledge).
Campbell, B. (1980) 'A Feminist Sexual Politics: now you see it, now you don't', *Feminist Review*. 5: pp. 1–19.
Chartham, R. (1969) *Mainly for Women* (London: Tandem).
Chesser, E. (1966) *Love and Marriage* (London: Pan). (Originally published in 1946.)
Comfort, A. (ed.) (1977) *More Joy of Sex* (London: Quartet Books).
Comstock. G. D. (1991) *Violence against Lesbians and Gay Men* (New York: Columbia University Press).
de Lauretis, T. (1987) *Technologies of Gender* (Bloomington, IN: Indiana University Press).
Dollimore, J. (1991) *Sexual Dissidence* (Oxford: Clarendon Press).
Ellis, H. (1967) *Psychology of Sex* (London: Pan). (Originally published in 1933.)
Faderman, L. (1985) *Surpassing the Love of Men* (London: The Women's Press).
Foucault, M. (1981) *The History of Sexuality*, vol. I (Harmondsworth: Penguin).
Jeffreys, S. (1986) *The Spinster and her Enemies* (London: Pandora).
Jong, E. (1977) *Fear of Flying* (London: Granada). (Originally published in 1974.)
Leeds Revolutionary Feminist Group (1981) 'Political Lesbianism: The Case Against Heterosexuality', in Onlywomen Press (eds) *Love Your Enemy* (London: Onlywomen Press).
Lees, S. (1993) *Sugar and Spice* (Harmondsworth: Penguin).
Marcuse, H. (1955) *Eros and Civilisation* (Boston, MA: Beacon Press).
Martin, B. (1992) 'Sexual Practice and Changing Lesbian Identities', in M. Barrett and A. Phillips (eds) *Destabilising Theory* (Cambridge: Polity Press).
Nestle, J. (1984) 'My Mother Liked to Fuck', in A. Snitow, C. Stansell and S. Thompson (eds) *Desire: The Politics of Sexuality* (London: Virago).
Pringle, R. (1992) 'Absolute Sex? Unpacking the Sexuality/Gender Relationship', in R. W. Connell and G. W. Dowsett (eds) *Rethinking Sex* (Melbourne: Melbourne University Press).

Rich, A. (1980) 'Compulsory Heterosexuality and Lesbian Existence', in C. Stimson and E. Spector Person (eds) *Women: Sex and Sexuality* (Chicago: University of Chicago Press).

Riley, D. (1988) *Am I That Name?* (London: Macmillan).

Segal, L. (1992) 'Sweet Sorrows, Painful Pleasures', in L. Segal and M. McIntosh (eds) op. cit., pp. 65–91

Segal, L. (1994) *Straight Sex* (London: Virago).

Segal, L. and McIntosh, M. (1992) *Sex Exposed: Sexuality and the Pornography Debate* (London: Virago).

Smart, C. (1992) 'Unquestionably a Moral Issue: Rhetorical Devices and Regulatory Imperatives', in L. Segal and M. McIntosh (eds) *Sex Exposed* (London: Virago), pp. 184–99

Stopes, M. (1923) *Married Love* (London: Putnams). (Originally published in 1918.)

Walkowitz, J. (1980) *Prostitution in Victorian Society* (Cambridge: Cambridge University Press).

Walkowitz, J. (1992) *City of Dreadful Delight* (Chicago, IL: University of Chicago Press).

Watney, S. (1987) *Policing Desire* (London: Methuen).

Weeks, J. (1985) *Sexuality and Its Discontents* (London: Routledge & Kegan Paul).

Wilkinson, S. and Kitzinger, S. (1993) *Heterosexuality* (London: Sage).

Index

active sensibility, care as, 3, 15, 26–33
Adler, Z., 181, 182, 190
adoption, and preservation of identity, 71–2
AIDS (Acquired Immune Deficiency Syndrome) *see* HIV/AIDS
Alistair, D., 210
Allatt, P., 3, 4, 38, 40, 41
Althusser, L., 38, 39
Anderson, M., 139
Apple, R. D., 102
Arber, S., 16
Archaud, D., 66
Armstrong, D., 124
Atkin, K., 16, 29
Austoker, J., 124, 125

Banks, M., 78, 79
Barrett, M., 184
Bart, P., 189
Barthes, R., 39
Batten, L. W., 102, 103
beauty, displacement of, 4
Becker, H. S., 25
Bell, N., 139
Bentley, P., 40–1
Berger, V., 178
Beveridge Report, 41, 50
Beveridge, W., 40
Bird, J. F., 138
Blaxter, M., 105
Bloor, M., 122
body
    discourses on the, 121–2
    and the menopause, 151–4, 155–7
    ownership and control of women's bodies, 8, 85–6, 129–31, 132–3
boys, and sexual harassment, 211–14
Bradshaw, J., 70

Brandes, S., 48
Brannen, J., 29
breast feeding, 6–7, 99–117
    and romance, 113–14
Brown, L. M., 80, 91
Brownmiller, S., 184
Bullock, A., 40
Bumiller, K., 182, 183
Burger, M., 125
Burghes, L., 66
Burkitt, I., 140
Buswell, C., 37
Butler, Josephine, 222
Butler, Judith, 11, 203, 205, 207, 236

Cadogan, William, 100, 102
Calder, A., 55
Callinicos, A., 140
Cameron, D., 173
Campbell, B., 173, 229
cancer, deaths from cervical, 124–5
capitalism, and sexuality, 230
Carabine, J., 168
Carey, Dr George, Archbishop of Canterbury, 65
caring, 2–3, 15–33
    as active sensibility, 3, 15, 26–33
    as a labour of love, 16–17
    as morality and ethics, 18–23
    and negotiation of commitments, 23–6
    for people with AIDS, 165
    as sentient activity, 3, 15, 26–33
Carter, A., 43, 44
Carter, P., 6, 7, 105
cervical screening, 7–8, 120, 123–33
Chambers, G., 181
Chesser, Eustace, 225
Chetley, A., 99
Child Support Agency, 63, 64
children
    adoption of, 71–2
    and parental responsibility, 72–3

242